Great
Awakenings

Great Awakenings

HISTORICAL PERSPECTIVES FOR TODAY

David Horn & Gordon L. Isaac, editors

HENDRICKSON PUBLISHERS

Great Awakenings: Historical Perspectives for Today

© 2016 by Hendrickson Publishers Marketing, LLC
P.O. Box 3473
Peabody, Massachusetts 01961-3473
www.hendrickson.com

ISBN 978-1-61970-767-2

Printed in the United States of America

First Printing — September 2016

Library of Congress Cataloging-in-Publication Data

Names: Horn, David, 1942- editor.
Title: Great awakenings : historical perspectives for today / edited by David Horn and Gordon Isaac.
Description: Peabody, MA : Hendrickson Publishers, 2016. | Includes bibliographical references and index.
Identifiers: LCCN 2016024510 | ISBN 9781619707672 (alk. paper)
Subjects: LCSH: Religious awakening--Christianity--History. | Revivals--History.
Classification: LCC BV3770 .G74 2016 | DDC 269.09--dc23 LC record available at https://lccn.loc.gov/2016024510

To a Gentleman and a Scholar

Garth Rosell represents the best qualities of scholar and gentleman. As our exemplar, mentor, colleague, and, most of all, friend, he has dedicated his entire academic life to the study of the subject matter of this book. With deep gratitude, we dedicate this volume to him.

Table of Contents

Introduction
The Surprising Work of God: Calling the Church to Spiritual Renewal

Gordon L. Isaac

Studying Great Awakenings

The book that you hold in your hands is about great awakenings, the kind that are produced by "the wonderful, free, and sovereign grace of God," to use the words of Jonathan Edwards.[1] When a great awakening arrives, it turns cold, formal religion and careless, performance-based Christianity into a lively and heartfelt exercise of the love of God that was the central teaching of Jesus Christ. It is manifest in repentance for sin and the conversion of life and practice. It eventuates in the praise of God, renewed worship, overcoming of old feuds, and care for neighbors.

As a subject of historical scholarship, the matter of great awakenings has produced a number of accounts that seek to explain the increased religious enthusiasm and fervor that has periodically evidenced itself in the cultural life of America. On the macro level, the work of William McLoughlin identifies a number of great awakenings that have played their role in shaping American culture. He sets out the following five awakenings:

The Puritan Awakening,	1610–40;
The First Great Awakening,	1730–60;
The Second Great Awakening,	1800–1830;
The Third Great Awakening,	1890–1920;
and The Fourth Great Awakening,	1960–90(?).[2]

---

[1] Jonathan Edwards, "*A Faithful Narrative of the Surprising Work of God*" in *The Works of Jonathan Edwards* Vol. 4, edited by C. G. Goen (New Haven and London: Yale University Press, 1972), 152. Hereafter cited as *WJE* with volume and page number.

[2] William G. McLoughlin, *Revivals, Awakenings, and Reform* (Chicago and London: University of Chicago Press, 1978), 10–11.

This periodization of the awakenings is approximate and McLough-lin's is not the only possible model to consider.[3] Further, there are those who would not embrace without qualification the sociological approach of McLoughlin.[4] When one is working on the macro level, nuance gained by individual studies on a particular awakening cannot be given full prominence.

What McLoughlin and other researchers would have us see is that awak-enings are certainly religious in nature, but should also be seen as coincid-ing with and contributing to the revitalization of culture. This approach highlights the complex social and intellectual causes as well as the religious causes of awakening. A sophisticated society is under constant pressure to adjust its central institutions in light of changing technologies, changing so-cial opinion, and moral/religious justifications that set the relation between institutions and the web of culture. A revival or great awakening begins when accumulated pressures for change produce such personal and corpo-rate stress that a shift is required for culture to proceed. At that moment the hard crust of custom must be broken through to sweep away blockages that would obstruct social structures that make for a new equilibrium.

When studying great awakenings from this vantage point, we can see that there is no separating the religious elements from the social elements. This is something that comes out as McLoughlin differentiates between two similar terms, that of "Revivalism" and "Great Awakenings."

> Revivalism is the Protestant ritual (at first spontaneous, but, since 1830, rou-tinized) in which charismatic evangelists convey "the Word" of God to large masses of people who, under this influence, experience what Protestants call conversion, salvation, regeneration, or spiritual rebirth. Awakenings—the most vital and yet most mysterious of all folk arts—are periods of cultural revitalization that begin in a general crisis of beliefs and values and extend over a period of a generation or so, during which time a profound reorientation in beliefs and values takes place. Revivals alter the lives of individuals; awaken-ings alter the world view of a whole people or culture.[5]

The great advantage of this definition is that it points out the differ-ence between a simple instance of religious fervor and the effects of a great awakening. While the first can be understood purely in religious terms—the effect of the word of God in the soul—a great awakening is a more complex reality with social as well as religious components.

---

[3]For example, Robert William Fogel, *The Fourth Great Awakening and the Future of Egalitarianism* (Chicago: University of Chicago Press, 2000).

[4]See the chapters in this volume by Hambrick-Stowe and Singleton.

[5]McLoughlin, *Revivals*, xiii.

The idea that a great awakening includes social components might be new to some, but it is standard thinking in the literature exploring the great awakenings. For example, in his work *From Puritan to Yankee,* Richard L. Bushman traces the deterioration of Puritan social institutions, especially from 1690 onwards. The internal stresses, including economic and social, pressed hard on the established patterns of authority. This atmosphere became the precursor for which the Great Awakening was the answer. When the awakening swept through Connecticut, it helped to seal a restructuring of the social contract. The Puritan compact was over, and a new (Yankee) structure for relating to authority (and the legitimization of the moral warrants for that structure) was set in place. In addition, the new structure made greater degrees of individualism, volunteerism, and democracy acceptable practices. All of these qualities helped prepare the colonies for the rigors of the Revolution. In fact, McLoughlin would argue that the First Great Awakening aided in the creation of the American republic.[6] The point of Bushman's work is not to detract from the reality of the religious experience of those involved, but rather to place it in the larger frame of reference of society as a whole.[7]

Jonathan Edwards and the First Great Awakening

Jonathan Edwards gives an eyewitness account of the beginnings of the First Great Awakening in his *Faithful Narrative of the Surprising Work of God.* When Edwards had taken up his post at the Northampton church as its third pastor, he noted that it was "a time of extraordinary dullness in religion." People were more interested in their own pursuits and the cares of daily life than in thinking about eternal matters. The young people were given to "night-walking, and frequenting the tavern, and lewd practices." This led to the corruption of morals and a general disregard for the authority structures in their families. Further, there was a significant division in the parish. As Edwards describes it, "There had also long prevailed in the town a spirit of contention between two parties, into which they had for many years been divided, by which was maintained a jealousy one of the other, and they were prepared to oppose one another in all public affairs."[8]

It was in this dark and dull time that tragedy struck. In 1734, a young man "in the bloom of his youth" was violently seized by pleurisy and died in about two days. Shortly after that, a young married woman who was very

---

[6] Ibid., 11.
[7] Richard L. Bushman, *From Puritan to Yankee: Character and Social Order in Connecticut, 1690–1765* (Cambridge: Harvard University Press, 1967), esp. 196–220.
[8] *WJE* 4, 146.

concerned about the salvation of her soul also fell ill. But before she passed away she "seemed to have satisfying evidences of God's saving mercy to her" and was able to warn and counsel others. Edwards rather stoically states, "This seemed much to contribute to the solemnizing of the spirits of many young persons: and there began evidently to appear more of a religious concern on people's minds."[9] Something new began to take place. In a settlement three miles from Northampton, a number "seemed to be savingly wrought upon."

Even more unexpected was the conversion of one of the young women who "had been one of the greatest company-keepers in the whole town." She was not known to be one interested in spiritual things yet, as Edwards put it, "By the conversation I then had with her, it appeared to me that what she gave an account of was a glorious work of God's infinite power and sovereign grace; and that God had given her a new heart, truly broken and sanctified. I could not then doubt of it, and have seen much in my acquaintance with her since to confirm it." Only after these events is the reticent Edwards able to say, in an allusion to Ezekiel 37, "The noise amongst the dry bones waxed louder and louder."[10] As Edwards describes the outpouring that takes place, he writes,

> There was scarcely a single person in the town, either old or young, that was left unconcerned about the great things of the eternal world. Those that were wont to be the vainest and loosest, and those that had been most disposed to think and speak slightly of vital and experimental religion, were now generally subject to great awakenings. And the work of conversion was carried on in a most astonishing manner, and increased more and more; souls did as it were come by flocks to Jesus Christ. From day to day, for many months together, might be seen evident instances of sinners brought out of darkness into marvelous light, and delivered out of an horrible pit, and from the miry clay, and set upon a rock with a new song of praise to God in their mouths.[11]

He goes on to report that this harvest of souls into the Kingdom had a profound effect on the community. "The town seemed to be full of the presence of God: it never was so full of love, nor so full of joy; and yet so full of distress, as it was then."[12] Some were weeping with sorrow for their sin, others were weeping for joy and love, and yet others were weeping with pity and concern for their neighbors.

Edwards reports that in one six-month period "more than 300 souls were savingly brought home to Christ." He goes on to tell how the surprising

---

[9] Ibid., 147–48.
[10] Ibid., 149.
[11] Ibid., 150–51.
[12] Ibid., 151.

work of God had touched other communities in the vicinity such as South Hadley, Deerfield, Hatfield, Westfield, and Enfield. He continues with accounts of revival at Guilford, Mansfield, Hebron, Bolton, and Woodbury. Farther distant are the movings of God's Spirit in New York and "the Jerseys," and in this connection Edwards mentions the names of important participants in the revival in the Mid-Atlantic states: William and Gilbert Tennent and Theodorus Frelinghausen.[13]

Edwards' account of these remarkable events was published in the colonies as well as in London and Glasgow. In this way, the surprising work of God became part of the public record. Other pastors sent in letters to the publishers to confirm the witness of Edwards. On this document, Garth Rosell offers the following comments,

> Woven into the fabric of Edwards' *Faithful Narrative* are the five distinctive threads of historic evangelicalism: the centrality of Christ's atoning work on the cross, the essential experience of religious conversion, the foundational authority of the Bible, the importance of spreading the gospel, and the possibility of individual and corporate renewal. Forged in the revival fires of the Great Awakening, these distinguishing marks remained at the center of the movement for more than three centuries.[14]

Rosell's comments show the degree to which the events of the First Great Awakening and the distinguishing marks are emblazoned on evangelical self-understanding.

Eventually the revival did subside. "In the latter part of May, it began to be very sensible that the Spirit of God was gradually withdrawing from us, and after this time Satan seemed to be more let loose, and raged in a dreadful manner." Unfortunately, one honorable man of strict moral sensibilities fell deep into the "disease of melancholy." He grew more and more discouraged and he was occupied with the thorny question of the state of his soul. "He was kept awake nights, meditating terror,"[15] and finally, under the suggestion of the Devil, took his own life. One is struck with the honesty of Edwards, who included the dark side of things as well as the thrilling portions of the Surprising Work.

The person who spends any time in this document cannot help but be impressed with the power of the personal stories of conversion and transformation. The experiential, or as they said in Edwards' time, the "experimental" aspect of evangelical faith is clear for all to see. The eyewitness account

---

[13] Ibid., 154–58.

[14] Garth M. Rosell, *The Surprising Work of God: Harold John Ockenga, Billy Graham, and the Rebirth of Evangelicalism* (Grand Rapids: Baker Academic, 2008), 35.

[15] *WJE* 4, 206.

brings one into close proximity to the gracious and winsome change that comes through the preaching of Christ and him crucified. Hearts were touched and sometimes filled with "new sweetnesses and delights; there seems to be an inward ardor and burning of heart that they express, the life to which they never experienced before."[16] This experience of the new birth would become central in the evangelical movement that would follow in the wake of this First Great Awakening.

The First Great Awakening in Later Historical Accounts

Jonathan Edwards wrote *The Faithful Narrative* as a pastor. He did not, in the strictest sense, write it as an historian. While he was clearly quite circumspect and careful in his organization, and of the material claims he set forward, he was all the while concerned to set down on the page the condition of the souls of the individuals he was writing about. A historical account of the First Great Awakening that featured some historical distance would have to wait for a later date. That time came in the next century, and the historical studies that followed create a rich and varied tapestry of opinion on what happened in Northampton and beyond.[17] We turn now to an account of the writing of history on the First Great Awakening.

In 1840, approximately 100 years after *The Faithful Narrative* was published, people gathered to consider the revival of religion of which Jonathan Edwards was a part. Some thought it was worthy of unmixed eulogy in public celebration, others spoke of it in more guarded and qualified ways, and there were some who thought that it should be mentioned rather with censure than otherwise. Seeing that no full-length study had been done on the Great Awakening, Joseph Tracy gathered what sources he had to hand and undertook the writing. It is no real surprise that central in his work is the position that the idea of "new birth" came to play. As he put it,

> The history of "The Great Awakening" is the history of this idea [the new birth], making its way through some communities where it had fallen in to comparative neglect, and through others where it was nearly or quite unknown; overturning theories and habits and forms of organization inconsistent with it, where it could prevail, and repelled by them, where it could not; working itself gradually clear in the minds of those who received it, and leading to habits of thought and practical arrangements in harmony itself. If the reader finds a

---

[16] Ibid., 208.
[17] In what follows I am indebted to Heath Mayo, "Religion in the Early Modern Atlantic World: A Historiographical Appraisal," blogs.brown.edu accessed 3/12/2016.

true and intelligible account of its various workings, the object for which this history ought to be written will be accomplished.[18]

Tracy's work spans over 300 pages and includes a significant amount of detail about the controversy between the New Lights, who were for revival, and the Old Lights, who remained skeptical about the matter. This passage highlights the centrality of the new experiential religion, and in particular the new birth. Tracy's history has a singular focus on a religious interpretation of the Great Awakening, yet in mentioning "overturning theories and habits and forms of organization," he alludes to the fact that there were structural changes that took place in light of the preaching of the new birth.

In the 1960s there were authors who sought to clarify and extend Tracy's work. C. C. Goen and Edwin Gaustad tend to view the Great Awakening in New England as a response to the decline of Puritan piety and the dull state of religion at the time. Like Tracy, Goen outlines the split between the New Lights, who insisted on the need for conscious conversion, and the Old Lights, who were not focused on the new birth and tended to accept more rationalist approaches to theology. He contends that it was the influence of Protestant pietism that brought about the revival of religion.[19] Gaustad's study features accounts of Whitefield, Tennent, and Davenport, along with a number of lesser revival preachers. He sees the Great Awakening as the watershed between the traditionalism of the seventeenth century and the new Protestant era. The study is focused on the religious aspects of the revival, and thus does not deal with the cultural aspects of the time.[20]

In the 1960s, Alan Heimart argued that the Calvinists who enjoyed a central role in the Great Awakening were instrumental in stimulating the democratic movement.[21] In the 1980s another set of authors sought to connect the Great Awakening with the individualism displayed in the American Revolution. These works contend that the religious fervor and the breaking down of old hierarchical structures encouraged a mindset in the colonies that made a break with Britain conceivable. David Lovejoy pursues a line of

---

[18] Joseph Tracy, *The Great Awakening: A History of the Revival of Religion in the Time of Edwards and Whitefield* (Boston: Published by Charles Tappan; New York: Dayton & Newman; Philadephia: Henry Perkins, 1845), xiii.

[19] C. C. Goen, *Revivalism and Separatism in New England, 1740–1800: Strict Congregationalists & Separatist Baptists in the Great Awakening* (London: Yale University Press, 1962).

[20] Edwin Gaustad, *The Great Awakening in New England* (New York: Harper & Brothers, 1957).

[21] Alan Heimert, *Religion and the American Mind from the Great Awakening to the Revolution* (Cambridge, MA: Harvard University Press, 1966).

thinking similar to Heimart, but instead of focusing on the Calvinists, his interest is in religious enthusiasm.[22]

Yale historian Jon Butler created a small sensation in Great Awakening studies when he contended that Joseph Tracy had invented the Awakening in the nineteenth century. He challenged the accuracy of the recorded accounts and asked questions of the historiography done up to that point. He was convinced that the revival in New England was 'erratic, heterogeneous, and politically benign.'[23] Bruce Hindmarsh, in reflecting on the provocative language of "fiction" as used by Butler and "myth" as used by John Kent in a similar critique on the revival in England, helps to place things in context:

> Principally, it seems to me, these writers are concerned that the religious and political consequences of revival in the period have been overstated. . . . However, despite their provocative language of 'fiction' and 'myth,' neither of these historians deny that participants themselves in eighteenth-century revivals often described their own experience in terms of larger solidarities that were transnational and transdenominational.[24]

Following up on Butler's contention is the work of Frank Lambert, who places the Old Lights and the New Lights in dialogue. The two sides had differing narratives of what was happening in townships and countryside, cities and outlying areas during the revival. In addition, Lambert tries to show the powerful role that the newly available print resources played in reporting and promoting the ideas of revival.[25]

An extremely important area of Great Awakening historiography is that which touches on the international or the transatlantic scope of the Awakening. At the forefront of this connection is W. R. Ward. He asserts that in spite of all the regional variations and geographical disparateness, revivals reflected the existence of a worldwide Protestant culture, a 'Protestant frame of mind.'[26] In his most recent book Ward sets out to show that there was a great deal of uniformity among the evangelical elite in the colonies, in England, and on the Continent. According to Ward, they had coherent

---

[22] David Lovejoy, *Religious Enthusiasm in the New World: Heresy to Revolution* (Cambridge and London: Harvard University Press, 1985).

[23] Jon Butler, "Enthusiasm Described and Decried: The Great Awakening as Interpretive Fiction" *Journal of American History* 69 (October 1982). Another more recent book along these lines is Thomas S. Kidd, *The Great Awakening:The Roots of Evangelical Christianity in Colonial America* (New Haven and London: Yale Univeristy Press, 2007).

[24] D. Bruce Hindmarsh, *The Evangelical Conversion Narrative: Spiritual Autobiography in Early Modern England* (Oxford: Oxford University Press, 2005), p. 62.

[25] Frank Lambert, *Inventing the Great Awakening* (Princeton: Princeton University Press, 1999).

[26] W. R. Ward, *The Protestant Evangelical Awakening* (Cambridge: Cambridge University Press, 1992).

answers to the general intellectual issues of the day, and their piety played an integral role.[27]

In addition to the works already cited, there is a new wave of focused studies that help us to understand particular aspects of the Great Awakening in context. I mention just two. Leigh Schmidt has written on some of the shared aspects of the revivals. Particular attention is given to "sacramental occasions" that would draw large numbers of people to festive participation in the Lord's Supper. Scottish evangelical Protestants brought this practice to the Kentucky revivals.[28] Also worthy of mention is the work of Linford Fischer, who has written on the interface of colonial culture and Native American culture. He shows that the "Indian Great Awakening" saw the faith indigenized by Native Americans in more than an imitative way. Yet, in the climate of violence and suspicion, the Awakening was not an altogether unmixed blessing to the Indians.[29]

What are we to make of this body of historical literature on the First Great Awakening? The wide array of approaches to the substance and the meaning of the First Great Awakening may be something of a surprise. In the first instance this is a testimony to the importance of the Awakening and the interest that it still generates. The varied studies give us a great deal to work with in providing a fuller account of the religious and the cultural connections in the phenomenon we call an Awakening, showing us not only "where we have been," but various ways of judging the significance of that past.

The Present and Future of Great Awakenings

The historical question regarding "where we have been" with great awakenings, while important, is not the only perspective represented in the following pages. To sit in contemplation of these historical moments, as important as that is, is not an end in itself. History gives perspective and greater knowledge, certainly, but it simultaneously raises questions about where we are going and what the future will look like. It is a historical fact that great awakenings have happened in numerous places and times. It is equally true that change and renewal were the result. Great awakenings by

---

[27] W. R. Ward, *Early Evangelicalism: A Global Intellectual History, 1670–1789* (Cambridge: Cambridge University Press, 2006).

[28] Leigh Schmidt, *Holy Fairs: Scottish Communions and American Revivals in the Early Modern Period* (Princeton: Princeton University Press, 1989).

[29] Linford D. Fischer, *The Indian Great Awakening: Religion and the Shaping of Native Cultures in Early America* (New York: Oxford University Press, 2012). Linford was a research scholar for Garth Rosell.

their very nature are surprising and a divine work, and so it is inevitable that the question should arise, "Can we expect God's awakening presence again?"

The question is made all the more poignant in the North American context of the twenty-first century. In our time, the post World War II generation has shaped Christianity in the United States in innumerable ways. The American Awakening of the 1940s and '50s produced the rebirth of Evangelicalism. In the wake of that powerful movement, a vast array of influential institutions were developed. From institutions of higher education to influential publications to international organizations, the sustaining structures of Evangelicalism have been built and have come of age. One could say that this burgeoning activity revealed a changed attitude and response to the world. It might be more accurate to say that the changed social reality allowed the Neo-Evangelical Movement to create these new structures to deal with a new reality. It may well be that some of these structures are in need of reinvention and/or revitalization. This comes at the same time when some are asking about the future direction of Evangelicalism.

It is in this context that the idea for a gathering focused on the great awakenings emerged. In October of 2015, a conference under the title "The Surprising Work of God: Calling the Church to Spiritual Renewal—Historical Perspective for Developing Future Expectations" was held in honor of Garth M. Rosell, whose varied career has spanned fifty years, thirty-seven of which have been at Gordon-Conwell Theological Seminary in South Hamilton, Massachusetts. Originally, Garth was brought to the seminary to serve as Academic Dean, a position he held for nine years. After leaving the dean's office, Garth not only returned to the classroom as Professor of Church History but he also served for seventeen years as chair of the Division of Christian Thought and as Director of the Harold John Ockenga Institute. In his well-attended courses, Garth always takes delight in introducing his students to the joys of historical studies and the wonder of church history. Many of them, inspired by his enthusiasm and redoubtable spirit, have gone on to their own studies and their own places in the church and academy. These students stand as an abiding testimony to Garth's legacy as a gifted teacher.

Dear to his heart, and central to his graduate level pedagogy, is the concept of spiritual renewal, something that he holds in common with his long time colleague Richard Lovelace. In *Dynamics of Spiritual Life: An Evangelical Theology of Renewal*, Lovelace sets forward biblical models of cyclical and continuous renewal, writing that "Under the Old Covenant the cyclical pattern of apostasy and spiritual renewal is one of the most obvious characteristics of the people of God."[30] The New Testament, on the other

---

[30] Richard F. Lovelace, *Dynamics of Spiritual Life: An Evangelical Theology of Renewal* (Downer's Grove, IL: InterVarsity, 1979), 61.

hand, seems to chart the possibility of a continuous renewal model. However, the church quite often finds itself repeating the experience of the Old Testament saints. The work of Lovelace is a comprehensive and disciplined proposal for congregational and denominational renewal that ultimately would help to revitalize evangelicalism and the church itself.

In his own work, Rosell has taken pains to point out to his students those places in church history where the decline of religion has made way for powerful renewal movements. Of special note are the Reformation, the Pietist renewal, the Methodist revival, and of course the great awakenings in North America. In his writings, Rosell has set out the contours of the leading character of the Second Great Awakening.[31] And in a more recent work that drew on the important archival material of Harold John Ockenga, he has told the story of how an American Awakening became a worldwide movement.[32] Whether it is telling the story of the new measures of a Finney or the compelling and fascinating story of the young band of evangelists with Billy Graham at the fore, Garth has always been fascinated with the spiritual renewal that can only come at God's prompting.

So when it came time to plan a conference in his honor, it was only fitting that the title should reflect the lifetime of scholarly interest and endeavor of Garth Rosell. The driving interest of the conference, which drew people from across the country, focused on understanding the phenomenon of great awakenings. In the first instance, attention was given to exploration of specific historical instances of awakening. In the second instance, the conference focused on expectations for the future extending out into the global realities of our time. Thus, it can be seen that, taken together, the emphases of the conference are nicely summarized by the subtitle of the book: "historical perspectives for today." If God has granted his special grace in specific times in the past with resulting awakenings, are we to expect that this will happen again? Are we living in a time in which the social structures are groaning under the stress? Are there signs of cultural realignment that make things ready for another great awakening? Would this take place here in America, or would it more likely take place in another portion of the global church? Are these unrealistic expectations?

The Structure of This Book

With such important questions in the air, it was determined that contributions representing a wide array of historical periods and different

---

[31] Garth M. Rosell and A. G. Dupuis, eds. *The Memoirs of Charles G. Finney: The Complete Restored Text* (Grand Rapids: Zondervan, 1989).

[32] Rosell, *The Surprising Work of God.*

awakenings should be enlisted. Only with adequate reflection on the history of God's action in the world is it possible to conjecture about possible scenarios in the future. In what follows, I would like to present the landscape of this collection of essays.

In first position is the presentation of Walter Kaiser Jr., who for eight years was President of Gordon-Conwell Theological Seminary. His many contributions to evangelical theology mark him out as an important voice in the movement. In the chapter entitled, "Why 2 Chronicles 7:14 Is the Paradigmatic Verse for the Revivals and Theology of the Book of Chronicles," Kaiser sets out his conviction that this single verse is the master text giving the organizing principle for several of the revivals recorded in Scripture. In addition, he sees the promises attached to this Old Testament verse as programmatic for our own time as well.

The next presentation is that of Adrian Chastain Weimer, "The Long Roots of Affective Piety in Early New England." Adrian is one of Garth Rosell's students, who presently teaches at Providence College and continues her studies in the Puritan period. Her work on what William McLoughlin called The Puritan Awakening demonstrates that Edwards and the leaders of the First Great Awakening "inherited a sophisticated language" for addressing the turning of the heart toward God, an inheritance that subsequent generations of the church have inherited in their turn.

You could perhaps expect that a presentation clearly settled on the first Great Awakening might follow, considering the outbreak of what we would call evangelicalism. But because we spent some time setting out a brief historiography and suggestions for reading in this introduction, the following chapters focus our attention forward.

Charles Hambrick-Stowe sets out an account of "Charles G. Finney and the Second Great Awakening." He does not demonize Finney as the source of all false doctrine as a few would have it; neither does he eulogize Finney as others might. But in a clear-eyed account, using the best of the most recent historical sources, Hambrick-Stowe traces the theological moves Finney was forced to make in the face of the changing religious landscape. Finney is presented for our consideration in fresh relation to Jonathan Edwards and the First Great Awakening, the emerging Holiness movement, and the political implications of his form of revivalism.

Kevin and Gwenfair Adams lovingly turn our attention to the Welsh Revival of 1905. Under the title, "From Calvinistic Coal Miner to Pentecostal Icon: The Surprising Story of Robert Evans, the Welsh Revival, and Azusa Street," we are treated to a front row seat to the curiously new, extraordinary, Spirit-filled atmosphere of the Welsh Revival. Who could have imagined that a Calvinist coal miner would be the forerunner of the Pentecostal out-pouring of Azusa Street?

In "Neo-evangelicalism and Renewal Since the Mid-Twentieth Century," George Marsden asks what keeps evangelicalism a discernable movement. In light of the fact that there is no headquarters to assure accountability in a widely divergent group, what holds the project together? Marsden asserts that there is a surprising degree of coherence among evangelicals. In the process of setting forward his answer to this matter, he also makes note of those characteristics of evangelicalism that may not wear well moving forward.

It is no hyperbole to say that Billy Graham has been the face of evangelicalism in the twentieth century. "Billy Graham and the Shaping of American Evangelism: Legacies" is the account by Grant Wacker that sets out the distinctive legacy of his ministry. Weaving his way through Graham's contribution to doctrine, evangelical culture, American politics, and the power of hope, Wacker paints a picture of the evangelical who spoke to more people face-to-face, with the possible exception of Pope John Paul II, than any other person in world history.

The presentation of Jim Singleton marks the pivot point in the conference presentations. His contribution, entitled, "Are the Surprising Works of God Completely Surprising?" explores the phenomenon of awakenings from a pastoral point of view. He points to the condition of our current cultural climate and asks, "Could there be any winds of revival on the horizon?" He offers several sustaining words as we assess our times.

The contribution of Ed Stetzer, not surprisingly, is meant to help us interpret some relevant data. "Transported to Oz: The Mission Field, Mission Force, and the Surprising Work of God in America" explains the meaning behind the new shift in mindset that has led to the growing number of individuals who declare "none" as their religious affiliation.

The contribution of Mark Noll, "The American Contribution to World-wide Evangelical Christianity in the Twentieth Century," works to explain why American-like forms of Christianity have grown so rapidly during the second half of the twentieth century. While the evidence shows that there has been a great effort expended by Americans in this regard, including showing the "Jesus" film to almost 5 billion viewers, the real answer to the question is not to be found by looking to American activity only. Rather, the phenomenon may have more to do with the changing world-social orders and the indigenous appropriation of Christianity.

The contribution of Timothy Tennent draws on field studies that give depth and meaning to demographic statistics. In his essay, "Emerging

Paradigm Shifts through the Global Revitalization of Christianity" traces three structural shifts of seismic proportions. The irrepressible shifting center of the World Christian movement is being reshaped in ways that touch upon Christian identity and the manner in which the message is shared.

Closing this volume, Todd Johnson and Cindy Wu ask the question, "What does the Global Christian family look like?" The answers given in "Awakenings and Revivals in the Context of Global Christianity" invite the reader to reflect on the demographic realities of our present and future with a vision that is as deep and wide as the work of God has been in the past.

The essays that you hold in your hand have been prepared to stimulate your thinking. They move from the text of Scripture to the seismic shifting outer boundaries of the World Christian movement. The offerings are widely different in topic and focus, but they all hold in common an interest in addressing our most heartfelt questions about great awakenings. These essays may not be the final word on this important subject, but it is my hope that in reading these contributions your awareness will be raised, your thinking sharpened, and the breadth of the discussion enhanced, as we continue to ponder and anticipate the surprising work of God.

1

Why 2 Chronicles 7:14 Is the Paradigmatic Verse for the Revivals and Theology of the Book of Chronicles

Walter C. Kaiser Jr.

Of the sixteen or more descriptions of revivals spread throughout the Old and New Testaments, 2 Chronicles 7:14 can be labeled as the master text that programmatically introduces at least five of the sixteen major revivals recorded in the Bible. By position, content, and emphases, these five revivals have become the ideal place from which to begin a study of the "surprising work of God" in revivals in ancient Israel, and his promise to replicate the same divine work all over the world. In fact, these five revivals can be viewed as central to the events in the days the Chronicler portrays, as well as one of the important keys to his theological argument in the second book of Chronicles. Moreover, just as these five revivals were central to the cleansing and restoration of the people of God in the times of the Chronicler, they are no less significant as forerunners of the work of God in our own times, for the same Lord calls on believers to repent and to turn back to him wholeheartedly.

Since it has been just over a century since God last visited our times with a revival, as he began to do in the country of Wales in 1905–1906 with a revival that eventually swept westward with the mighty power of God's forgiveness and restoration of believers, surely it is time for another such movement of the grace of our Lord. In that former day it brought a revitalization and a return of new life in Christ that believers had originally possessed; but it also was a time when the church sought God to "Revive [his church once] again" (Ps 85:6).[1] In the wake of this Welsh revival, some nine hundred

---

[1] Unless otherwise noted, Scripture quotations in this chapter are the author's translation.

thousand converts were added to the name of Christ in Central and South America when this movement of God swept southward during the entirety of the twentieth century, after reaching the western part of the United States around 1905. It is important, then, that 2 Chronicles 7:14, often looked to for other reasons, be recognized as a verse that is at the heart of the study of revivals, not only in the book of 2 Chronicles, but in the whole Bible.

H. G. M. Williamson legitimately observed:

> It is quite extraordinary that none of the [previous] commentators has seen the vital significance of this verse [of 2 Chronicles 7:14] for the Chronicler's theology. . . . Four avenues of repentance [as evidenced in the four impera-tives in this verse] are mentioned, which will lead God to forgive and restore, and these are taken up at various points in the remainder of the narrative and illustrated, often with one of the remarkable [and "surprising"] interventions of God. . . . That this is deliberate is shown by the fact that whenever these terms occur in the earlier narrative they are quite neutral theologically and do not mark similar miraculous turning-points [as found later in 2 Chronicles].[2]

In the context of 2 Chronicles 7:12–22, the appearance of the Lord to Solomon for a second time is also highlighted for us (1 Kgs 9:2; 2 Chr 7:12). The first time, of course, was when God appeared to Solomon at Gibeon just after he had been named as king. In that appearance, the Lord invited Solomon: "Ask for whatever you want me to give you" (2 Chr 1:7 NIV). In that first appearance of the Lord, Solomon asked for "wisdom" rather than wealth, or success in battle, or anything of that sort. In this second nocturnal appearance, however, God approved of Solomon's dedicatory prayer upon his completion of building the temple of God (1 Kgs 8:22–53; 2 Chr 6:12–40) by sending down "fire . . . from heaven" (2 Chr 7:1) to ignite the burnt of-fering and the sacrifices on the altar, indicating his acceptance of the king's worship and prayer of dedication.

This section of Scripture included in 2 Chronicles 7:13–15, with our key text in verse 14 on revivals, is not found in the parallel passage of 1 Kings 9:2–9, for the purpose of the writer of Chronicles was somewhat different from the purpose that the writer of Kings had in mind when he recorded the same event. Therefore, these seemingly intrusive verses in 2 Chronicles 7:13–15, which might seem to interrupt the account as similarly recorded in 1 Kings 9:3, actually supply the answer to Solomon's prayer, included in chapter 6 of 2 Chronicles. However, in introducing this pivotal text of 2 Chronicles 7:14, the preceding verse 13 makes reference once again (as Solomon made reference in his prayer in 2 Chr 6:22–39) to several calami-

---

[2] H. G. M. Williamson, *The New Century Bible Commentary: 1 and 2 Chronicles* (Grand Rapids: Eerdmans, 1982), 225.

tous situations that God might send to Israel if they did not walk with him, such as a divinely sent drought, an invasion of locusts, or a plague that would bring illness. But then, thanks be to God, he introduced the great divine promise announced in 2 Chronicles 7:14–16:

> If my people, who are called by my name, will humble themselves and pray and seek my face and turn from their wicked ways, then I will hear from heaven, and I will forgive their sin and will heal their land. Now my eyes will be open and my ears attentive to the prayers offered in this place. I have chosen and consecrated this temple so that my Name may be there forever. My eyes and my heart will always be there. (NIV)

The fact that this text is embedded in a context that refers to three calamitous catastrophes reminds us of the eight outstanding characteristics found in most revivals, which Wilbur Smith outlined for us as early as the middle of the twentieth century.

1. Revivals usually occur in a time of deep moral darkness and national depression where Biblical ethics have been overturned and morality and justice have been distorted.

2. Often revivals begin in the heart of one consecrated servant of God who becomes the human energizing stimulus behind the revival.

3. Revivals rest on a return to the bold preaching of the word of God with power and faithfulness to what is written in the whole text of Scripture.

4. Revivals are marked by the destruction of all idols or any other competitors to the living God.

5. Revivals also witness a return to the worship and adoration of the Lord God in a new and fresh way.

6. There is a decisive determination to separate oneself from all known sin in each revival.

7. Revivals result in the experience of exuberant joy and gladness by the people of God.

8. Revivals are followed by a period of divine blessing on the church and a general improvement in the prosperity of all the culture.[3]

---

[3] Wilbur M. Smith. *The Glorious Revival under King Hezekiah* (Grand Rapids: Zondervan, 1954), 7–8. Smith actually listed nine characteristics, but included "A return to offering blood sacrifices," which applies more directly to Old Testament times even though the principle still applies in our day. However, one might also note the significance of the doctrine of the atonement in all revivals just as well!

It is from the environment of characteristics such as these eight features that God gave his answer to the dedicatory prayer of King Solomon. The Chronicler, under the inspiration of our Lord, sets out an outline and an agenda for the theology of revival. He then illustrates its use in the lives of five Davidic kings in Judah, who each exhibit one of the four divine commands given to the following kings in these chapters in 2 Chronicles: King Rehoboam (2 Chr 11–12; "humble one's self"), King Asa (chs. 14–16; "seek my face"), King Jehoshaphat (chs. 17–20; "pray"), King Hezekiah (chs. 29–32; "turn from our wicked ways"), and King Josiah (chs. 34–35; "humble one's self"). To be even more precise, fifteen of the Chronicler's thirty-six chapters are devoted to illustrating the soundness of the four commands (to "humble yourselves, pray, seek my face, and turn from your wicked ways"). God gave these instructions to Solomon and his successors, and then he showed him how observance of these commands would result in the three outcomes God promised in this programmatic verse of 2 Chronicles 7:14—God would hear their prayers, he would forgive their sin, and he would heal their land!

But who are the persons called "my people" in this text? Were they limited to the Jewish people of that day, or are they the people of God who would live in all future times? And if they were only addressed to the Jewish people of Solomon's day, then what about the Gentiles? Were they excluded from this text? Or was God's surprising work of revival meant to cover them as well?

Who Are the People of God?

It is a fact that not all readers of the Scriptures are convinced that those addressed in 2 Chronicles 7:14 were all the peoples who were on earth at that time, or even Jewish believers as well as the Gentiles who would come to faith in the future. For example, Fredrick J. Mabie, writing in the esteemed, conservative Zondervan *Expositor's Bible Commentary,* explained:

> What is perhaps one of the most well-known verses of Chronicles and the OT as a whole (v. 14, "If my people, who are called by my name. . . .") is also one of the most misappropriated verses in the Bible. In short, this verse is not a promissory statement being made to the United States or any country apart from the ancient covenant community of Israel. This statement is situated within the covenantal particulars related to the Deuteronomic covenant (cf. v. 13), matters of temple theology (and the interwoven Israelite sacrificial theology; cf. vv. 15–16), and the Davidic covenant (cf. vv. 17–22). Note that all these features are directly applicable to the nation of Israel located within the specific area of the Promised Land featuring a functioning temple in the city of Jerusalem and having a Davidic king on the throne. Moreover, the Chronicler

is retelling something that had been told to Solomon about four centuries prior to the time of writing.[4]

This is not a new or otherwise unheard-of criticism against (what some would regard as) an enlarged use of this text as a revival Scripture for all times and all believing peoples around the globe. It is usually protested on Dispensational grounds that this text was addressed solely to Israel and therefore is part of their mail, but it is not a word addressed directly to Gentiles at large.

In reply, it must be said that what this view fails to notice is that the phrase "my people" has an appositional clause (or epexegetical clause) alongside of it that explains what the writer intended to communicate when he quickly added to the condition "If my people" that they were the ones "who are called by my name." When God called his name over anyone or anything, that person or thing belonged to him exclusively (2 Sam 12:28; Jer 25:29; Dan 9:19). This was true whether it was the temple (1 Kgs 8:43; Jer 7:10–11, 14, 30; 32:34; 34:15) or men and women (Isa 4:1; Jer 14:9; 15:16). Thus, when David called his name over a city, he owned that city and it became part of Israel.

What is more, this text is being recorded by the Chronicler possibly 400 years after the day God originally gave it to Solomon, as Mabie himself observed in the citation above. Thus, it had a continuing address to both Israel and to all who had God's name called over them later on (and who were thus also owned by God), for, as Paul taught: all Scripture is profitable and useful for teaching, reproof, rebuke, and making one wise to salvation!

This conditional promise of 2 Chronicles 7:14 had the same broad application that the "New Covenant" (Jer 31:31–34) had, for it too was specifically and directly addressed to "the house of Israel and the house of Judah" in both the OT (Jer 31:31 NKJV), and in its NT citation (Heb 8:8, 10), yet New Testament believers were meant to participate in the "blood of the New Covenant" (Matt 26:28 NKJV) and some were called "ministers of a new covenant" (2 Cor 3:6 NKJV). When they too believed in that coming Man of Promise, they were grafted into the Olive Tree of Israel (Rom 9:11–24). According to Galatians 3:29, all who believe in Messiah are part of God's "people," for "If [we] belong to Christ, then [we] are Abraham's seed, and heirs according to the promise" (NIV). Thus, this promise has both a "now" aspect for ancient Israel and a "not yet" aspect for the Gentiles who would be part of the future one "people of God," whether believing Jew or Gentile. Even more to the point of Mabie's objections, the temple was to be open to the prayers of any and all aliens or foreigners, as Solomon had prayed (2 Chr 6:32–33).

---

[4] Frederick J. Mabie, *The Expositor's Bible Commentary: Revised Edition, Vol 4, 1 Chronicles–Job* (Grand Rapids: Zondervan, 2010), 192.

And as for David's prayer in 2 Samuel 7, did he not thank God for the fact that the Covenant he was receiving, which promised a "throne, a dynasty and a kingdom" to him, would be "a charter/instruction for all humanity" (2 Sam 7:19)? This word in 2 Chronicles 7:14 was not a chauvinistic decree reserved for Israel alone, as if they were the "pets" and the exclusive recipients of the promises of God in the Old Testament; it was open to all mortals who would humble themselves and repent!

But what were the four commands that make up the conditional part of this promise in 2 Chronicles 7:14? Each needs to be investigated in turn.

1. The Call to Humble Ourselves

The first command God gave to those whom he called his people was for them to "humble [themselves]," just as 1 Peter 5:6 teaches: "Humble yourselves under God's mighty hand. . . ." The verb to "humble" ourselves (Hebrew *kana'*) appears 36 times in the Old Testament. But half of those uses exhibit sacred or spiritual instances of the verb, with Chronicles using 14 of the 18 instances with this meaning. It signified the act of bringing oneself low before our Lord. Biblical humility, then, was a modesty which replaced vanity, pride, and arrogance. Thus, the humble person was not one who was wise in his or her own eyes, for they recognized that all that they had was indeed received from the Lord (1 Cor 4:7). The humble person turned to God with a contrite and receptive heart.

So important was this imperative verb that its illustrations in the book of Chronicle form a literary stylistic form known as an "inclusion," wherein King Rehoboam, Solomon's son, who followed him on the throne of David in 931 B.C., belatedly "humbled himself" (2 Chr 12:6, 7 [2x]) when he was already under attack from Pharaoh Shishak. Thus God gave him "some" relief even after the year 925 B.C., when Shishak had carted off what we estimate to be about 130 tons of Solomon's gold from Judah!

At the other end of Judah's 345-year occupation in the land (931–586) was the new, eight-year-old King Josiah, who began to reign in 640 B.C., ruled for thirty-one years, and who likewise "humbled himself," especially when he heard the word of God read to him for the first time after that word was found in a temple cleaning event in 621 B.C. (2 Chr 34:27). His grandfather, King Manasseh, had ruled for over 50 years; however, he did not humble himself until he was almost at the end of his days (2 Chr 33:12, 19). Neither did King Amon, Manasseh's son and the father of young Josiah, "humble himself" (2 Chr 33:23); however, Josiah did "humble himself," and thus he was richly blessed by God.

The second of the four commands instructed men and women to pray.

2. The Call to Pray

The Chronicler illustrates the second divine command, to "pray," by pointing to the actions of the Judean King Jehoshaphat in 2 Chronicles 20. Jehoshaphat was a godly, pious, and successful leader of the nation, even though his weakness, which he unfortunately exhibited repeatedly, was to join with the forces of unrighteousness without first consulting the Lord for wisdom. He would first act and then seek the counsel of God!

At one point in his reign, Jehoshaphat was confronted by three nations that vastly outnumbered his army and his ability to cope with them (2 Chr 20:1–30). As the people of Judah came together to seek help from the Lord, the king took the lead by standing up before the people of Judah in front of the new courtyard of the temple in Jerusalem, where he began to pray. The entire population—the men, their wives, and their children, including even their little ones (20:13)—gathered together and listened as their king led them in prayer.

His prayer acknowledged that God alone rules on the basis of his ancient promise to the Jewish patriarchs, for all power and might were in his hands, therefore "no one [could] withstand" him (20:6)—not anyone, not even the three kings who were confronting Judah. What is more, God delighted to do exactly as he promised, i.e., give the land to the nation as Israel's home forever (20:7–11), for had he not said as much to his "friend Abraham" (Gen 17; 2 Chr 20:7; and in James 2:23; Isa 41:8 where he also was called the "friend" of God)? Thus, God would judge all attackers against Judah and King Jehoshaphat (2 Chr 20:12). This attack by these three nations of Moab, Ammon, and the Meunites, moreover, had been unprovoked. Therefore the eyes of faith in Israel would be on the Lord. This would be the solution: all who trusted in the Lord and called on him in prayer would be delivered by the hand of God.

All of this dependence on a supernatural deliverance may seem fantastic and unreal. Some doubters might have felt similarly about the way Israel went about bringing down the walls of Jericho. Was the strategy used in Joshua's day likewise too hard to believe? Skeptics must consider a similar, but more contemporary, miracle that took place in Leipzig, Germany, after World War II. Today, at the St. Nicholas Church (founded in AD 1165), stands a memorial to what happened on that very spot on October 9, 1989.

To get the context for this event, back up in time to August 13, 1961, when the Communist part of the recently divided city of Berlin began construction on the Berlin Wall to separate the East Germans from the western part of the city. From 1961, fast forward to June 12, 1987, when the President of the

United States, Ronald Reagan, stood at the Brandenburg Gate in Germany and demanded, "Mr. Gorbachev, open this gate. Tear down this wall." An even earlier proclamation by another US President, John F. Kennedy, on June 26, 1963, had about the same effect: nothing happened! Both proclamations by both presidents, along with all the United States' foreign policy, did little to tear down the Berlin Wall and bring the two Germanys together.

However, a prayer meeting begun by Pastor Christian Fuhrer had been meeting every Monday for some seven years, and by then had more than two thousand people regularly attending and praying to God for his divine intervention. Yes, government spies had infiltrated the meeting, and the pastor had once been left in the snow to die as his punishment for fomenting trouble. Some church members had indeed lost their jobs and were punished, but their places in the prayer meeting (which they had vacated) were quickly filled by the younger generation, who joined in their prayers to God for relief from this wall that divided the two Germanys. This group had no political agenda—their prayer was only that God would intervene and remove the Berlin Wall. This little-remembered prayer meeting culminated in a peaceful protest on October 9, 1989.

On that night, almost the entire town of one hundred thousand Leipzig citizens joined the two thousand prayer warriors carrying candles as they led a march in their streets. The East German military was prepared for a head-on conflict with riot gear, rifles, and tanks lined up on one side of the street. It must be recalled that only months before this, the Chinese government had put down a student protest in Tiananmen Square. Thus, the Germans were ready to face anything—except prayer and candles. The two thousand prayer warriors began to offer the East German army their candles and, amazingly, the soldiers began to take them, dropping their weapons to take the lights into their hands.

The next week the general of the German army, General Henecker, resigned his post. Four weeks later, on November 9, 1989, the Soviet authorities in charge of East Germany announced the Berlin Wall no longer guarded the people: they were free to leave the eastern sector if they wished. People began tearing down the wall and poured through to meet their West German relatives. God had intervened and once again the wall had come down—by prayer offered to Almighty God—just as Jericho's walls had fallen in an earlier time!

Today, a tower stands in front of the Leipzig Church. On that tower are inscribed palm branches, the symbol of peace. It stands as a testimony to the fact that God answers prayer.

The third imperative of the four calls us to seek the face of our Lord.

3. Seek My Face

This command is one of the favorite expressions of the Chronicler: "to seek him" or "to seek his face" (2 Chr 14:4, 7 [2x], 15:2, 4, 12, 13, 15; 16:2) as well as the parallel term "to rely on the Lord" (14:11; 16:7, 8). This principle motif of the Chronicler called for a revulsion against sin, a refusal to rely on anything other than the Lord, and a wholehearted desire to follow the Lord.

To illustrate the call to "seek the face of the Lord," the writer used the life and experiences of the Davidic relative, King Asa. But what was unusual about the national revival during King Asa's time was the fact that it did not follow a period of religious decline, but a time of reformation instead. Contrary to most revivals, where a time of spiritual refreshment and renewal would come after a time of national adversity, calamity, or deep moral decline, this revival had a different type of origin. When King Asa ascended the throne, a spiritual reformation was already in progress. The law of God was heeded and an active campaign against idolatry was being enforced. As a matter of fact, this reform movement went on for fifteen years before the revival actually arrived, even though it was taking place in the year of 896 B.C., some thirty-five years after the division of the kingdom (into Israel and Judah) and the death of King Solomon in 931 B.C.

During this time, King Asa actively pursued all that was good and right in the eyes of the Lord (14:2). He assailed pagan idolatry with a vengeance as he tore down foreign altars, smashed sacred stones, and cut down the poles erected to the goddess Asherah (14:3–4). Accordingly, God blessed the country with unusual prosperity. Construction was evident all over the land, with new walls, new towers, and new gates going up to secure the land on all sides (14:6–7). Even when the threat came from Zerah, the Ethiopian, and Judah was completely outnumbered, King Asa confidently called on the name of the Lord, and the Lord granted him a national victory in these extraordinary circumstances. Thus, Asa illustrates the importance of the concept that described him exactly: "he sought the Lord," a phrase that was used 9 times in the 48 verses describing his reign (14:4, 7 [2x]; 15:2, 4, 12–13, 15; 16:12).

Some may ask: What does it mean to seek the Lord? Seeking can be described in both a negative and positive manner. For example, to take the negative form first, Leviticus 19:31 shows that "seeking out" mediums or wizards can defile a person. Not seeking the Lord would be evidence that someone was disqualified from being a member of the community of faith. The positive illustration reveals that to seek God was equivalent to a summons to repentance as Amos 5:4–6 urged: "Seek me and live." This can also be seen in 1 Chronicles 16:11 (cf. Ps 105:4 NKJV)—"Seek the LORD and His strength; Seek His face evermore." One of the best texts with this expression is Jeremiah 29:12–13, "You will seek me and find me when you seek me with all your heart" (cf. Isa 55:6–7 NIV). God used these same verses from Jeremiah to call Charles Finney, the great revivalist of the nineteenth century, to come to faith in Christ. Finney dropped his plans to be a lawyer and called this nation to repentance instead!

The final appeal was for believers to turn from their wicked ways.

4. Return to the Lord

One of the most sudden revivals in the history of such works of God came in King Hezekiah's time. He had just begun his work as a reforming leader, hardly one month into his reign as the Davidic king of Judah. Within two months, however, the whole land was overcome with a beautiful spiritual enthusiasm. Surely, this suddenness, with the genuine fervor it raised, could only be attributed to the special visitation of a surprising work from God. Of course, one could not attribute such a positive historical influence to King Hezekiah's father, King Ahaz, for his sixteen years as leader epitomized the essence of evil. It may be said with some confidence that Ahaz had done more to poison the spiritual life of the nation than few others, if any (2 Chr 28:1–27). Ahaz's worship of Baal was bad enough, but combine that with burning his children as a sacrifice to Molech (28:3), and one has a sure recipe for unspeakable carnality, sensuality, and evil.

If he had such an evil father, where did Hezekiah get his spiritual leanings from? Is it possible to blame some of our failures in the spiritual realm on our parentage and upbringing, or must we give an account for our own failures before God? Certainly, Hezekiah did not have the heritage of a godly father, yet he still served God exclusively and wholeheartedly.

In fact, no word typifies all sixteen writing prophets more than the Hebrew word *shuv*, "to turn," "return"—the OT word for "repentance"! Zechariah 1:3 summarized all the prophets who had preceded him (and he was the next to last prophet), saying, "Return to me, says the LORD." He claimed that this was exactly what the former prophets had urged as well: "Return to the LORD." This "turning" called for a 180 degree reversal in the direction one was headed. I heard a pastor once get so excited as he taught this truth that he went a bit overboard in his excitement. He urged, "Brethren, we need to turn back to the Lord, we need to turn 360 degrees!" Actually 180 degrees will be just fine!

If we want our Lord to turn to us, we must turn to him with an unqualified trust and belief (2 Chr 30:6). If we want to avoid becoming despicable, we need to turn to God with a wholehearted obedience (30:7). If we want to avoid being the objects of his anger, we need to turn to him with glad service (30:8). And if we want to experience his favor, presence, and blessing, we need to turn to our God with unceasing prayer (30:9).

5. The Promised Results

Once again, let us address the fear that the promised results listed in 2 Chronicles 7:14c are limited to the Jewish people of that former day, when God said, "Then I will hear from heaven, and I will forgive their sin and will heal their land" (NIV).

The results promised here are relevant to all repenting peoples on earth. Consider, for example, the instruction that God gave to the prophet Jeremiah, telling him to go down and visit the potter's house in Jeremiah 18. As the prophet watched the potter work with the clay on the wheel, something happened that caused the potter to interrupt his work. Something was wrong in the lump of clay, but not with the potter; the clay might have been too wet, too dry, or it might have picked up a piece of grit mixed in with the clay. Surprisingly, the potter did not swipe that batch of clay off the flat surface of the wheel he was working on with a complaint that you just can't get good clay anymore. No, he took the *same* lump of clay and *remade it*, after he removed the offending cause. God immediately attached a principle to what Jeremiah had just seen. This was what the word of God taught the prophet Jeremiah, not only about Israel but also about any nation or kingdom in any historical period:

> "Can I not do with you Israel, as the potter does?" declares the LORD. "Like clay in the hand of the potter, so are you in my hand, Israel. If at any time I announce that a nation or kingdom is to be uprooted, torn down, and destroyed, and if that nation I warned repents of its evil, then will I relent and not inflict on it the disaster I had planned. And if at another time I announce that a nation or a kingdom is to be built up and planted, and if it does not obey me, then I will reconsider the good I had intended to do for it."

So it is important to notice that our Lord began with the nation of Israel, which he mentions twice in the beginning of this quotation from Jeremiah 18:8–10, but then he quickly shaped it into a general policy that covered all nations and kingdoms—and apparently in all times of history! Because our Lord is sovereign over all nations and kingdoms, he uses the same principles in governing and judging them all. Thus, the same principle is especially true during times calling for revival in any of those nations!

This is the reason why the interpreter must not treat the instructions in the Old Testament that come from the Lord as if they were addressed strictly and exclusively to Israel. There is no limiting context to suggest that fact.

Who can hear our cries for help like our Lord? Who can forgive sin like our God? Who can heal even the land overloaded with sin and guilt except the Lord, who rules over it all? As a matter of fact, had not the prophet Haggai taught the same truth concerning the land? Before the people returned to building the second temple again, after an unplanned hiatus of sixteen years, the prophet asked if they noticed how they were planting more but harvesting less; how they were eating more, but enjoying it less; how often they were drinking more, but staying thirsty; or even how they were wearing more clothes, but still feeling cold. They were also earning more, but seemingly they were putting the increase in a purse or wallet that had holes in it (Hag 1:5–6). But when they turned to the Lord in obedience twenty-four days later as they got started on rebuilding the temple, the drought God had called on the work of their hands (Hag 1:11), and on all the labor of their arms, changed with the blessing of God. Wasn't that also a healing of their land? This is another reason why God calls for revival in our times as well.

Conclusions

1. The thesis and theology of 2 Chronicles is fairly stated and summarized in the programmatic verse of 2 Chronicles 7:14. It is time we and our nation turned back to God!

2. This divine response to Solomon's prayer of dedication for the temple opened the avenue of restoration for a revitalization of life in the Spirit with God, not only for the nation of Israel, but for all whom God had called by his name among the nations of the world.

3. Five Judean Davidic kings illustrated the blessings that await all of the people of God anywhere in space or time, if they too rely on him and act favorably on his four commands.

4. God promises that he will respond to repentance, forgiving the sins of his people and acting to heal their lands wherever they are.

2

THE LONG ROOTS OF AFFECTIVE PIETY IN EARLY NEW ENGLAND

Adrian Chastain Weimer

The colonists of early New England believed it was possible to generate a map of the soul. Along with English Puritans, they developed a rich language, a sophisticated lexicon, for talking about the interior life. Puritan vocabularies for the heart undergirded at least two hundred years of American Protestant devotional life. They were indispensible to the awakenings of the eighteenth century.

For these zealous reformers, spiritual health was something that could be assessed and measured. This measurement was not in a strict sense empirical. Yet, there were ways to measure affect, to discern whether the heart was hot or cold, to see in which direction it was oriented—toward God or toward idols.

"Affective piety" is about the transformation of the heart, but it is not limited to the emotions. Puritans understood that feelings come and go. More than emotions, affections are the overall orientation of the soul, the deepest longings of the heart, understanding, and will together. The Puritan language of affective piety, a language of experience and discernment, was refined by ministers and laypeople throughout the seventeenth century.

Some of the most crucial periods for the development of the language of affective piety in New England were the 1630s, when many new churches were being formed; the 1660s, when a new generation of devotional manuals gained popularity; and the 1680s and 1690s, when churches were revitalized through covenant renewals.

Migration Experiences

The first group of immigrants to Massachusetts Bay often expressed utter relief that they could worship freely. Back in England, Archbishop

William Laud was driving Puritan ministers out of the Church of England and the universities. Puritans had agonized over the decision of whether to stay in England as suffering witnesses, or to flee. Many decided that it was better to be useful than rot in prison. When they arrived in the New World, colonists were immensely relieved at being able to worship with liberty. They were hungry for good preaching. In the new towns cropping up around Salem and Boston in the 1630s, people flocked to godly sermons.

A layperson named Roger Clap from Dorchester, Massachusetts, left a testimony of these early years. He wrote,

> The Lord Jesus Christ was so plainly held out in the Preaching of the Gospel unto poor lost Sinners, and the absolute Necessity of the *New Birth*, and God's holy Spirit in those Days was pleased to accompany the Word with such Efficacy upon the Hearts of many; that our Hearts were taken off from *Old-England* and set upon *Heaven*.[5]

Clap noted with some surprise that people were not talking about how hard life was in the colonies, wishing for the comforts of England. Some emigrants did go home, but many instead were asking,

> *How shall we go to heaven? Have I true grace wrought in my heart?* . . . O how did Men and Women, young and old, Pray for Grace, beg for *Christ* in those Days; and it was not in vain: Many were Converted, and others established in Believing: many joined unto the several Churches where they lived, confessing their Faith publickly, and shewing before all the Assembly their Experiences of the Workings of God's Spirit in their Hearts to bring them to *Christ*: which many Hearers found very much Good by. . . . Oh the many Tears that have been shed in *Dorchester* Meeting-House at such times, both by those that have declared God's Work on their Souls, and also by those that heard them. In those days, *God, even our own God*, did *Bless* New-England.[6]

The excitement of the early years was marked by vivid preaching, intense prayer, spiritual searching, and tears. Clap notes that participation was multigenerational. People who had been going to church their whole lives experienced religion in a new way. The fervor was sustained by testimonies. People told the story of their own experiences of the Holy Spirit in a way that had a profound effect on others.

These religious experiences were not uniform, however. Clap listened carefully to these public testimonies. He continued on to say, "God doth

---

[5] Roger Clap, *Memoirs of Capt. Roger Clap* (Boston, 1731), 4. While, as some scholars have noted, Clap's narrative was written later in his life, there is no compelling reason to doubt its authenticity.

[6] Clap, *Memoirs*, 4–5.

work divers ways upon the Hearts of Men, even as it pleases him; upon some more sensibly, and upon others more insensibly; verifying that Text [John 3:8] . . . *The Wind bloweth where it listeth . . . So is every one that is born of the Spirit.*" Clap knew that the Spirit had come, but was reluctant to systematize its work. He admitted that his own experience of grace did not happen in a discrete moment—he could not name "the Time when, the Place where, the manner how" as some other colonists could.[7] Yet he knew the Spirit was working, and rejoiced.

Thomas Shepard and the Parable of the Ten Virgins

As Clap, a layperson, attempted to explain the workings of the Holy Spirit in the 1630s, Thomas Shepard, one of the most learned men in the colonies, undertook a similar task. Shepard was one of those ministers silenced by Archbishop William Laud in England. Laud told him, "Spare your breath; I will have no such fellows prate in my diocese."[8] Shepard's own spiritual life had been a rocky one, but when Laud suspended him from the ministry, his faith solidified. Unemployed for a time, he found refuge among Puritan nobility, but eventually had to go into hiding in England. He came to the New World in 1635, at age 30. He was quickly chosen as minister of Cambridge, Massachusetts.

An accomplished mentor, Shepard influenced a whole generation of Harvard seminarians. He expected a great deal of himself as a spiritual guide. He later advised his son in the ministry to

> emprove your own meditations for the drawing up the heads of your sermon before you consult any authour that treats upon that text or subject. So that you may make experiment of the serviceableness, & faithfullness of your own Judgment.[9]

It is reasonable to assume that Shepard was praying and meditating over the biblical texts he preached on, and practicing the methods he described.

Shepard's sermons reflecting on the religious excitement of the 1630s were based on the biblical parable of the ten virgins. He preached them on lecture days, which were mid-week gatherings, between 1636 and 1640. He was responding to a radical spiritist movement, the Antinomians, led by Anne Hutchinson, whom he considered dangerously unorthodox. He was

---

[7] Clap, *Memoirs*, 5–6.

[8] Michael McGiffert, *God's Plot: Puritan Spirituality in Thomas Shepard's Cambridge* (Amherst: University of Massachusetts Press, 1994), 51n23.

[9] John Sparhawk Ms. Notebook, American Antiquarian Society, Worcester, Massachusetts.

also responding to the needs of laypeople like Roger Clap, who were trying to interpret their experiences.

Shepard's *Ten Virgin* sermons were considered a model of mapping the heart in their own time and for at least the next four generations. Jonathan Mitchell, also a Cambridge pastor, introduced the work in its printed version in 1660:

> why should we not desire and hope that the sutable solemn counsels and warnings here given to these Churches by this *Seer in Israel*, in reference to the main matters of life and godlinesse, may now be of living, awakening and soul-instructing use to them (Oh that it may be!) unto many Generations![10]

In the next century, Jonathan Edwards would turn more often to Shepard than any other author. Of Shepard's works, *Ten Virgins* was Edwards' favorite.[11]

Ten Virgins is essentially a treatise about mapping the heart, a method for recognizing true Christian experience. Its driving question is: how can we discern the work of the Holy Spirit from its counterfeits? In the middle of this fervent time, when churches were being founded and men and women were having intense experiences of grace, Shepard knew it was important that his flock have a way of talking about affective piety. He wanted to help people discern between true piety that flowed from the Spirit, and shallow piety that was disconnected from the source. He wanted to help people understand their hearts.

According to Shepard, affections were central to true piety. The deep desires of the heart, for a Christian, would be oriented toward God. Christians are in trouble, he wrote, when they "confess sin without sorrow or shame, petition without thirsting, live without love, do without life, because there is no spring, but a dry heart within."[12] Yet spirit-generated piety and self-generated piety could look very similar. Those operating in their own power could have a moral conscience; they could have good theological knowledge; they could get caught up in the good news of the gospel. The mark of a true Christian, for Shepard, was "satisfying grace, or that grace which brings them to full rest, and satisfying sweetness in God, not only to their consciences but to their hearts; not carnal, but spiritual." Some of Shepherd's writing is so dense it reads best as verse. He meditates on this grace that satisfies:

---

[10] Jonathan Mitchell, Epistle to the Reader, in Thomas Shepard, *The parable of the ten virgins* (London, 1660), A3v.

[11] John Smith, "Introduction," in *Jonathan Edwards: Religious Affections* (New Haven: Yale University Press, 1959), 54.

[12] Thomas Shepard, *The parable of the ten virgins opened & applied* (London, 1660), I:177.

If ye eat my flesh and drink my blood, there is life,
if not, no life
eating and drinking, is not sipping and tasting
many may eat and drink in his presence . . .
but yet not feed at all on his person
this makes the soul glad in God,
and in all the days of his life;
where any creature is at rest,
there it is in the proper place;
it is a token the Lord is the proper place of the soul . . .
when it is at rest there;
and this is the last end, and fruit of the redemption of Christ . . .
so satiate as not to desire other things, but there to stay,
though the heart doth oft feel not the same sweetness.[13]

Satisfying grace means feeding on Christ and resting in Christ. Shepard knows that feelings are fleeting. Yet paying attention to the deep desires of the heart is a path to discernment.

If someone were to ask Shepard, *what can people do to encourage this kind of resting, satisfying grace?* he might say: "Look that you make your Vessels clear. It hath been said of old, and I beleeve tis a truth still, that the Lord will never send his Spirit to dwell in an unclean heart. Doves build not their habitations on dunghills."[14] Shepard reminded his hearers over and over again: not taking sin seriously enough, not feeling sin as "exceeding bitter," would truncate the spiritual life. And by sin he meant primarily greed—not caring for orphans and widows. The best way to know if hearts are clean is to "look to their love to the people of God."[15] Those who are filled and satisfied with God have love to pour onto their neighbors. Right knowledge is inseparable from purity of life and abundant affection for those in need.

Signs of Grace

This concern for discerning true affective piety from its counterfeits also appears in lists of signs of grace found in Puritan diaries. These lists of signs or marks of grace were treasured and passed down in families. One that survives is by the concordance writer Samuel Newman, who lost his teaching position under Archbishop Laud and fled to Rehoboth, Massachusetts.[16] His marks of grace assess the affections, the heart's deepest desires and fears.

---

[13] Shepard, *Parable of the ten virgins*, II:81.
[14] Shepard, *Parable of the ten virgins*, I:226.
[15] Shepard, *Parable of the ten virgins*, II:84.
[16] David Wilson, "Samuel Newman," *Oxford Dictionary of National Biography Online.*

I find I Love, and desire to Love God principally and for Himselfe
A desire to requite & power in some measure to reward evill with good
A Looking up to god to see Him and his hand in all things that befall Mee
A greater fear of displeasing god than all the World
A Love to such Christians I never saw or received any good from[17]

The language of affective piety in these marks of grace is typical of the first generation of Puritans in New England.

Samuel Newman acknowledged he found these signs in himself in "weak measure." He did not have an easy time as minister of Rehoboth. Cotton Mather called him a man of "invincible patience" who "held out, under the scandalous neglect and contempt of the ministry" (this probably means his congregation did not pay his salary on time). However, in Cotton Mather's glowing formulation, "[h]e loved his church as if it had been his family, and he taught his family, as if it had been his church."[18] Newman and his family set aside annual times for fasting, self-examination, and thanksgiving. Newman's marks of grace, a method for mapping the soul, were treasured by his grandson John Sparhawk. As a young minister in Bristol (at that point part of Massachusetts), Sparhawk copied them over in his diary, and may have used them himself.

Church Membership

In the period between the 1630s and the 1680s, church membership did not stagnate. It increased, as it has in almost every period of American history. Our best studies of church membership in early New England show that over the long term it was cyclical—there were regular times of lower affiliation and then regular times when people came back in more numbers. We also know that most people joined the church after the birth of their first child. The main exceptions to the cyclical pattern were the 1630s and the 1740s (the Great Awakening), when numbers increased dramatically, and the revolutionary era, when numbers dropped significantly, though the drop seems to persist only for men.[19] However, there is also an important, if smaller, increase in

---

[17] Sparhawk Ms. Notebook.

[18] Cotton Mather, *Magnalia Christi Americana* (London, 1702), III: 114.

[19] Edwin Scott Gaustad and Philip L. Barlow, *New Historical Atlas of Religion in America* (NY: Oxford University Press, 2001), 7–9; David D. Hall and Anne S. Brown, "Family Strategies and Religious Practices" in *Lived Religion in America: Toward a History of Practice* (Princeton, NJ: Princeton University Press, 1997), 41–68; Harry Stout and Catherine Breckus, "Declension, Gender, and the 'New Religious History'" in *Belief and Behavior: Essays in the New Religious History*, ed. Philip R. Vandermere and Robert P. Swierenga (Brunswick:

church membership in the 1680s and 1690s. How then did people living in a time between phases of more rapid church growth respond to their situations?

Ministers in the 1650s and 1660s were concerned that the children and grandchildren of the first generation were not having the same kinds of intense experiences that their grandparents had undergone. They were not coming forward to join the church in the same numbers. In 1662, the ministers met together in order to think about ways to awaken the church. They came up with the idea of the half-way covenant, which simply said that the grandchildren of full church members could be baptized. So even if their parents had not been able to speak about a transformative experience of grace, the children would not be penalized. It was a way of making the church more welcoming to young people.

The half-way covenant was a plan by the ministers, and at first most laypeople were not on board. It took a few decades before congregations started to participate, and to see real change. In the meantime, people who cared about the church made sure that the culture was saturated with good books—lively, awakening books.

Awakening Books

One of the bestsellers of the 1660s and 1670s was the English devotional writer John Flavel's *A Saint Indeed*. The book claimed to be "a seasonable and proper expedient for the recovery of the much decayed power of godliness." In Flavel's preface to the work, he quoted the great medieval preacher Bernard of Clairvaux, "in reading Books, regard not so much the science as the savour."[20] There were some books that were technically orthodox, but deadening. Puritans recognized that books like Flavel's had the savor of life, serving as a vehicle for spiritual power.

Flavel's treatise was an often-used guide to mapping the heart. Its advice was based on Proverbs 4:23: "Keep thy Heart with all diligence, for out of it are the Issues of Life." Like Shepard, Flavel defined the heart not so much as emotions as "the seat of Principles, and fountain of Actions." Also like Shepard, he was concerned with the problem of how to nurture authentic Christian experience and how to discern hypocrisy. By hypocrisy, Flavel

---

Rutgers University Press, 1991), 15–37; Robert G. Pope, *The Half-way Covenant: Church Membership in Puritan New England* (Princeton, NJ: Princeton University Press, 1969); Gerald F. Moran, " 'Sisters' in Christ: Women and the Church in Seventeenth-Century New England," in *Women in American Religion,* ed. Janet Wilson James (Philadelphia: University of Pennsylvania Press, 1980), 47–65.

[20] John Flavel, *A Saint Indeed* (London, 1668), A8r-A8v.

meant both those who think they are Christians but are not, and those Christians who cause harm to the gospel by sinning. "The greatest difficulty in Conversion," he wrote, "is to win the heart to God, and the greatest difficulty after Conversion is to keep the heart with God. Here lies the very pinch and stress of Religion." *A Saint Indeed* was mean to provide "Direction and help in this great work" of winning hearts and keeping them with God.[21]

Flavel insisted that keeping hearts with God involved both "means and duties"—a consistent program of spiritual exercises involving reading, meditation, prayer, holy conversation, and acts of charity. Only ongoing diligence would keep people from sinning, and "maintain" the soul's "sweet and free communion with God."[22] In Flavel's diagnosis, each aspect of self-orientation had a corresponding spiritual prescription.

> *Self dependence* is removed by Faith
> *Self-love,* by the love of God
> *Self will,* by subjection and obedience to the Will of God
> *Self-seeking,* by self-denyal
> The darkned understanding is again illuminated . . .
> The refractory will sweetly subdued . . .
> The rebellious appetite . . . gradually conquered
> And thus the Soul which sin had universally depraved,
> Is again by grace restored. . . .[23]

Flavel said that deep, affective piety involved self-examination or "self-conference" and "frequent observation of the frame of the heart." Those who could not map their interior worlds had reason to worry about their spiritual lives. He reflected with sadness, "there are some men and women that have lived forty or fifty years in the world, and have scarce had one hours discourse with their own hearts." Flavel insisted that Christians needed to keep track of the state of their hearts like accountants keep track of their bank accounts. Self-examination involved both repentance and petitions: "deep humiliations for heart evils and disorders" and "earnest Supplications . . . for heart-purifying and rectifying Grace."[24] In the middle of writing his treatise he broke out into prayer:

> Oh, for a better heart!
> Oh, for a heart to love God more!
> To hate Sin more,
> To walk more evenly with God

---

[21] Ibid., 1.
[22] Ibid., 3.
[23] Ibid., 8.
[24] Ibid., 8–11.

Lord deny not to me such a heart,
What ever thou deny me;
Give me an heart to fear thee,
Love and delight in thee
If I beg my bread in desolate places.[25]

Manuals like Flavel's were the most common reading for New Englanders in the 1660s and 1670s.

Another popular manual was William Dyer's *A Cabinet of Jewels*. The title might sound like it is holding out a promise of wealth for the godly, but that couldn't be further from the truth. If Max Weber had read a few more Puritan sermons, he would have known that individual wealth was almost never linked with God's favor or personal salvation. Dyer's jewels, rather, were twenty things that people could do to invite the Holy Spirit to awaken their hearts. The list, predictably, begins with repentance and moves on to desire:

Loath Sin, and leave Sin
Put off the old man, and put on the new man.
Make your peace with the Prince of Peace. . . .
Desire better hearts, more than better times.
Grow downward in humility, and inward in sincerity.
Do good to those that be good.[26]

In this last jewel Dyer is referring particularly to charity for Christians who are suffering in prison, persecuted, or oppressed. Incredibly popular, Dyer's text went through eighteen printings in the later seventeenth century. The ability to speak the language of affective piety, to evaluate one's spiritual experience, was expected of laypeople as well as ministers.

Heart Language and the Rising Generation

Increasingly, as attention turned to teenagers and twenty-somethings who were not joining the church as full members, people wondered: were they able to speak this language of the heart? Were Christian knowledge and Christian desire something young people could articulate? One pastor in Chelmsford, John Fiske, decided to find out. Fiske's own life was marked by tragedy—his mother had died on the voyage to New England, and then his wife went blind. However, he had an extraordinary commitment to his flock.

---

[25] Ibid., 12.
[26] William Dyer, *A Cabinet of Jewels* (Boston, 1704), 192–220.

When he was recruited from Wenham to Chelmsford in 1654, the majority of his church decided to move with him.[27] Fiske left a remarkable journal chronicling the history of the church for the later seventeenth century.

The journal deals mostly with run-of-the-mill issues of organization and discipline—church members insulting each other, adultery, people forgetting to pay their tithes, escaped cows eating up neighbors' gardens. However, the records for 1663 show that Fiske's church voted that he should interview all the children in the town about their "knowledge of the doctrine of faith" and also about their "experiences" of faith. And he was supposed to start with his own family (!). Fiske's children got mixed reviews—Sarah passed with flying colors; John Jr. "merely as to understanding." Youth in other families ranged from "very loathe" to "very ignorant" to "more in the letter as to understanding" to "competent upon his desire."[28] The interviews demonstrate a shared expectation that young people had a vocabulary with which to talk about their hearts. Interestingly, Fiske found that the young people appreciated his attention to their spiritual journeys.

The 1670s were stained by the devastation of King Philip's War, in which many towns were burned to the ground, and the native tribes of southern New England were all but wiped out. It was a gruesome war, and to many of the clergy it was clear that the colonists were far from innocent. As congregations focused on rebuilding their shattered churches, there were fast days to repent of atrocities committed during battle, and to seek God's will going forward. Fiske's interviews were an important precedent for a practice associated with fast days that would become the hallmark of the 1680s and 1690s: covenant renewals.

Covenant Renewals

Covenant renewals represented a new urgency about connecting with young people. They involved a series of preparations. First, a church would do the kinds of interviews that John Fiske engaged in. Then they would hold special classes, usually with a freshly written catechism, in order to help young people develop an understanding of doctrine and Christian experience. Then they invited the youth (and anyone else) to participate in

---

[27] Wilson Waters, *History of Chelmsford, Massachusetts* (Lowell, Mass., 1917), 17.

[28] John Fiske, *The Notebook of the Reverend John Fiske, 1644–1675*, ed. Robert G. Pope (Boston: Colonial Society of Massachusetts, 1974), 187. Eleazer Mather is another example of a minister actively concerned about his congregation's aptitude for heart religion and capacity to be "affected by the gravity or joy of the Gospel promises." Philip F. Gura, "Preparing the Way for Stoddard: Eleazer Mather's Serious Exhortation to Northampton," *The New England Quarterly*, Vol. 57, No. 2 (Jun., 1984), 245.

a covenant renewal ceremony. This was a special part of the fast day service when people came forward to sign a covenant. Covenants were newly written documents which said, in summary, "we will walk in God's ways" and "we will try to get along with each other."[29]

Norwich, Connecticut and Plymouth held successful covenant renewals in 1676. In 1678, the Commissioners of United Colonies recommended a fast day to be held by all the colonies in order to pray that "a spirit of conversion may be poured out upon our children, that they may give up themselves and their seed after them to be the Lord's, willingly subjecting themselves to all his holy rules and government in his house."[30] When the Massachusetts ministers met in a synod, later called the Reforming Synod, in 1679, they decided that covenant renewals might be a way to awaken the church. They agreed that they should be promoted throughout the colony.

Covenant renewals were understood as preparation rather than manipulation. Only the Spirit could change hearts:

> Inasmuch as a thorough and heart Reformation is necessary, in order to obtaining peace with God, Jer. 3. 10. and all outward means will be ineffectual unto that end, except the Lord pour down his Spirit from on High, it doth therefore concern us to cry mightily unto God, both in ordinary and extraordinary manner, that he would be pleased to rain down Righteousness upon us. . . . Amen![31]

Increase Mather did the work of laying the theological foundation for covenant renewal ceremonies, looking mostly at the Old Testament. "[T]his renewal of Covenant" he wrote, "is the great Scripture expedient" for "Reformation among a professing people." Mather and many other ministers were convinced that in the Bible, covenant renewals were the way "any notable reformation was effected in the Church."[32]

---

[29] David D. Hall, *The Faithful Shepherd: A History of the New England Ministry in the Seventeenth Century* (Chapel Hill: Institute of Early American History and Culture/University of North Carolina Press, 1972), 243–44; Charles Hambrick-Stowe, *The Practice of Piety: Puritan Devotional Disciplines in Seventeenth-century New England* (Institute of Early American History and Culture/ University of North Carolina Press, 1982), 130–32. Hambrick-Stowe notes that Fiske and others had practiced covenant renewals earlier in the century. However they became a widespread practice in the 1680s.

[30] David Pulsifer, ed., *Records of the Colony of New Plymouth in New England* (Boston, 1859), X: 398–99.

[31] Boston Synod, The necessity of reformation with the expedients subservient thereunto . . . Agreed upon by the elders and messengers of the churches assembled in the Synod at Boston in New-England (Boston, 1679), 15.

[32] Increase Mather, *Renewal of covenant the great duty incumbent on decaying or distressed churches* (Boston, 1677), 10. Historians have debated whether covenant renewals were lay-driven or a ministerial initiative. It probably varied by region. See Paul Lucas, *Valley of Discord: Church and Society along the Connecticut River, 1636–1725* (Hanover, NH: University Press of New England, 1976), 90–95.

The fast day rituals with which covenant renewals were paired were already an important means of nurturing piety. Fast days happened on weekdays when people took off work and abstained from food until the later afternoon. The events involved corporate humiliation, or repentance, and intense expectation for the Holy Spirit to come with power.[33] Often multiple churches joined together, and the fasts were coordinated throughout colonies and even entire regions. Coming together for fast days was like a later revival meeting in many respects.

Covenant renewals often involved a commitment to more frequent celebration of the Lord's Supper. The later seventeenth century saw a revitalization of sacramental piety, piety focused on preparing for and meditating on the Eucharist.[34] Covenant renewals were not the same thing as joining the church. They provided a rite of passage, however, an intermediate step that often led to full church membership. And so a pattern of church growth developed through the 1680s and 1690s. In Hartford in 1695, 192 young people participated in a covenant renewal. Some were already full church members, but chose to renew their commitment in this way.[35] These covenant renewals helped younger people who did not have the same kind of religious experiences as their parents and grandparents, or who could not commit with the same certainty, take a step toward membership in the church.

The Great Awakening's Long Roots

The revivalists of the eighteenth century knew their history. They were deeply aware of the spirituality of the seventeenth century. Thomas Prince, one of the most important publicists of the Great Awakening, printed Roger Clap's memoirs describing the piety of the 1630s. Edwards also mentioned Clap's ecstatic experience of the Holy Spirit as a way of defending the eighteenth-century revivals. Prince also printed the "Meditations and Spiritual Experiences of Mr. Thomas Shepard" in 1747, asking the missionary David Brainerd to write the preface.[36] Brainerd thought Shepard's life

---

[33] See, for example, *On a day of publick fasting and prayer* (Boston, 1727), a reprinting of the 1680 Malden covenant renewal document; Mather, *Magnalia Christi Americana*, II: 332–33; William DeLoss Love, *The Fast and Thanksgiving Days of New England* (Boston: Houghton, Mifflin, 1895), 218–19.

[34] Lucas, *Valley of Discord*, 94; Hambrick-Stowe, *Practice of Piety*, 206–18; E. Brooks Holifield, *The Covenant Sealed: The Development of Puritan Sacramental Theology in Old and New England, 1570–1720* (New Haven: Yale University Press, 1974), chs 6–7.

[35] Lucas, *Valley of Discord*, 116.

[36] Charles Hambrick-Stowe, " 'The Spirit of the Old Writers': The Great Awakening and the Persistence of Puritan Piety" in Francis J. Bremer, ed. *Puritanism: Transatlantic Perspec-*

and work demonstrated "true Religion . . . in its own native Excellency, Worth, and Beauty." He knew that models were important for encouraging affective piety.

John Flavel was considered such an authority on affective piety that he was used on both sides of the debates on revivalism. Though Flavel had died in 1691, two opposing tracts printed in Boston in the early 1740s extracted parts of his works. Additionally, Edwards used a story from Flavel about a man who had an experience of "heavenly joys" so intense that he didn't know where he was for a time.[37] When Charles Chauncy, who opposed the revivals, rebutted Edwards point by point, he wouldn't touch Flavel: "The Account from Mr. Flavel," he wrote, "I leave as it stands."[38]

It is also important to notice the living figures who bridged the piety of the seventeenth and eighteenth centuries. When George Whitefield came to New England, he met Nathaniel Clap (unrelated to Roger Clap), one of the last of the generation of preachers who had come of age in the covenant renewal movement, and a great promoter of affective piety. Whitefield recalled that he was "the most venerable man I ever saw in my life. He looked like a good old Puritan, and gave me an idea of what stamp those men were, who first settled in New England. His countenance was very heavenly, and he prayed most affectionately for a blessing on my coming to Rhode Island.[39] Clap's affectionate prayers impressed even Whitefield.

Much more than the younger revivalists, Clap was the spiritual advisor to Susanna Anthony and Sarah Osborn, who spearheaded the Great Awakening in Newport.[40] Sarah Osborn wrote that she "went to hear Mr. Clap; who told me the very secrets of my heart in his sermon"—a crucial step in her spiritual journey.[41] At a moment of spiritual confusion, she finally asked Clap directly if she was a hypocrite. In Osborn's words, "he said, he never thought so; and put me upon renewing covenant engagements with God, and giving myself up to him *then;* and perhaps I should find I had done so

---

tives on a Seventeenth-Century Anglo-American Faith (Boston: Massachusetts Historical Society, 1993), 288–89.

[37] The Great Design and Scope of the Gospel Opened: An Extract from the Rev. Mr. Flavel's England's Duty (Boston, 1741); A Word to the Well-Wishers Of the Good Work of God in this Land (Boston, 1742); Jonathan Edwards, Some Thoughts Concerning the present Revival of Religion in New-England (Boston, 1742), 28–29.

[38] Chauncy continued, "with only saying that good Men may differ in their Sentiments as to the *Cause* of such *Effects.*" Chauncy, *Seasonable thoughts on the state of religion in New-England* (Boston, 1743), 92.

[39] George Whitefield, *Journals* (Edinburgh: Banner of Truth Trust, 1960), 452.

[40] Susanna Anthony, The life and character of Miss Susanna Anthony (Hartford, 1799), 4.

[41] Sarah Osborn, *Memoirs of the Life of Mrs. Sarah Osborn* (Worcester, 1799), 21. For an excellent treatment of Osborn's career, see Catherine Brekus, Sarah Osborn's World: The Rise of Evangelical Christianity in Early America (New Haven: Yale University Press, 2013).

before." Covenant renewals were still an important method for nurturing piety in the middle of the Great Awakening. Clap personally encouraged Osborn in her ministry to students and African-Americans.[42] Both Clap and Osborn's letters of spiritual counsel are rich manuals of affective piety.

Edwards and other eighteenth-century preachers inherited a sophisticated language of affective piety. The third part of Edwards' *Treatise on Religious Affections* consists of a list of signs of grace. These signs are remarkably similar to earlier lists such as Samuel Newman's. Edwards drew directly on Shepard for the idea that a small dose of self-manufactured religious intensity could be a spiritual disaster. Edwards also thought about affections in new ways. For him, true affections were exercises of the inclination or will, which were both sensible and vigorous—so vigorous that they could actually bring the self out of its indifference.[43]

Much of the culture of the Great Awakening—optimism about spiritual discernment, promoting books with the "savour of Life," sharing testimonies and models, communal gatherings for prayer and fasting, creativity in incorporating young people—have long roots in early New England. Seventeenth- and eighteenth-century Protestants experienced a continuous tension, a biblical tension, between waiting for the Spirit and actively preparing for the Spirit's arrival. Though their understanding was neither perfect nor complete, Puritans understood that ultimately it is the Spirit who awakens the church, and the Spirit who enables people to know their hearts.

[42] Osborn, *Memoirs*, 44, 63.
[43] Smith, "Introduction," 12.

3

Charles G. Finney and "The Second Great Awakening"

Charles E. Hambrick-Stowe

Charles G. Finney's *Memoirs* of his evangelistic career, published in 1876, the year after his death, effectively relaunched his ministry posthumously for generations to come. With the title *Autobiography of Finney* on the spine, the book was enormously successful, appearing in edition after edition and in many languages abroad throughout the following century. The well-worn copies on my bookshelf, salvaged from boxes in dusty church basements, testify to their wide distribution among general readers, who read them almost to tatters. Along with the enduring influence of his *Lectures on Revivals of Religion* (1835), the *Memoirs* secured Finney's reputation both as "the father of modern evangelism" and as a culminating figure in the period of American religious history known as "the Second Great Awakening."[1]

By their very nature, memoirs are an exercise in looking back in time with the conviction that the author's version of the past is somehow significant for the future. With the post-Civil War challenges of an aggressively expansionist, rapidly urbanizing, industrial America before them, and as the leaders of antebellum religious movements were coming to the end of their lives, colleagues felt with some urgency the need for Finney's own account of what they considered archetypal evangelistic work. Bowing to pressure to complete the project while he was still mentally and physically capable, Finney himself understood the purpose of the book as an effort to revive the spirit of the old revivals.[2] American society had changed a great

---

[1]Charles G. Finney, *Memoirs of Rev. Charles G. Finney, Written by Himself* (New York: A. S. Barnes & Company, 1876).

[2]In this sense, publication of Finney's *Memoirs* may be compared to Thomas Prince in the 1740s founding the evangelical periodical, *The Christian History*, to circulate archival material from the seventeenth century to inspire the work of revival by demonstrating that the new revivals stemmed from Puritan spirituality, that "the pious Principles and Spirit" of

deal in the fifty years since 1825 when Finney first made his mark, however. In order to shape the manuscript for modern readers, James Harris Fairchild, Finney's successor as president of Oberlin College, exercised a strong editorial hand. The Fairchild version served extraordinarily well as inspiration and guidance for generations of Protestants, ministers, and laity alike.

One could say further that, together with notable works of Jonathan Edwards from the Great Awakening of the eighteenth century, Finney's *Memoirs* and other writings on revival contributed to America's role in the creation of a global evangelical movement. Finney's influence abroad predated his first British tour by a decade, thanks to publication of a Welsh translation of his *Lectures on Revivals of Religion*. In 1840, letters of appreciation from clergy associations in Wales reported that the book, "under the blessing of God, has been the means of rousing the dormant energy of our churches." They went so far as to describe the recent awakening in that region as "Finney's Revival," suggesting that it could be "attributed in great measure to the reading of your works." Translations of Finney's sermons, lectures, and *Memoirs* were published in many editions in countries around the world, from the mid-nineteenth through the twentieth century. His influence spread through the work of missionaries as well, including scores of Oberlin graduates who served as missionaries in Africa, India, and East Asia. A sterling example of Finney's global impact is the fact that as a young man V. S. Azariah, the great Christian leader in India, co-authored with George Sherwood Eddy a biography of Finney in 1899 based on the *Memoirs*, and went on to translate portions of *Lectures on Revivals* into Tamil.[3]

Finney also lives in infamy, of course, as a foil or whipping boy for more conservative evangelicals of a strictly Calvinist bent. A quick internet search reveals the astonishing vehemence with which, even today, Finney is demonized in some quarters as the font of theological error, the source of much that's gone wrong with American Protestantism and evangelical Christianity generally.

---

the "Old Writers" were "at this Day revived" in the Great Awakening. You can find more of my work on this subject in Charles E. Hambrick-Stowe, "The Spirit of the Old Writers: The Great Awakening and the Persistence of Puritan Piety," in Francis J. Bremer, ed., *Puritanism: Transatlantic Perspectives on a Seventeenth-Century Anglo-American Faith* (Boston: Massachusetts Historical Society, 1993), 277–91.

[3] Charles G. Finney, *The Memoirs of Charles G. Finney: The Complete Restored Text*, ed. Garth M. Rosell and Richard A. G. Dupuis (Grand Rapids, MI: Zondervan Publishing House, 1989), 74–77. Charles E. Hambrick-Stowe, *Charles G. Finney and the Spirit of American Evangelicalism* (Grand Rapids, MI: William B. Eerdmans Publishing Co., 1996), 229. Susan Billington Harper, *In the Shadow of the Mahatma: Bishop V. S. Azariah and the Travails of Christianity in British India* (Grand Rapids, MI: William B. Eerdmans Publishing Co., 2000), 70.

In any case, it was not until the masterful annotated critical edition of Finney's complete original text by Garth M. Rosell and Richard A. G. Dupuis that Finney's narrative in his own words became fully available. The Rosell-Dupuis edition of *The Memoirs of Charles G. Finney* is essential for any new effort to understand Finney in relation to the revivals of his own day, their roots in the previous century, and their ongoing legacy.

Apart from perhaps a few of its first readers, the many who have been spiritually awakened, converted, called to ministry, or renewed in their sense of direction in ministry by means of reading the *Memoirs*, and then his other writings, never heard Finney preach. But in the imagination of countless readers his stirring voice, his direct delivery, his piercing gaze, and his compelling charisma have lived on. While not usually identifying themselves as "Finneyites" (a term employed in his lifetime as both badge of pride and vilifying epithet), those influenced by his example did typically go on to pray for and seek to replicate in their own time and place the experience of something like a Finney-style revival.

As a legendary "father of modern evangelism," Finney has commonly been portrayed as the first in a string of American revivalists in succeeding generations, most notably Dwight L. Moody, Billy Sunday, and Billy Graham, among scores of lesser lights. That was certainly the view of Lewis A. Drummond, whose somewhat hagiographic biography, *The Life and Ministry of Charles G. Finney* (1985), was first published in England as *Charles G. Finney and the Birth of Modern Evangelism* (1983). Drummond testified that in his own case, reading the "old autobiography" as a seminarian, "Finney's account of what had erupted in his volcanic ministry flowed as fiery lava before my spiritual eyes. I was captivated, challenged—and *changed*."[4] With Finney as his "idol in the ministry," Drummond's vocation was settled. Over the course of his career as a pastor and seminary president, Drummond taught as Billy Graham Professor of Evangelism at several Southern Baptist seminaries and directed training programs for the Billy Graham Evangelistic Association. Appropriately, Graham himself wrote the foreword to Drummond's biography of Finney, asserting that "the lessons and insights of his life are as applicable today as they were in his own age."[5] It may seem unlikely that a "new Finney" or a "new Billy Graham" of such iconic stature is possible in the twenty-first

---

[4]Lewis A. Drummond, *The Life and Ministry of Charles G. Finney* (Minneapolis, MN: Bethany House Publishers, 1985; orig. Hodder and Stoughton, 1983), 10. Other recent biographies are Keith J. Hardman, *Charles Grandison Finney, 1792–1875: Revivalist and Reformer* (Syracuse, NY: Syracuse University Press, 1987); and Charles E. Hambrick-Stowe, *Charles G. Finney and the Spirit of American Evangelicalism* (Grand Rapids, MI: Wm. B. Eerdmans Publishing Company, 1996).

[5]Drummond, *The Life and Ministry of Charles G. Finney*, 6.

century, but many Christians continue to pray for a fresh outpouring of the Spirit in a new wave of widespread national revival. Is the age-old paradigm of extended periods of pervasive moral and spiritual reform through a massive surge of individual conversions led by the evangelistic preaching of high-profile ministers no longer viable in an overwhelmingly pluralistic society? If that is the case, what does the example of Charles G. Finney have to offer for the present and future of the church in America and abroad?

Preachers and historians have reinforced the interpretive model of successive periods of revival, with Finney occupying a pivotal spot in the early nineteenth century's Second Great Awakening. In the decades of the 1950s–1970s, prominent Brown University scholar William G. McLoughlin made the same connection as Drummond in *Modern Revivalism: Charles Grandison Finney to Billy Graham.*[6] In *Revivals, Awakenings, and Reform*, McLoughlin went on to develop a scheme covering all of American history that imagined five periodic awakenings as "revitalizations of culture," times of "fundamental social and intellectual reorientation" with ramifications beyond the evangelist's call for sinners personally to turn to Christ.[7] Such efforts to identify a series of discrete revival periods, however, prove problematic. McLoughlin's attempt to squeeze the American experience into precise, thirty-year segments of awakening followed by forty to sixty years of equilibrium or decline, for example, is simply too neat to describe the more messy reality of history. Whether or not it is accurate to fit the First Great Awakening into the period 1730–1760 and the Second Great Awakening into the slot 1800–1830 (which, we now know, it does not fit), identifying a "Third Great Awakening" with the years 1890–1920 and a more religiously diverse "Fourth Great Awakening" beginning in 1960 and projected through the 1980s seems naïve in retrospect, at least from the vantage point of the second decade of the twenty-first century. Subsequent, more nuanced historiography notwithstanding, the tendency to retain this traditional template remains strong, especially for teaching purposes, because of its straightforward clarity and narrative power.[8] The problem, however, is that this hoary paradigm does not provide the most accurate and helpful way to understand the significant legacy of revivalism in American history.[9]

---

[6] William G. McLoughlin, *Modern Revivalism: Charles Grandison Finney to Billy Graham* (New York: Ronald Press, 1959)

[7] Ibid., *Revivals, Awakenings, and Reform: An Essay on Religion and Social Change in America, 1607–1977* (Chicago: University of Chicago Press, 1978), 10.

[8] The very reasons this framework is included in the introduction to this volume.

[9] See, for example, Thomas S. Kidd, *The Great Awakening: The Roots of Evangelical Christianity in Colonial America* (New Haven, CT: Yale University Press, 2007); Frank Lambert, *Inventing the "Great Awakening"* (Princeton, NJ: Princeton University Press, 1999); Catherine

The relationship between the Great Awakening of the eighteenth century, associated with Jonathan Edwards, George Whitefield, and Gilbert Tennent among others, and the revivals of the early 1800s is not as tidy as has been portrayed by those preachers and historians who employ a hermeneutic of periodization. The similarities and overlap suggest episodic but continuous development over time—rather than the regular cycle of awakening-declension-awakening that has been such a satisfying interpretive fiction.[10] In the awakenings of both centuries, evangelists preached the urgent need for a personal conversion experience, rebirth included a civic or social reform dimension (sometimes associated with establishment of or advancement toward the kingdom of God), and revivals were linked with similar events in Britain and Europe. As Edwards had inveighed against Enlightenment rationalism, post-Revolutionary churches battled the more radical, now even antireligious, rationalistic Enlightenment ideology emanating from France and the writings of erstwhile patriots Thomas Paine and Ethan Allen. If the Great Awakening had presaged the American Revolution by promoting both a socially fracturing spiritual independence and a shared national spiritual experience throughout the colonies, revived churches in the new nation reorganized, founded numerous interdenominational voluntary associations focused on specific mission and social reform issues, and expanded west in the social context of religious freedom. All of this exhibited the distinctively American blend of competition and cooperation even more strongly than in the previous century. As Alexis de Tocqueville famously put it in his 1835 *Democracy in America*, "Anglo-American civilization . . . is the product (and one should continually bear in mind this point of departure) of two perfectly distinct elements which elsewhere have often been at war with one another but which in America it was somehow possible to incorporate into each other, forming a marvelous combination. I mean the *spirit of religion* and the *spirit of freedom*."[11]

A. Brekus, *Sarah Osborn's World: The Rise of Evangelical Christianity in Early America* (New Haven, CT: Yale University Press, 2013).

[10] The same case can be made with regard to the flow of developments from seventeenth-century Puritanism to the revivals in the Connecticut River valley in the eighteenth. In his excellent study of Thomas Hooker, Baird Tipson overturns the common narrative of the Great Awakening arising "almost miraculously from the corpse of colonial churches": "Hooker's preaching documents a vital stage in the development of Protestantism from the Reformation to the great Evangelical Revivals of the eighteenth and early nineteenth-centuries. . . . Hooker's theology differed in vital areas from that of the later evangelicals, but as he attempted in his preaching to put core Reformation teachings into practice, he startlingly anticipated much of what was to come." Baird Tipson, *Hartford Puritanism* (New York: Oxford University Press, 2015), 4.

[11] Alexis de Tocqueville, *Democracy in America*, ed. J.P. Mayer, transl. George Lawrence (Garden City, NY: Anchor Books, Doubleday, 1969), 46–47.

Historians also point to obvious differences, of course, between the two periods. The early nineteenth century, shaped by a "market revolution" that transformed not only the economy but every aspect of culture, was in many ways a changed world from that of colonial America. Evangelists in the 1730s and 1740s believed, in the words of Edwards, that "the surprising work of God" could not be manipulated. The Calvinist or Reformed theology that held sway among the Congregational, Presbyterian, and Baptist preachers that dominated the period emphasized the sovereignty of God while minimizing the human role in effecting salvation. Preachers of revival in the Early Republic, however, typically modified their Calvinism to make more room for human effort and response, or were evangelical Arminians. Examples include Francis Asbury and the hundreds of Methodist evangelists he was instrumental in organizing; New School Presbyterians and Congregationalists (cooperating under the 1801 Plan of Union) such as Timothy Dwight and then Lyman Beecher and Charles Finney; Restorationists like Barton Stone and northern New Englander Abner Jones; and hosts of Baptist farmer-preachers throughout the land. Vehicles of the early-nineteenth-century revivals included the camp meeting (introduced earlier by Presbyterians but now appropriated by Methodist circuit riders and local preachers, who made it their own) and its urban counterpart, the protracted meeting that Finney made famous. The advent of cheap print technology, popular religious music, public involvement of women, interdenominational voluntary societies for temperance, world and domestic mission, Bible and tract distribution, female education, Sunday schools, and other social reforms, including abolitionism, also emerged. By the early 1800s, revivals were *organized*, with the goal of Christianizing the nation's social fabric. As Finney so provocatively put it in his *Lectures on Revivals*, "religion is the work of man," so that, even though it depends on the work of the Holy Spirit, "a revival of religion is not a miracle" but the "purely philosophical result of the right use of constituted means."[12]

The roots of these developments, however, can still at least be traced to the Great Awakening period of the eighteenth century. Most notable were the organized tours, oratory, and mass publicity campaigns of George Whitefield and the pioneering evangelical periodical *The Christian History*, published in Boston in the 1740s, which collected transatlantic revival news. And, of course, Finney's "constituted means" must be understood at least

---

[12] Hambrick-Stowe, *Charles G. Finney and the Spirit of American Evangelicalism*, 156. A modern critical edition of Finney's *Lectures on Revivals of Religion* was edited by William G. McLoughlin (Cambridge, MA: Harvard University Press, 1960). A version "edited for today's reader" is also available (Minneapolis, MN: Bethany House Publishers, 1988).

to some extent in continuity with the "means of grace" in seventeenth-century Puritanism. Lines between the periods blur even more upon closer examination. Edwards' "New Divinity" disciples preached for conversion through the 1750s and 1760s, and were rewarded with occasional revivals. As one Edwards scholar has recently written, "The pulsating heart of Edwards' theology was God's great work of redemption, in which revival was the lifeblood" and "Edwards' immediate disciples certainly shared his vision for God's work of redemption being accomplished through revivals." Despite the fact that another "great" revival did not break out until after the Revolution, in towns like Bethlehem, Connecticut, under the preaching of Joseph Bellamy, and elsewhere, "that vision became a local reality." A particularly vivid example was in Newport, Rhode Island, when Sarah Osborn's 1766–1767 home meetings attracted hundreds of both blacks and whites, especially young people. As she wrote, in this interracial revival it seemed as if "all things were new and astonishing." Black Congregational minister Lemuel Haynes, who was already preaching as a young soldier at Ticonderoga in 1776, delivered the gospel with an evangelistic zeal and Edwardsian evangelical Calvinist theology that drew large crowds in western New England and Vermont after the Revolutionary War.[13]

The transatlantic Methodist movement, meanwhile, was added to the American religious mix in the 1760s and 1770s with its itinerant preachers and local class meetings, simmered during the Revolution, and came quickly to a boil after the war. In 1755, New England Baptists Shubal Stearns and Daniel Marshall—and Marshall's wife, herself a powerful preacher—carried evangelicalism to North Carolina. By the 1770s, the culture of revival had spread throughout the south. All these evangelists and the churches they spawned were products of the Awakening of the previous decades. Equally if not more auspicious for the future, the number of African Americans embracing the evangelical message began to rise by the 1780s. In effect, a constantly developing century-long American Awakening persisted from the 1730s through the century and continued both to shape religious life and to be shaped by the cultural changes wrought in the New Republic. As American religious historian Thomas S. Kidd has recently concluded, "there

---

[13] David W. Kling, "Edwards in the Second Great Awakening," in Oliver D. Crisp and Douglas A. Sweeney, *After Jonathan Edwards: The Courses of the New England Theology* (New York: Oxford University Press, 2012), 130–31. See also my chapter, "The New England Theology in New England Congregationalism," which traces the organized effort to spread Edwardsian evangelical Calvinism throughout New England, in the same volume, 165–77; and my chapter, "All Things Were New and Astonishing: Edwardsian Piety, the New Divinity, and Race," in David W. Kling and Douglas A. Sweeney, *Jonathan Edwards at Home and Abroad: Historical Memories, Cultural Movements, Global Horizons* (Columbia, SC: University of South Carolina Press), 121–36.

was simply no clear break" between the revivals of the eighteenth century and those traditionally identified as a "Second Great Awakening."[14]

Kentucky's 1801 Cane Ridge revival, the largest camp meeting of the era with many thousands attending, exemplified the movement traditionally identified as a "Second Great Awakening" in the west and south. Weeklong outdoor gatherings like this significantly predated 1800, but the camp meeting as a religious practice took on new life with Cane Ridge. Continuous interdenominational and interracial preaching often produced emotionally ecstatic religious behavior, sparking church growth and proliferation, and cementing a pattern of American popular religion. Within decades, the Methodist and Baptist churches overshadowed older denominations in size, while the revival spirit gave rise to countless sectarian groups. A remarkable element of some of these revivals in the early nineteenth century was their interracial character. Slaves and free blacks found in evangelical Protestantism a religious form in which African traditions in some measure survived, slavery's horror could be endured or resisted, and the hope of freedom found expression in a blend of biblical and indigenous imagery. Northern blacks also embraced Methodism as leaders like African Methodist Episcopal Church founder Richard Allen and female evangelist Jarena Lee arose. White Methodists and Baptists were influenced by African American converts and preachers, sharing experiences like the shout and spiritual visions, although by the 1830s whites more often disassociated themselves from, and feared, black evangelicalism as leaders of slave revolts emerged from this tradition.

This was the religious culture into which Charles Finney was born in Connecticut in 1792. After the Revolution, spiritual awakening was in the air everywhere in the new United States, fueled both by the perceived threat of antireligious rationalism and by the exhilaration of the expansionist new century in a new nation. At Yale in the late 1790s and early 1800s, president Timothy Dwight's preaching sparked a campus revival with national impact as graduates took his activist Calvinism west, founding churches and schools. Dwight himself, as a grandson of Jonathan Edwards, personally bridged the previous and rising generations of evangelical Calvinists coming out of New England. His student Lyman Beecher, a sometime nemesis of Finney who nevertheless welcomed Finney to Boston in 1831, made the voluntary society a hallmark of the nineteenth-century expression of the movement. Meanwhile, Nathaniel William Taylor, pastor of the prestigious Center Church in New Haven and professor of theology at Yale from 1822, further developed an adapted version of theology in the Reformed tradi-

---

[14] Kidd, *The Great Awakening*, 321.

tion designed to support evangelistic preaching in the new environment. It was especially in the "burned over district" of central and northern New York State that Taylor's modified Calvinism provided a theology that, in the hands of Charles Finney and other New School Presbyterians and Congregationalists, fueled revival among the traditional denominational churches.

The portrayal of Finney as a frontier preacher is a common trope, but Finney never in his life set foot on the frontier, except to the extent that central and northern New York State was new territory for white settlement in the mid-1790s when his family moved there. Finney returned to Connecticut as a student at Warren Academy and taught school in New Jersey between 1814 and 1818, all within the orbit of New England and mid-Atlantic "Presbygationalism." In his *Memoirs* and elsewhere, Finney severely disparaged the preaching he heard growing up and as a young adult, and Fairchild downplayed his early religious influences even further, all to highlight his uniqueness. Nevertheless, Finney was the heir of a culture thoroughly steeped in zeal for the gospel and imbued with the expectation that mass spiritual awakening was possible. When he began to preach in the north country up along the St. Lawrence River following his conversion in 1821, Finney mixed Taylor's "New Haven Theology" with the Baptist and Methodist evangelistic urgency with which he was impressed. When delivered with Finney's powerfully direct style of preaching, honed in part through his experience with oratory as a teacher and young lawyer, Taylor's theology proved highly effective as a narrative framework for revival. When Finney took his ministry to the burgeoning new cities along the Erie Canal in the mid-1820s, his campaigns produced revivals with a contagion that spread from town to town and in ever-wider circles. The momentum was made possible not only by Finney's ability to work a crowd but also by his appeal among the business and professional class of civic leaders and the network of revival-minded ministers in the traditional denominations. Finney was never a lone operator, but always worked with teams of like-minded believers.

In Oneida County Finney organized revivals in Utica, Rome, and nearby villages, using such "new measures" as neighborhood canvassing, nightly meetings, lay (sometimes female) testimony, prayer for individuals by name, and the call for immediate conversion. In league with New School Presbyterian pastors and civic leaders, he preached from Auburn in the west to Troy in the east in 1826, gaining national attention as well as opposition in Old School Presbyterian and more conservative New England Congregational quarters. As early as 1828–1829, Finney launched his first campaigns in eastern cities like Wilmington, Philadelphia, and New York. This epic phase of his career was capped with his most influential campaign, from September 1830 to June 1831 at Rochester, New York. It was there that he introduced the "anxious seat" for penitent sinners to come forward at the call to turn to Christ (adapted from camp meeting methodology and replacing his older method of meeting separately for spiritual counseling and prayer after the dismissal). Also at Rochester, Finney married the revival to the temperance crusade, making explicit the evangelical connection of personal salvation and social reform, causes that also included antislavery, sabbatarianism, and women's rights, among others.

After a successful Boston revival in 1831–1832, evangelical philanthropist businessmen Arthur and Lewis Tappan established Finney at his own New York City church in the renovated Chatham Street Theater. It was there that he published *Sermons on Various Subjects* and delivered and published *Lectures on Revivals of Religion* in 1835. The next year, his wealthy New York City patrons built a new church for Finney, and installed him as pastor of Broadway Tabernacle. The kinship between Finney's message and that of Nathaniel William Taylor at Yale had long been apparent to Old School Presbyterians who were sticklers for detailed adherence to the Westminster Confession. When Lyman Beecher and other prominent ministers began to be charged with heresy for espousing the New Haven Theology, Finney abandoned his nominal affiliation as a Presbyterian and officially, however loosely, became a Congregationalist.

Taylor was born in 1786 so, like Finney, his coming-of-age in the new nation might have rendered the eighteenth-century experience irrelevant to his thinking, but this was not the case. He entered Yale in 1800, at the height of President Dwight's historic preaching. True to the example of his mentor, he understood his ministry as a battle for what he considered the true legacy of colonial New England, and most especially the spiritual mantle of Jonathan Edwards. The immediate threat was the emergence of Unitarianism as an organized denominational force and, like his contemporary Lyman Beecher, Taylor opposed disestablishment of Congregationalism in Connecticut. After that cause was lost in 1818, Lyman Beecher memorably acknowledged that it was for the best, because it threw the churches back on their own resources and on the power of God. Taylor was disturbed that, as it seemed to him, the chief proponents of Calvinist orthodoxy in New England, notably Leonard Woods of Andover Theological Seminary in Massachusetts, were failing in the war against articulate Unitarians like Henry Ware of Harvard and William Ellery Channing, who portrayed the God of Calvin, the Puritans, and Edwards as arbitrary, unreasonable, unjust, and cruel. By the late 1810s, Taylor, along with Lyman Beecher and others, had begun to undertake a restatement of Calvinism in progressive terms keyed to popular assumptions about freedom, voluntarism, and divine benevolence in tune with the ethos of the young republic. When a theological department was established at Yale in 1822 as a rival seminary to Andover, Taylor was installed as one of the professors. Preserving what he considered at least the spirit, if not the letter, of the Westminster Confession and employing the Scottish common sense philosophy he had learned from Dwight, Taylor upheld the doctrine of "entire moral depravity," but denied that God creates in people a sinful nature and then damns them for the very nature he creates. In his moral government of the universe, God creates people as free moral agents. Although every person will sin as Adam did, guilt only comes with each person's actual sin, the selfish free choice of some object other than God as chief good. Individuals are responsible for their own sin and, although it is certain that they will in fact sin, they do possess power to the contrary. Taylor's moral government theory of the atonement, with the cross making God's pardon of repentant sinners possible, preached well at a revival meeting. The Holy Spirit worked through the means of the spoken word, not by compulsion but by persuasion, as people got "a new heart" of obedience to God's moral law and joined in the moral reform of society.

Finney's wholehearted embrace of this "Taylorite" reformulation of the New England theology is indicative of his place in the nineteenth-century revivals. The theology and the geography of his ministry were both integral to the mission of a "Greater New England" to shape the moral and spiritual future of American society. More specifically, Finney's career, conducted as it was primarily in New York State and Ohio, must be understood as an expression of the Connecticut diaspora and an extension of the revival tradition associated with Jonathan Edwards.

For Taylor and those who followed his line of thinking, including Charles G. Finney, the legacy of Jonathan Edwards continued to matter. For them it was not about the grandeur of Edwards' theology, some points of which they were willing to jettison as outmoded. Finney himself was vocal about his opposition to Edwards' ideas on the will, and to those who preached what he considered a calcified version of Edwardsian theology. Conservative New England Calvinism, like the Old School Presbyterianism of the mid-Atlantic region, was useless for the purpose of revival according to Finney, because all it did was tell people to wait and wait for God to act. What mattered was the evangelistic spirit of the Great Awakening, preaching for conversion, the "religious affections," intense personal piety, and the goal of promoting widespread revivals. In his *Memoirs*, Finney compared his own personal experience of times when "the Lord was pleased to visit my soul with a great refreshing" with the model of Edwards' intense piety. Once, for example, "after a season of great searching of heart," God "gave me much of that divine sweetness in my soul of which President Edwards speaks as an experience of his own soul."[15] He criticized the blandness of evangelical preaching by Boston Congregationalists, asserting that "the prevalence of Unitarianism and Universalism there, has kept them back from preaching and holding forth the danger of the impenitent as President Edwards presented it."[16] Theological conservatives disagreed with this focus on experience, upholding Edwards the theologian rather than Edwards the evangelistic preacher. The "New Haven Theology" drew the ire of New England conservatives, who attacked it as unCalvinist, and of Old School Presbyterians, who fought Taylor's "Arminian" influence among New School evangelicals, especially in New York State. The contest was essentially about which version of Reformed-tradition evangelicalism carried forward the spirit of the Great Awakening most faithfully.

In 1827, the New Lebanon Convention was convened in a small town east of Albany in New York State, just a few miles from the Massachusetts border. Its purpose was to iron out differences between the more boisterous "western" revivalists of the Mohawk Valley and New England evangelical Congregationalists. The premier New England evangelist of the time, Asahel Nettleton, served as standard bearer for the legacy of the New Divinity developed by Edwards' immediate followers, and stood opposed to Finney's theology and methods. The gathering at New Lebanon was emblematic of the persistence of the Edwardsian tradition broadly understood, and Finney's part in it. Finney and his colleagues were largely vindicated at New Lebanon, opening the way for him to campaign in New England. In similar fashion, with regard to Presbyterian adherence to the Westminster Confession, the evangelical- and social reform-minded New School party that dominated central New York convened at Auburn in 1837 to refute the Old School charge of infidelity to that core standard. The sixteen errors condemned in an Old School "Testimonial and Memorial" were largely associated with the New Haven Theology of Taylor, most significantly that Finneyite New School preachers diluted the doctrines of original sin and atonement for an elevated view of human ability to keep the moral law and choose salvation. By this time, Finney himself had moved the center of his work to Oberlin, Ohio, while continuing to mount campaigns in large eastern cities, but he remained symbolic of all that was either right or wrong with the evangelical tradition. The Auburn Declaration's response that the New School's "true doctrines" affirmed the essence of the Westminster standards while not excluding other influences did not avert the denominational

---

[15] Finney, *Memoirs*, ed. Rosell and Dupuis, 393, 465.
[16] Ibid., 465.

split that then occurred. What it did, however, was reaffirm the rootedness of nineteenth-century evangelistic work in the earlier period.

In 1835, with the Broadway Tabernacle still under construction, Finney initiated his move to Oberlin, Ohio, where he would teach and preach for the rest of his life. He served as both professor of theology (and later president as well) of the college and pastor of the town's Congregational church. It was from that base in Connecticut's old Western Reserve that, in addition to his regular duties, he would conduct evangelistic campaigns elsewhere in the northern United States and Great Britain until 1860. While limiting his activities to Oberlin for health reasons after that, he continued to preach for revival locally and to teach his pastoral theology course almost until the end of his life.

Despite the longevity of his career, it is the first ten or twelve years that receive the lion's share of attention among both historians and preachers. If Finney's evangelistic work in northern New York State, the Mohawk Valley, and elsewhere in the 1820s is typically cited as the last phase of the "Second Great Awakening," it is his ministry over the next three decades that reinforces a broader understanding of evangelism and revivals in the religious history of America. For one thing, those who saw to the publication of his *Lectures on Revivals of Religion* and *Sermons on Various Subjects* in 1835 would have been surprised to learn that the great revival had concluded five years earlier. Furthermore, Finney's own thinking about evangelism, conversion to Christ, the work of the Holy Spirit, the life of holiness, and the importance of the church in all of this underwent significant development in the mid-1830s. During the transition period when he had one foot in New York City and one at Oberlin, he delivered a series of lectures that were published in *The New York Evangelist* and then as a book, *Lectures to Professing Christians* (1837). Here already Finney put forth his understanding of holiness as "Christian perfection," prayed for the church to be a fellowship of love and learning, and spoke on "Christ the husband of the church." Finney and his Oberlin colleagues shifted their theological focus to include the life of faith beyond repentance and conversion (the first stages of the old scheme of salvation, which had formed the basis for evangelistic preaching since the seventeenth century), that is, to the later stage of sanctification. Oberlin became famous, or infamous in the eyes of opponents, for its emphasis on holiness, which Finney defined as righteous obedience to the law of God. Finney lost some old friends when he adopted the language of "perfection" and to speak of a post-conversion experience of "entire sanctification," but for Finney this was an extension of, not a departure from, the enduring themes of his ministry.

Writing in the periodical *The Oberlin Evangelist*, Finney and his colleagues developed the theme of the "baptism of the Holy Ghost" in sanctification as the necessary spiritual outcome of the conversion experience. From a modified Reformed perspective, this coincided with the beginnings of the Holiness movement within Methodism, exemplified by Phoebe Palmer among others, and anticipated the eventual birth of Pentecostalism. Oberlin's holiness doctrine also undergirded the college's pioneering work in such areas as antislavery, coeducation for women, and admission and integration of black students. Finney argued that, while the earlier revivals may have emphasized individual experience and were often characterized by emotion, true religious experience was a deep reorientation of the soul away from self-centeredness to God- and other-centeredness. The holiness doctrine in Finney's theology was, in essence, a further expression of the Edwardsian theme of Christian faith as a life of "disinterested benevolence," which Finney had inherited from the New Divinity of the late eighteenth century and espoused throughout his career. Finney's theology and its Edwardsian roots had political implications. Always an advocate for the common social good, Finney was never a Jacksonian individualist. To the contrary, he not only stood with the Whig party in opposition to Jacksonian politics, he branded the individualistic commercial values of "The Age of Jackson" as essentially selfish, the very definition of sin.

At Oberlin, Finney came to a fresh appreciation of the role of the church in the Holy Spirit's work of sanctification. In 1845 and 1846, he wrote a series of "Letters on Revivals" in *The Oberlin Evangelist* that specifically acknowledged that revival was impossible apart from the church. While his earlier campaigns had always depended on networks of evangelical ministers and civic leaders, and he had always preached in local churches, Finney now confessed that in the flush of those exciting years, he had underestimated the essential need for the church as the fellowship in which believers would steadily grow in faith and holiness. Without a spiritually vital church, converts easily backslid into sin or, at best, lukewarm faith. He now argued that it was the church itself that needed revival in order for individuals to come to Christ and develop in holiness, and, more broadly, for the nation to be reformed.[17] It should be noted that Finney's "Letters on Revivals" appeared as a corrective addendum to *Lectures on Revivals* at precisely the time when John Williamson Nevin published his blistering attack on revivalism in *The Anxious Bench* (1843) and Horace Bushnell published the first edition of *Christian Nurture* (1847). In other words, Finney's emphasis from 1836 through the 1840s on the ministry of the church as the environment

[17] Finney's 1845–1846 "Letters on Revivals" in *The Oberlin Evangelist* have been published as Charles G. Finney, *Reflections on Revival*, ed. Donald Dayton (Minneapolis, MN: Bethany House Publishers, 1979).

within which believers grow in Christ shared at least some kinship with the ecclesiology of theologians that criticized the individualism of earlier revivals. While Finney and Nevin never connected directly, Bushnell welcomed Finney to preach in Hartford in 1852, and the two enjoyed a warm personal friendship for the remainder of their lives. Moreover, Finney's ministry during that revival in Hartford brought churches together and helped heal rifts among the ministers related to controversy over Bushnell's theology. Finney's campaigns in the 1850s continued to spark episodes of conversions and church growth. Building on this latter decade of Finney's revival work, the evangelical ministers and Congregational churches of Boston banded together to engage him as the lead preacher in their city during the "Businessmen's Revival" which swept the urban centers of the North in 1857–1858.

The long evangelistic career of Charles G. Finney ought to put to rest the old paradigm of a "Second Great Awakening" from 1800 to 1830, or however the period may otherwise be defined. There were indeed remarkable waves of "great" revival during the early nineteenth century, and the religious and cultural identity of the new nation was most certainly shaped in large measure by evangelistic work across the denominational spectrum in those decades. But, just as there was no clear break between the revivals of the eighteenth century and the renewed energy of evangelical preaching after the Revolution, Finney and others like him showed no sign of slowing down in the decades from the 1830s to the Civil War. Finney was not the culminating figure in a Second Great Awakening, therefore, but rather a great revival preacher in an enduring American tradition of evangelistic preaching. The narrative of his *Memoirs*, composed at the very end of his life, conveys the consistency in his ministry as times changed, even as Finney himself developed over time. His move to Oberlin coincided with his reconsideration of the essential role of the church in the post-conversion Christian life of personal holiness and social reform, but it is equally the case that his direct call for sinners to turn immediately to Christ for salvation never wavered.

Whether Finney may be considered "the father of modern evangelism" is an open question, partly because George Whitefield in the previous century is also sometimes given that honor. More relevant to ask is what that work of evangelism, and the revival tradition that Finney exemplified, might look like in the twenty-first century. Here it is helpful to remember that in Finney's own lifetime American society was dramatically transformed, from an overwhelmingly Protestant religious culture in the 1820s to one marked by great religious variety by the middle of the century, with significant Jewish and especially massive Roman Catholic immigration. The generations of evangelists that followed Finney in the late-nineteenth and twentieth centuries dealt with the loss of Protestant hegemony and the fact of religious variety in various ways, from reactionary resistance to creative accommodation. Now, the religiously pluralistic, secular-minded, and vaguely "spiritual but not religious" ethos of the early twentieth century makes the notion of a "Christian America" created through a new "Great Awakening" problematic, to say the least. On the other hand, the situation today is but a further development of what it has been from the 1730s to the Revolution and then in the early national and antebellum eras of Finney—a fiercely competitive religious marketplace in which preachers must win their right to be heard, make their case in a way that is both biblically faithful and socially engaged, and strive to influence the wider culture with their understanding of the values of the gospel.

If we now know that a regular series of "Great Awakenings" that periodically transformed society is not the best way to understand American religious history, this fact should relieve Christians from the pressure to produce one in their own time. This does not, however, relieve the urgency for believers to communicate the faith and to pray for spiritual renewal and moral reform. If anything, the fact that the evangelical tradition, of which Charles G. Finney is an exemplar, has endured and developed so steadily since at least the the eighteenth century indicates that every generation must receive its own call to respond afresh to the Great Commission. In his ministry, Finney was rewarded with powerful episodes of revival that influenced the course of American society, and he persevered in that ministry through many dire and difficult challenges over the course of four decades of American history. Whether there can be a "new Charles Finney," or even a "new Billy Graham," of giant stature in today's pluralistic society may be irrelevant. What matters is that, in the very different world of the twenty-first century, ministers and churches must discern what it can mean today to stand in this enduring tradition of gospel proclamation. It is a tradition that has continually both shaped and been shaped by three centuries of the American experience. It is a tradition that lives on with spiritual intensity and indigenous vitality in many parts of the world. In remarkable and surprising ways, the tide of evangelical awakening in the southern hemisphere, in Africa and in Asia, is returning to the United States via immigration and inspirational example. With all of this, the witness of Charles G. Finney has enduring relevance for the life and ministry of today's global church.

4

From Calvinistic Methodist Miner to Pentecostal Icon: The Surprising Story of Evan Roberts, the Welsh Revival, and Azusa Street

Gwenfair Walters Adams and D. Kevin Adams

The present world-wide revival was rocked in the cradle of little Wales.

Frank Bartleman[1]

In 1904, another "great awakening" broke out. This time, it started in the tiny country of Wales, a land of sheep-bedecked mountains, poetry, and coal mining. Within one year, in a population of about one million, one hundred thousand Welsh people would convert to Christianity. The awakening would spread around the world to other parts of Britain, continental Europe, India, Asia, Africa, Latin America, and the United States. In the United States, it would enter a small white building at 312 Azusa Street in Los Angeles, California. From there, Pentecostalism would emerge and become the largest Protestant Christian movement in the world today.

This essay argues that the Welsh Revival of 1904 helped to shape early Pentecostalism, especially through the key revivalist Evan Roberts' inspiration of Frank Bartleman, an important leader at Azusa Street. After a brief overview of previous revivals in Wales, we will first examine the development of Evan Roberts' revival services as he left Calvinistic Methodist formalism to embrace a spontaneous, Spirit-led model of worship. Second, we will explore the particular ways in which Frank Bartleman was exposed to and influenced by this model and by Roberts' life story, teachings, and passion for revival.

---

[1] Frank Bartleman, *Azusa Street* (S. Plainfield, NJ: Bridge Publishing, Inc., reprint, 1980; originally published in 1925), 19.

Together the two parts comprise the surprising story of a young former coal miner, training for ministry as a Calvinist Methodist pastor, who ended up as an icon for the largest Protestant Christian movement in history.

Background of the Welsh Revivals

By the time of Roberts' entry into the Welsh revival tradition, Wales could look back at a long history of the growth of Christianity.[2] Christianity had taken root early in the Roman period and had expanded under the influence of larger-than-life monastic leaders during the sixth to the eighth centuries. The most well-known, St. David, is still seen as the patron saint of Wales. The medieval period, especially after the Norman Invasion of 1066, saw a revival in church building and Romanesque architecture, accompanied by a tighter church bureaucracy, which worked to conform the more charismatic Welsh to European norms of ecclesiastical law and order.

The Henrician Reformation of the sixteenth century again brought change, yet it was often external and poorly understood by the (then less-educated) populace. The Tudor period, however, did produce one thing that was to be key in fueling future revival fires: a Welsh translation of the Bible by Bishop William Morgan in 1588. Luther's German translation of the Scripture shaped German language and culture; the same was to be true of Morgan's masterpiece. The DNA of all Welsh revivals can be traced back to this, for having the Scriptures in the people's own language provided the fuel for the awakenings of the future.

Small spiritual brushfires were experienced in a few localities during the ascendancy and short reign of the Puritans, but it was not until the eighteenth century that Wales experienced a national revival. The Methodist Awakening in Wales, although contemporaneous with the Great Awakening in the American colonies, began independently of Jonathan Edwards' influence. A trinity of Methodist leaders—Howell Harris, Daniel Rowland, and William Williams—came to faith and leadership in the mid to late thirties of the eighteenth century. Predating George Whitefield, Howell Harris' passionate and zealous preaching and organizing began to awaken the dormant spirituality of the day. As an organizer, Harris was the Welsh John Wesley. As a preacher, Daniel Rowland was the Welsh Whitefield, and as a hymnist, William Williams was the Welsh Charles Wesley. Thousands listened in churches and in

---

[2]For an overview of the history of Christianity in Wales, see Gwyn Davies, *A Light in the Land: Christianity in Wales 200–2000* (Bryntirion, Wales: Bryntirion Press, 2002); Glanmor Williams, *The Welsh and their Religion: Historical Essays* (Cardiff: University of Wales Press, 1991), 1–72.

the open air to the fresh enthusiasm of these young leaders. Methodist societies grew into Methodist chapels throughout the century, becoming their own denomination in 1811.[3] Their charisma and enthusiasm, spilling over into both Baptist and Congregational churches, created a new, contagious culture of Welsh Nonconformity that dominated Wales for the next 150 years.

The Welsh continued to pray for revival and expect it locally, in the confines of a single congregation, or more widely, on a national level. This hope was strengthened by actual awakenings, great and small, such as the Beddgelert Revival of 1817 and the 1859 national revival, inspired by the 1857 American Prayer Revival beginning at Fulton St., New York.

The revivals were chronicled in the myriad religious and denominational newspapers of the day, and in the numerous ministerial biographies published during the period. Revival was expected, experienced, and printed on the consciousness of a chapel- and church-going nation. To be Welsh—especially for those who spoke Welsh—was to live in a land of revival, a land of "white gloves" (signifying that often during revivals the crime rate was so drastically reduced that the circuit judge had no cases to try, occasions when a pair of white gloves would be presented to the court).[4]

Of course, the Christianizing of a nation had its own problems. Churchgoing could easily become nominal, hiding spiritual decline behind ornate religiosity. This could be true of both congregational singing and preaching, which were the staple diet of the Nonconformist consumer. The Welsh rhetorical methodology in preaching, "the Hwyl" as it was called, was professional and poetic, yet often at the expense of being spiritually nourishing to the hearer. This, though, for many, only increased the longing for yet another national revival that might recalibrate and resurrect a more vital Christian experience, and a number of prayer initiatives were born throughout the land.[5]

1904 Revival

The prayers seemed to be answered in November of 1904 when chapels and churches in the small town of Lougher, South Wales, filled from night to night with hundreds of people making either recommitments or

---

[3] Methodist societies were small groups of converts made accountable to one another spiritually. For insight into their spirituality, cf. Bethan Lloyd Jones, trans., William Williams' *The Experience Meeting: An Introduction to the Welsh Societies of the Evangelical Awakening* (London: Evangelical Press, 1973).

[4] Eifion Evans notes, "Between 1762 and 1862, there were at least fifteen outstanding revivals in Wales. Separately, each had its own characteristic and together they seemed to justify for that period at any rate the appellation given to Wales as the land of revivals." Eifion Evans, *When He is Come: The 1858–1860 Revival in Wales* (Evangelical Press: 1967), 10.

[5] Cf. Jesse Penn-Lewis, *The Awakening in Wales* (1905).

fresh commitments to Christ. For the next six months, news of the revival dominated the religious press, crossing over to the national secular press and making headline news, day by day, week after week.[6]

At the heart of the interest was the most prominent leader of the revival, Evan Roberts, a 26-year-old former coal miner. On November 17, 1904, two weeks after the revival became public, Roberts gave an interview to the *Llanelly Mercury*, a local newspaper. Under the heading, "A GREAT RE-VIVAL / Remarkable Scenes near Llanelly / Collier's Wonderful Preaching / All Night Meeting," the unnamed reporter noted, "The whole of south Wales has been thrilled by the remarkable scenes . . . ones not seen in over 20 years, unparalleled since 1859." Then he went into some detail about Evan Roberts himself, the Revival's public face and perceived leader. It was immediately clear that the Revival story would be closely linked with the spiritual persona of this unusual young man. The reporter, seeking to describe Roberts' spiritual zeal, referred to him as the "modern Howell Harries [sic] . . . [having] the eyes of an enthusiast and the tenacity of purpose and strength of will of which martyrs are made." Then he compared him to the preachers and chapel ministers of the day, starkly contrasting the professional clergy with this young, charismatic revivalist:

> He also believes thoroughly in himself not as a preacher or an orator, but as a humble instrument guided and led by a higher Power. This it is which explains the marvelous hold which he exercises over his hearer. He is not a great orator in the ordinary sense of the term. What cannot but strike the listener, however is the tremendous faith that is in the man. Disdaining the tricks of the pulpit beater, he speaks straight out to the heart in simple language. He tells the 'old, old story' as he would to a child, and instead of striking terror into the hearts of his audience, he wins them over by appealing to the conscience and all that is best in man. At later stages of his meetings, however, when the air is charged with electricity, Mr Roberts himself becomes powerfully moved, and walks up and down the aisles of chapel in a state of ecstatic fervour.[7]

Again, the extraordinary newsworthiness of Roberts was found in his mystical demeanor and his claims of direct access to God's leading, so different from the clergy of his day. What was already present in this early account were hints of three of the characteristics of Roberts' services that, combined, would set them apart from many of the earlier revivals' services: the empha-

---

[6] For example, see the seven supplements of *Western Mail* news reports in *Religious Revival in Wales* (Western Mail). These will be quoted from and referred to below as the *Western Mail Supplement* [=WMS]. They have been more recently published as *The Religious Revival in Wales: Contemporaneous Newspaper accounts of the Welsh Revival of 1904–05 published by the* Western Mail (Quinta Press, 2004).

[7] *Llanelly Mercury*, November 17, 1904.

sis on the leader being guided by the Holy Spirit in the moment, resulting in spontaneous, free-flowing services; a less prominent place for preaching; and intense emotion that came from aspects of the service beyond preaching.

In attempting to trace the influences on Roberts' services, one could look in many directions, but none quite captures the particular combination of qualities. Quakers and Plymouth Brethren had the unstructured, leaderless meetings, but not the emotional excitement of Roberts' services. And it is not known how familiar Roberts would have been with them; there was a Plymouth Brethren congregation in Llanelli (four miles to the west) at the time, but it is unlikely that he visited. The Great Awakening had some of the overt spiritual enthusiasm and extreme manifestations of the 1904 Welsh Revival, but the strong emotional responses were connected more directly to the preaching, and the preaching was more central than in the Welsh Revival.

Another possible set of influences may be Roberts' reading habits. There is no definitive list of all that Roberts had read before the revival, but we know that he had been studying the earlier Welsh Revivals, and there is strong evidence that he was familiar with Charles Finney's writings.[8] There were striking parallels, for example, between the chapter on the Holy Spirit in Finney's *Lectures on Revivals Of Religion* and Roberts' directives on the Holy Spirit.

In addition to what he read, though, it was Evan Roberts' spiritual journey that seems to have shaped his theology, his message, and, therefore, his guiding of the revival.[9]

Evan Roberts' Theology Shaped by Spiritual Experience

Evan Roberts[10] was born on June 8, 1878 at Lougher, eight miles west of Swansea, in southwest Wales. After a basic education, he left school at twelve

---

[8] On Roberts' reading, D. M. Phillips notes four key books: The Bible, a Calvinistic Methodist catechism, *Pilgrim's Progress*, and the Calvinistic Methodist hymnbook. *Evan Roberts: The Great Welsh Revivalist and His Work* (London: Marshall Brothers, 1906), 65–66. Thomas Frances, a local minister who interviewed Evan Roberts during the Revival, adds two more to the list: A. A. Hodge's *Outlines of Theology* and the Welsh Encyclopedia. *Y Diwygiad a'r Diwygwyr* (E. W. Evans, Dolgellau: 1906), 26. Roberts would have read all of them in Welsh. Finney's *Lectures on Revivals* were translated into Welsh in 1839 and were influential in the Revivals of 1840 and 1859. For Finney's influence on the earlier revivals, see, for example, Thomas Rees, *History of Nonconformity in Wales* (John Snow and Co., London: second edition, 1883), 429.

[9] Evan Roberts would write, "I have merely preached the religion of Jesus Christ *as I myself have experienced it.* God has 'made *me* glad,' and I am showing others the great joy of serving him, a joy so great and so wonderful that I shall never be able to express it in its completeness" [emphasis added]. Evan Roberts, "A Message to the World" quoted in Arthur Goodrich et al, *The Story of the Welsh Revival* (Revell, 1905), 5–6.

[10] For more detailed accounts of his life, cf. D. M. Phillips, *Evan Roberts*; Kevin Adams, *Diary of Revival: The Outbreak of the 1904 Welsh Awakening* (Farnham, Surrey: CWR, 2004).

to assist his father as a coal miner at a nearby pit. As a child, he attended his parents' Calvinistic Methodist chapel, Moriah, where he became a faithful and involved member. Evan Roberts dated his conversion to sometime before his thirteenth birthday, and throughout his adolescence and early manhood, his growing faith was manifested in his regular attendance and engagement with church life, as well as his commitment to the weekly prayer meeting. He was also an avid theological reader, and took great interest in the history of revivals in Wales, once saying, "I could sit up all night to read or talk about revivals."[11] And, for over thirteen years, he prayed for a national revival.

By late fall, 1903, Roberts began to feel an increasing call to full-time Christian ministry and, therefore, for further education. He planned to attend the preparatory college at Newcastle-Emlyn, which equipped candidates for ministerial college. Before he entered the school in September 1904, however, Roberts experienced four months of what he called 'deep communion with God.'[12]

Then, during the months of September and October of 1904, the 'revivalist' Evan Roberts was born. While listening to the evangelist Seth Joshua— at a nearby conference for the deepening of the Christian life on September 29—he heard the evangelist say, "Bend us," that is, a prayer of submission to God, and he believed that these were words that God was speaking directly to him. Within two hours, while still at the conference, Roberts felt a "living force" growing within him, until in the end he burst forth in prayer:

> I cried, "Bend me! Bend me! Bend us!" Then "Oh! oh! oh! oh!" . . . "O wonderful Grace!" What bent me was God commending His Love, and I not seeing

---

[11] Shaw, *Great Revival*, 76.

[12] Evan Roberts on December 28, 1904 stated:

"One Friday night last spring, when praying by my bedside before retiring, I was taken up to a great expanse—without time and space. It was communion with God. Before this a far-off God I had. I was frightened that night, but never since. So great was my shivering that I rocked the bed, and my brother, being awakened, took hold of me, thinking I was ill.

"After that experience, I was awakened every night a little after one o'clock. This was most strange, for through the years I slept like a rock and no disturbance in my room would awaken me. From that hour I was taken up into the Divine Fellowship for about four hours. What it was I cannot tell you, except that it was Divine. About five o'clock I was again allowed to sleep on till about nine.

"At this time I was again taken up into the same experience as in the earlier hours of the morning until about twelve or one o'clock . . . it was too Divine to say anything about it. This went on for about three months." *WMS*, iii, 30. Hollenweger interprets this experience of Roberts as his baptism of the Spirit. [Walter J. Hollenweger, *The Pentecostals: The Charismatic Movement in the Churches* (Minneapolis: Augsburg, 1972), 179]. Roberts, however, never refers to *this* experience as his receiving of the Holy Spirit. Rather, he regards his experience of September 29, 1904 as his "filling of the Spirit." See below.

anything in it to commend. After I was bent a wave of peace came over me
. . . [And] I thought of the bending at the Judgment Day, and I was filled with
compassion for those who would be bent on that day, and I wept.[13]

This is what Evan Roberts saw as his baptism in the Spirit. A young lady
sitting next to him remembered the experience:

> The Spirit worked within him in all its power and while his whole body quivered
> with emotion . . . Then later, he rose and in a torrent of new born eloquence he told
> the astonished gathering how the Holy Spirit for which he had been praying for the
> last 13 years had now descended on him in all its plenitude of grace.[14]

Recommitted, spiritually energized, and filled with compassion for the
lost, Evan Roberts wrote the next day, "I was on fire with a desire to go
through Wales and if it were possible, I was willing to pay God for allow-
ing me to go!"[15] From then on, his personal experience of the Holy Spirit
became his autobiographical theology for the coming revival.

The next month at Newcastle-Emlyn brought many mystical visions,
including specific, prophetic words concerning a mighty revival where one
hundred thousand would be added to the churches in Wales. By October
31, Roberts could wait no longer and returned to his own church to spread
the message.

For two weeks, he brought together first the young people, but then all
ages, to respond to his simple four-point plan. Writing to his fellow student at
Newcastle-Emlyn, Sydney Evans, he explained his theological methodology:

> This is the plan:—We begin by asking someone to read, another to give out a
> hymn, and another to pray. Then I say a few words. This is what is said every
> night:—

1. We must confess before God every sin in our past life that has not
   been confessed.

2. We must remove anything that is doubtful in our lives.

3. Total surrender. We must say and do all that the Spirit tells us.

4. Make a public confession of Christ.

That is the plan that the Spirit revealed to me.[16]

---

[13] *WMS*, iii, 31.

[14] November 24, 1904, *Llanelly Mercury*, p. 6. D. M. Phillips, Evan Roberts' major biographer, notes of this meeting, "This is the wonderful history of how Evan Roberts was
filled with the Spirit." D. M. Phillips, *Evan Roberts: The Great Welsh Revivalist and His Work*
(London: Marshall Brothers, 1906), 125.

[15] *WMS*, iii, 31.

[16] Letter quoted by D. M. Phillips, *Evan Roberts*, 225.

These points were the creators of the type of revival service that Roberts led during most of the revival.[17] Though simple when enacted and responded to, these points gave the revival meetings of Evan Roberts their curiously new, mystical, even extraordinary and 'Pentecostal' (i.e. reminiscent of Acts 2) manner. Here was the message and the Spirit-filled messenger that created the atmosphere and response that was to go "viral" in Wales during the first few months of the Revival.

A typical chapel (Nonconformist) service before the revival would include a short opening prayer followed by a hymn, then a Scripture reading, then another hymn, a prayer—not written—announcements, collection, hymn, sermon, hymn. This became known as the "hymn sandwich."[18] The services of the 1904 revival were quite different, the change being remarked upon by writers and journalists. Early on, the *Western Mail* reported:

> Instead of the set order of proceedings to which we are accustomed at the orthodox religious service, everything here was left to the spontaneous impulse of the moment. The preacher, too, did not remain in his usual seat. For the most part he walked up and down the aisles, open Bible in hand, exhorting one, encouraging another, and kneeling with a third to implore a blessing from the Throne of Grace.[19]

Another witness noted, "Formality is excluded! No big paid choirs! No pipe organs to entertain! Jesus is enough! Joy in every heart! Everybody prays, prays through, gets to God; gets the 'Witness of the Spirit' for himself . . . The Comforter has come!"[20] And a third stated, "Mr. Roberts was speaking of obedience to the Spirit of God, when the big congregation seemed to be utterly incapable of restraining themselves any longer. One would sing a verse, another recite a stanza, whilst others would be engaged in prayer, and all this would culminate in an outburst of song."[21]

---

[17] An anecdote that illustrates that individuals responded directly and immediately to the points, is reported in the *Western Mail*: "While Mr. Evan Roberts was speaking on implicit obedience to the Spirit, and summarizing the point into four words, 'You must do anything and everything, anywhere, and everywhere. . . . There was a stir in the aisle and three young people marched up towards the 'big pew.'" [*WMS*, i, 25.]

[18] Looking back, five years later a revival convert named David Hughes noted the change in level of formality: "The first continuing blessing that we observe is, the successful and beneficial way found of raising the meetings out of formalism. The constant complaint was that the meetings [before the revival] had fallen into this mechanical formalism." [Quoted in Brynmor P. Jones, *Voices from the Welsh Revival, 1904–1905* (Bryntirion: Evangelical Press of Wales, 1995), 160.]

[19] *WMS*, i, 4.

[20] The *Life-Line* quoted in S. B. Shaw, *The Great Revival in Wales* (Originally published in 1905; reprint, Pensacola, FL: Christian Life Books, 2002), 181.

[21] Sunday, December 18, 1904 at Pontypridd; *WMS*, ii, 12.

Besides being personal to Roberts, the four points were the keys to the liberation of believers and non-believers alike from the well-known, well-worn chapel customs of the day. The old chapel wineskins were far too inflexible to hold the new wine of Roberts' approach.

This was due partially to the simplicity and immediacy of his message, one that called for a quick response by his listeners. This wasn't something to be just listened to and appreciated. This was a call to obey and surrender completely to the will of Christ. Roberts was seeking to bring his congregation to share what he had undergone on September 29: a moment of giving himself fully to God, of bending his will to God's, of praying as Jesus prayed, "Not my will be done, but thine," and receiving the baptism of the Spirit.[22] Speaking about his experience, Roberts noted, "I was baptized with the Spirit. He has led me as He will lead all those who, conscious of their human weakness, lean upon Him as children upon a father."[23]

Roberts confronted the congregation with a clear choice. They could remain apathetic or reach out for freedom and a new spiritual dawn. For many, it was the challenge to move from a nominal Christianity to one that took holiness and the deeper spiritual life much more seriously. Roberts exhorted them to remove "things doubtful" (step 2 of his 4 points). In practice, this included abstaining from smoking, alcohol, playing and watching sports, swearing, and bad language. These then became behavioral markers of the converts, symbols to family, friends, and coworkers of the growing community of the "children of the Revival."

It was these converts who went on to practice the next two steps: instant and prompt obedience to what the Spirit might lead them to do (step three), and public confession of Christ (step four). Evan Roberts modeled

---

[22] "Later on he dwelt upon the importance of praying for *a baptism of the Spirit*, to infuse life and to invest each person with some power to work for the Lord" [emphasis added] *WMS*, i, 15. Many of his hearers followed his advice. "One man in the gallery said he had been a member of the Baptists and a 'saved man' since he was fifteen, but he had not received the Holy Ghost into his heart until recently. He said he was not a drunkard, or a swearer, or a bad man in the ordinary acceptation of the term, but the baptism of the Spirit had not come to him until lately. Since then, he had for the first time, conducted family worship in his own house, he had done what he could to tell his fellow-workmen about salvation, and he had gone about the public-houses of his neighborhood delivering tracts, and was ready to do anything he could" [*WMS*, i, 21]. It is important to note that Roberts' use of the term "baptism of the Spirit" was not primarily a theological one. Nor did it denote a specific "second experience" marked by the speaking of tongues, as would be later delineated by Pentecostal theology. Rather, he used the term descriptively of personal spiritual revival leading to greater power for service. Nevertheless, his use of the term acclimated future Pentecostals for its use by them in their own developing theology. (Cf., for a contemporary explanation of Evan Roberts' view, cf. Chapter 17 of D. M. Phillips, *Evan Roberts*, 115ff.)

[23] Evan Roberts, "A Message to the Church," *Homiletic Review,* Vol. 49 (1905), 173.

this himself in the revival services by saying and doing what he felt the Spirit might ask him to do. This meant the death, in many quarters, of the regular Sunday pattern of hymn, reading, hymn, prayer, announcements, hymn, sermon, and hymn.

Evan Roberts' services could be long and unpredictable, filled with impromptu congregational hymn singing, spoken testimonies of Christ's power, and individual prayers of intercession or praise. On occasion, Roberts might give a short word of exhortation by taking a line from a hymn or a Bible text. At other times, he would even remain silent, letting the meeting be led by the Spirit through other people. Sometimes he would feel that God had given him supernatural knowledge about individuals in the service.[24] Here was someone who didn't just preach a sermon. Here was a messenger who seemingly had direct and clear communication with the divine during the service itself.[25] God was speaking, and Evan Roberts knew what God wanted to say and how they, the congregation, should respond. An accompanying team of young lady singers helped to lead the worship while being, themselves, led by the Spirit.

Impact on Early Pentecostalism

A modern Pentecostal or charismatic leader might find themselves very much at home in a typical service with this young Calvinist Methodist coal miner in the revival years. This is, at least in part, because Evan Roberts became a prototype for early Pentecostal leaders and, therefore, helped shape future Pentecostal services.

---

[24] Although he did not use the term "words of knowledge," his practice would immediately be understood by a modern, charismatic believer. In one service (Jan 26, 1905) he felt there were individuals who came as "wolves in sheep's clothing" with the express purpose of putting an obstacle in his way, even feeling compelled to identify him by name ("Startling Announcement" in *WMS*, iii, 27). Feeling that the meeting was getting cold, Evan Roberts' diagnosis included supernatural insight into individuals in the congregation: "One of you must ask God's pardon" . . . "There is someone here now who is moved to recite a verse" ("Great 'Haul' at Maesteg" on February 13, 1905, *WMS*, iv, 12); "The meeting had not proceeded far before Mr. Evan Roberts said: 'There is an obstacle here which must be removed, and the Spirit tells me what it is. There is a person in this congregation who does not speak to his brother. If you are honest you will rise and say so, that the meeting may go on. God wishes you to rise and say so. If you do not, there is a terrible time awaiting you. It is not I who is asking. You may go through this service without saying it, but you may rely upon it. There is a time awaiting you." A long pause followed, after which a voice was heard saying, "Better say it in English lest he be an Englishman." Mr. Roberts: "No, he is a Welshman." The story continues at length until the person in question responds ("Revivalist's Predictions" in *WMS*, iv, 18).

[25] For example, cf. *WMS*, iii, 8.

As people who visited the revival meetings returned to their towns and villages, and even other countries, to describe what they saw; as journalists reported on them in newspapers and religious journals; and accounts were quickly put together in books and tracts, interest in the revival grew. And in the years following the revival, these accounts were to have a significant impact on the future dawning of Pentecostalism—in Wales, the United States, and worldwide. With their emphasis on the need of a baptism of the Spirit, "soon-to-be-Pentecostals" were influenced by Roberts and sought to imitate his methodology and example. And his services offered a template: free-flowing, Spirit-led, and emotionally intense.

Of the estimated one hundred thousand additions to the church in Wales due to the Revival, a number found it hard to go back to church as usual. By the summer of 1905, the general excitement of the Revival was coming to a close, and many established clergy—some of whom had been silently skeptical of Roberts' more extreme statements and actions—were quietly glad that they could get back to their preaching and regulated services. Yet thousands of members were no longer able to fit into the religious confines of the pre-Revival era. It was these who rejoiced in the rediscovered priesthood of all believers, and now formed their own groupings. Some joined open Plymouth Brethren Assemblies because of their emphasis on the leading of the Spirit and their absence of official clergy. Others formed gatherings that eventually became known as mission halls. And other groups would associate themselves with the soon-to-be-forming Pentecostal movements.

Roberts would be an inspiration to the Pentecostals in his own nation, the leaders of which were all influenced by the Revival. Edmund Owen underlines the direct link between the "children of the revival"—that is, the converts—and the growth of the Pentecostal movement: "Out of the 'children of the revival' therefore came the initial growth of the Welsh Pentecostal movement, and it was those who were converted during that revival that became the prominent leaders of the three Pentecostal denominations in Britain after 1912: the Apostolic Church, the Elim Churches, and the Assemblies of God."[26] In this sense, Owen continues, there is some truth in saying that a section of the Pentecostal blessing came from the revival in Wales. Owen further notes that Dan P. Williams, or Pastor Dan, as he became known, was converted at 22 years old, listening to Evan Roberts in Lougher on Christmas Day 1904. He was later to be the first apostle of the Apostolic Church in Wales.[27]

---

[26] Edmund Owen, "Pentecostaliaeth a'r Neuaddau," in Noel Gibbard, ed., *Nefol Dan (Heavenly Fire): Agweddau ar Ddiwygiad, 1904–1905* (Gwasg Carreg Gwalch, 2004), 200; English translation by Kevin Adams.

[27] Gibbard, ed., *Nefol Dan,* 200.

Converts of the Welsh Revival found a warm and welcoming home in the new Pentecostal movement after 1906. And as has been noted, this wasn't just in Wales. Roberts' influence was also seen and felt internationally, from France to India to Korea and the United States, where the news of Evan Roberts and the Welsh Revival would become a seminal influence at the core of the burgeoning Pentecostal movement.[28]

Frank Bartleman's Icon

The international influence of Roberts affected the birthplace of the twentieth-century Pentecostal movement: Azusa Street itself. Impressed by the Welsh Revival, many of the founders saw Roberts as a template for the future leadership of a new, worldwide Pentecostalism. A key example of how Evan Roberts influenced this is seen in the story of Frank Bartleman, an American Holiness preacher who became involved at Azusa Street as a leader and promoter of the new movement.[29]

Bartleman got to know about the Welsh Revival for the first time in either late March or early April of 1905, according to his own testimony.[30] On April 8, he heard the well-known preacher and devotional writer F. B. Meyer describing the revival, one which he himself had visited and during which he had met Evan Roberts personally.[31] Bartleman was enthused: "My soul was stirred to its depths, having read of this revival shortly before. I then and there promised God He should have full right of way with me, if He could use me."[32]

In early May, Bartleman read the newly published book *The Great Revival in Wales*, by S. B. Shaw.[33] This was a compilation of newspaper reports, both secular and religious, concerning the revival in Wales, written by journalists and ministers, chronicling the spread of the awakening. The articles were positive and greatly enthusiastic about the outbreak. An article from the *Methodist Recorder* began: "Wales is in the throes and ecstasies of the most remarkable religious revival it has ever known."[34] It went on to quote

---

[28] Noel Gibbard, *The Wings of a Dove: The International Effects of the 1904–05 Revival* (Bryntirion: Bryntirion Press, 2002).

[29] For an overview of the events at Azusa, see Robert M. Anderson, *Vision of the Disinherited: The Making of American Pentecostalism* (Peabody, MA: Hendrickson Publishers, 1992), 62–78.

[30] Bartleman, *Azusa*, 27.

[31] Ibid., 7. For F. B. Meyer and the Welsh revival, cf. Shaw, 98–105; *WMS*, iii, 10; *Voices*, 14–16, 252; Shaw, *Great Revival*, 79f (1905 ed.).

[32] Bartleman, *Azusa*, 7.

[33] Ibid., 9.

[34] Methodist Recorder quoted in Shaw, *Great Revival*, 17.

the Welsh Mr. Lloyd George, a Member of Parliament, and later to become Prime Minister of Britain, describing the revival as "this remarkable upheaval which seems to be rocking Welsh life like a great earthquake."[35] There were regular references to Pentecost. G. Campbell Morgan, the then minister of Westminster Chapel, London, noted, "If you ask me the meaning of the Welsh Revival, I say *it is Pentecost continued . . ."* [36] Another writer added, "Surely this is Pentecost! It is not only an awakening of sinners, but the church being brought back by God Himself to her primitive and rightful condition."[37]

On reading Shaw's collection, Bartleman remarked, "The Spirit, through the little book set me on fire . . . My burden was for a revival."[38] So moved was he by the book that he began to sell it in the churches he visited in Pasadena and Los Angeles, where "God wonderfully used it to promote faith for a revival spirit."[39] He also distributed a tract by Campbell Morgan, entitled *The Revival in Wales.*[40] Here Campbell Morgan echoed the voice and theology of Evan Roberts' four points: "Let us listen for the Spirit, confess Christ, be absolutely at His disposal."[41] At one time, Bartleman was even gifted with five thousand of these Campbell Morgan pamphlets, which he distributed among the churches. "They had a wonderful quickening influence," he noted.[42] Not only did these writings become an inspiration to churches and to Bartleman himself, it is also clear that very soon the Welsh Revival, and Evan Roberts specifically, became a standard for him by which all real revivals were to be judged. Shaw's book was not just an instigator but also a manual of how revivals, and specifically revivalists, should conduct themselves. The history, in Bartleman's hands, became an illustrative how-to, a reference work—you might even say a twentieth-century Finney-like guide on how to lead a revival—as edited by Shaw. Much of that narration centered around Roberts himself. His story inspired other "non-professional clergy," who felt that they could do the same.[43]

---

[35] George T. B. Davis, "Thirty-four Thousand Conversions in Wales" in *New York Weekly Witness* excerpted in Shaw, *Great Revival,* 50.

[36] Sermon of December 25, 1904; excerpted in Shaw, *Great Revival,* 110.

[37] H. S. Hallman, "The Great Revival in Wales" in *Gospel Banner,* excerpted in Shaw, *Great Revival,* 168.

[38] Bartleman, *Azusa,* 10.

[39] Ibid., 11. In 1907, Bartleman would preach at S. B. Shaw's mission in Chicago [103].

[40] Ibid., 11. The tract was a sermon, "Lessons of the Welsh Revival" by the Rev. G. Campbell Morgan, D. D., delivered in Westminster Chapel on Sunday evening December 25, 1904. It was contained in Shaw, *Great Revival,* 107–28.

[41] Shaw, *Great Revival,* 125.

[42] Bartleman, *Azusa,* 19.

[43] Evan Roberts' story was narrated three times in Shaw's compilation, p. 20–25 Evan Roberts' call from God, 20–25; story, 75–59; early life, 145–50. The book also reported in detail many of the revival services and Roberts' sayings.

Another avenue through which the Welsh Revival affected Azusa Street was the ministry of Pastor Smale, of the First Baptist Church of Los Angeles. He had just returned from visiting the revival in Wales and desired to see something similar happen in Los Angeles. Attending Smale's meetings regularly, Bartleman wrote in June, 1905, "A wonderful work of the Spirit has broken out in Los Angeles . . . Already these meetings are beginning to run themselves. Souls are being saved all over the house, while the meeting sweeps on unguided by human hands . . ."[44] Bartleman described the meetings as "impromptu," "spontaneous," "[beginning] some time before pastor arrived," words that easily summed up most of the services in the revival in Wales.[45]

By September 1905, Smale resigned, as the church officials "tired of the innovations" sought to return to normality, putting pressure on him to "either stop the revival, or get out."[46] He got out and began his own assembly, The New Testament Church, where he might have more freedom. Smale's eyewitness accounts of the revival in Wales, along with the publication of Shaw's work, influenced Bartleman, and others who were to be the foundational members of the Azusa St. Mission.

Another connection of Evan Roberts to Frank Bartleman was through a brief series of letters. Bartleman, probably unable to afford an Atlantic crossing, wrote to the evangelist at least three times, and received three letters from the man who was becoming an iconic hero to him. The first was undated, while the other two were written on August 7, 1905 and November 14, 1905. Evan Roberts' responses to Bartleman were short and general in nature. During the revival, Roberts was bombarded with letters from all over the world, asking for prayer and advice.[47] Roberts' responses to Bartleman showed his eagerness to keep praying for a worldwide revival, which he believed was occurring. In a meeting in early January 1905, a *Western Mail* journalist reported Evan Roberts praying, "that the Spirit which prevails so large in Wales today would spread not only to England but throughout the world."[48]

The three short letters from Roberts included advice such as, "Congregate the people together who are willing to make a total surrender. Pray and wait. Believe God's promises. Hold daily meetings."

---

[44] Bartleman, *Azusa*, 16.

[45] Ibid., 20.

[46] Ibid., 26.

[47] "He was receiving letters from England, Scotland, Ireland, Norway, France, Spain, America, and Africa, asking them to remember them in their prayers." January 10, 1905 in *WMS*, iii, 13.

[48] "I believe that the world is upon the threshold of a great religious revival, and pray daily that I may be allowed to help bring this about. . . . The world will be swept by His Spirit as by a rushing, mighty wind." Evan Roberts quoted by Bartleman [*Azusa*, 34].

In the second letter, Roberts wrote, "I was exceedingly pleased to learn the good news of how you are beginning to experience wonderful things. Praying God to continue to bless you."[49]

The third letter was a little longer and concentrated on the "terrible fight" between the kingdom of God and the "kingdom of the evil one." Roberts emphasized the need for prayer and true worship, which meant giving oneself to God and pleasing God, not self. He referred to the "mighty downpouring of the Holy Spirit" in Wales and emphasized that he would continue to pray to God to keep Bartleman's "faith strong, and to save California."[50] Bartleman later commented concerning the prayers from the revival in Wales, "I feel their prayers had much to do with our final victory in California."[51]

Although some historians describe Bartleman as having an epistolary relationship with Evan Roberts, *relationship* is perhaps overstating it. Roberts' missives were well-wishing letters that were similar to what he probably wrote to hundreds of people around the globe. Roberts didn't know Bartleman in any intimate way. Yet the letters, for Bartleman, were a significant inspiration and encouragement that he was now personally linked with the world-renowned revivalist of Wales. As Bartleman got involved in the new Azusa St. Mission where the power would fall on April 9, 1906, and the baptism of the Spirit would be followed by speaking in tongues, he would define true revival in terms of Evan Roberts and the Welsh awakening.

Being a key personality and publicist of the new move of God, Bartleman introduced the spirit of the Welsh revival and its chief revivalist into the new Pentecostal stream flowing out of Azusa. Edmund J. Gitre sums up the mix: "Leaders in the emerging pentecostal revival directly mimicked Welsh spirituality and practices. Most notably, they too refused to acknowledge human leadership; they, too, refused to set the order to service. Anyone was free to speak, dance, exhort or pray. More to the point, elsewhere as in Wales the emphasis on the omnipresent Holy Spirit was most pronounced."[52]

The message that Evan Roberts gave to an American journalist over breakfast in Swansea on January 4, 1905, would come to fruition in ways that Roberts could not have imagined. Once again, he had repeated his four points, but this time directed at America:

> The prophecy of Joel is being fulfilled. There the Lord says, "I will pour out my spirit upon all flesh." If that is so, all flesh must be prepared to receive. 1. The past must be clear: every sin confessed to God, any wrong to man must be put right.

---

[49] Ibid., 25.

[50] Ibid., 33.

[51] Ibid.

[52] Edmund J. Gitre, "The 1904–05 Welsh Revival: Modernization, Technologies, and Techniques of the Self," *Church History* 73:4, December, 2004: 826–27.

2. Everything doubtful must be removed once for all out of our lives. 3. Obedience prompt and implicit to the Spirit of God. 4. Public confession of Christ. Christ said, "I, if I be lifted up will draw all men unto me." There it is, Christ is all in all.[53]

These four points, and especially being open to the Spirit, became embodied in what would become the largest Christian movement in history: Pentecostalism.

Conclusion

The spiritual journey and prominence of Evan Roberts during the Welsh revival became a theological and spiritual endowment that influenced the first wave of Pentecostal beginnings in Los Angeles. And his legacy would live on among the Pentecostals of the twentieth and twenty-first centuries, who still come in droves to visit his home church and his grave at Lougher. Although never a Pentecostal himself—he wrote strongly against speaking in tongues, for example[54]—his insistence on being open to the Holy Spirit, in the moment, while leading worship services; the need for being filled and baptized with the Spirit; and the passionate focus of the heart on God helped to shape the newborn Pentecostalism.

Although Evan Roberts retired from the public gaze in 1906, giving himself to a ministry of intercessory prayer, his public image as a worldwide revivalist leader endured in the Christian consciousness.[55] He continued to be important not only to the converts of the revival, but also to those who had shared his dreams and longed for a deeper experience of the Holy Spirit and the Christian life. The onetime Calvinistic Methodist leader remains a charismatic and Pentecostal icon to this day. And perhaps no one would be more surprised than Evan Roberts himself.

---

[53] New York Weekly Witness excerpted in Shaw, Great Revival, 53.

[54] Jesse Penn-Lewis with Evan Roberts, War on the Saints (Leicester, 1912).

[55] For his later years, see The Religious Revival in Wales (Quinta Press), 497–539; Brynmor Pierce Jones, An Instrument of Revival: The Complete Life of Evan Roberts, 1878–1951 (South Plainfield, NJ: Bridge Publishing, 1995), 163–252.

5

Neo-evangelicalism and Renewal Since the Mid-Twentieth Century

George M. Marsden

Several decades ago, when evangelicals were much in the news, one of my evangelical friends remarked that he would like to resign from evangelicalism, except that he did not know where to send the letter. The comment points to one of the movement's major characteristics. There is no headquarters or single standard-bearing agency to which to refer to see if one is being truly evangelical.[1]

Harold Ockenga and the other leaders of the "new evangelical" movement of the mid-twentieth century were eager to define and reshape evangelical identity in a way that would promote renewal. In this chapter I want to reflect on those efforts and on what they might be able to teach us as we think about possibilities for evangelical renewal in the twenty-first century. The point of departure for understanding the renewal dynamics of the Neo-evangelical movement is Garth Rosell's illuminating treatment in *The Surprising Work of God: Harold John Ockenga, Billy Graham, and the Rebirth of Evangelicalism.*[2] What I say here is a sort of gloss on that work.

The distinctively Neo-evangelical project was to rebuild the interdenominational evangelical movement that, while vigorous in some respects, was reeling from the fundamentalist controversies of recent decades. The rise of theological modernism and the ensuing controversies disrupted the relationships between evangelicalism and the major denominations that had sustained much of it prior to 1920. Fundamentalist evangelicalism was an extraordinarily decentralized and many-sided movement. Much of it was also marked by simplistic theological responses to the challenges of

---

[1] The present essay overlaps in a few places with my article "How Evangelicals and Fuller are Shaped by Their Traditions," published originally in *FULLER magazine* 2 (2015), 40–43, and those passages are used with their permission.

[2] (Grand Rapids, MI: Baker Academic, 2008).

modernity. The role of Ockenga and his allies was to help rebuild it on two fronts. One was organizational, marked especially by the founding of the National Association of Evangelicals in 1942. The other was theological and intellectual. Ockenga organized scholars' conferences in the 1940s. He was instrumental in the founding of Fuller Theological Seminary in California, and later in the reorganization of what became Gordon-Conwell Theological Seminary. He also played a leading role in founding *Christianity Today* in 1956 and in overseeing it as the semi-official voice of the movement.[3]

As I said, evangelism was always the number one goal, and Ockenga's degree of success in revitalizing parts of that movement depended on having a dynamic base of revivalism to build on. The fundamentalist movement had already energized evangelicalism in this respect. Dispensationalism, while intellectually simplistic, helped build a sense of urgency in response to the challenges of modernity. With the signs pointing to the end being so near, the most urgent need was to evangelize—both at home and in missions abroad—so as to promote the rescue of as many souls as possible. One of the most helpful dimensions of Garth Rosell's account of Ockenga's work is that it shows that Billy Graham emerged as just the most prominent of a band of brother revivalists who were already in the field. Ockenga and Neo-evangelicalism did not have a lot to do with establishing this revivalist dynamic; it was already there. The same could be said of bands of evangelical missionaries spreading throughout the world, especially after World War II. Ockenga and his Neo-evangelical allies could build on those tremendous dynamics and try to give them some coherence and a degree of theological-intellectual sophistication.

So far as shaping an evangelical identity is concerned, it is now commonplace to observe that the Neo-evangelicalism of Ockenga, Carl Henry, and *Christianity Today* did not speak for all of evangelicalism. Their movement had a Reformed bent, was politically conservative, and differed in a number of ways from various Holiness, Pentecostal, Mennonite, and African-American traditions.[4] In later decades evangelicalism would continue to grow in unanticipated ways, as in the charismatic movement, the Jesus People, youthful rock styles of worship for everyone, giant TV ministries, the prosperity gospel, and varieties of mega churches. Around the world, the varieties have been even more bewildering. No one group or

---

[3] I have dealt with some of these issues in more detail in *Reforming Fundamentalism: Fuller Seminary and The New Evangelicalism* (Grand Rapids: William B. Eerdmans, 1987). See also Joel Carpenter, *Revive Us Again: The Reawakening of American Fundamentalism* (New York: Oxford University Press, 1997).

[4] Molly Worthen, *Apostles of Reason: The Crisis of Authority in American Evangelicalism* (New York: Oxford University Press, 2013), emphasizes this point.

coalition of evangelicals can speak for the whole. There is no evangelical headquarters.

One way to understand the proliferation of the bewildering varieties of evangelicalism is to see it as an expression of spiritual free enterprise in the modern world. Evangelicalism arises in the eighteenth century around the same time as the emergence of the new market economy. Both take advantage of modern techniques, such as those facilitating travel, print communication, advertising, and innovative patterns of organization. Traditional and more hierarchical modes of organizing society are breaking down and giving way to new consciousness regarding individual authority and initiative. When they perceive a need or an opportunity, enterprising leaders establish new institutions with no need to consult ecclesiastical bureaucracies. These institutions and their leaders thrive on competition with each other, sometimes in friendly competition among allies, other times in sharp rivalries that accentuate differences. Such institutions are to some degree dependent on the constituencies they cultivate. The institutions provide leadership and guidance for such communities, but community opinion also acts as a constraint on what is to be taught and tolerated. As Mark Noll points out, since these traits of evangelicalism first developed when modern economies were emerging in the Western world, they have proved effective more recently in the global South, where there is similar social mobility and breakdown of traditional cultures.[5]

The amazing degree of success of these evangelical movements in the past half century is not something that has been managed or directed by anyone, so in that sense it has been a truly surprising work of God. Who in the mid-twentieth century would have guessed that by the early twenty-first century the center of gravity of evangelicalism would have moved away from the West into Africa, Latin American, China, and other parts of the world? Western missionary efforts, including Neo-evangelical efforts, certainly contributed to those successes, but the real story is about countless indigenous efforts.

If there is no headquarters, and not even an informal magisterium, what gives this bewilderingly complex movement any coherence whatsoever? What keeps it from blowing apart into thousands of fragments moving further apart from each other as each develops peculiar teachings and practices? I have Roman Catholic colleagues from Notre Dame who are fond of arguing that such is the inevitable fate of Protestantism. Brad Gregory, in *The Unintended Reformation,* for instance, argues that the Protestant principle of "the Bible alone" inevitably opens the door for an endless number

---

[5] *The New Shape of World Christianity* (Downers Grove, IL: InterVarsity, 2009).

of competing interpretations of what the Bible teaches, and hence for ecclesiastical anarchy, countless heresies, and ultimately an individualism that
destroys Western civilization.[6] Or Christian Smith, a graduate of Gordon
College and a convert to Roman Catholicism, argues in *The Bible Made
Impossible* that claims to biblical authority are inconsistent and incoherent.[7]
There is a plausible case for such accusations, and it is sometimes disheart-
ening to contemplate the popularity of various heretical teachings among
those who might be identified as evangelical.

In spite of all that, however, I want to suggest that there is a much more
remarkable historical phenomenon hidden in that story: that is, the degree
of *coherence* in evangelicalism. How are we to explain that?

Here is an organizationally chaotic worldwide movement with thousands of virtually independent leaders of competing agencies. Each of these
leaders, groups of leaders, and organizations claims "the Bible alone" as
its authority. All of them are operating in a modern world that is shaped
by rampant individualism as well as by all the inborn human vices such
as cupidity, pride, and self-aggrandizement. So one might expect that the
overwhelming pattern would be to use the slogan of "the Bible alone" to
justify whatever one wants to find in the Bible or whatever might attract
a large following. The result would be that world Protestant Christianity
would have by now degenerated into countless heresies, and that anything
resembling the traditional gospel would have been all but entirely choked
out by the overgrowth of superficially attractive and easier false teachings.
Perhaps one who is narrowly precisionist in theology might read what has
happened that way. In that case the number of true Christians around the
world is very small. But I think that if one is at all generous and ecumeni-
cal in the spirit of Harold Ockenga, or let's say a C. S. Lewis or a John Stott,
then the astonishing fact is that, despite all the aberrations and deviances,
in most of evangelicalism around the world one can find a core gospel being
preached that George Whitefield would have recognized. Or we might say
that around the world we can find an evangelicalism that David Bebbington
can recognize according to his now-famed quadrilateral. It is conversionist,
Biblicist, and crucicentric in that it puts emphasis on the atoning work of
Christ on the cross, and is activist in the sense that every believer is to be
actively engaged in the work of the church and sharing the gospel.[8] Granted,

---

[6] *The Unintended Reformation: How a Religious Revolution Secularized Society* (Cambridge: Harvard University Press, 2012)

[7] *The Bible Made Impossible: Why Biblicism Is Not a Truly Evangelical Way of Reading
Scripture* (Waco: Brazos Press, 2012).

[8] *Evangelicalism in Modern Britain: A History from the 1730s to the 1980s* (London:
Unwin Hyman, 1989), 2–17.

it may often come packaged with a lot of extra-Christian, sub-Christian, and/or heretical messages (such as the prosperity gospel) attached to it, but in the long run the core message, much like that which Whitefield preached, seems to survive better than any of the eccentricities.[9]

How do we explain this remarkable historical phenomenon? We can say that it is the work of the Holy Spirit, part of the truly surprising work of God, but the Holy Spirit works through means, and so one way that we historians can make ourselves useful is to try to identify the means used. As the great historian of spiritual dynamics, Richard Lovelace, has remarked, what we are observing "is as confusing as a football game in which half the players are invisible." Our job is to try to identify players and other forces that are visible, and to offer suggestions as to which alignments of these may be most conducive to the positive work of the whole.[10]

Some of the identifiable dynamics are impersonal forces. On the negative side are the natural centrifugal forces that seem inevitable consequences of decentralization: competitive, free, populist demagoguery and encouragement of personal readings of Scripture. These would seem to encourage fragmentation, spiritual eccentricities, and heresies. Yet they seem to be countered by other natural centripetal forces that help decentralized evangelicalism to survive as an identifiable and not entirely incoherent movement. One very important mundane centripetal factor is the market force that is part of the spiritual free enterprise system. What works in one place is soon being borrowed and used everywhere, as one sees in styles of music or prayer. Hence, despite institutional fragmentation, evangelical churches of every sort of denomination and non-denomination typically resemble one another. Then we can combine that mundane force of the market with what I would argue is an inherent luminosity in the central gospel message of sin, grace, and salvation through the loving work of Christ on the cross. That is a message, to put it mundanely, that works. And it works in all sorts of cultures and eras because it speaks to the human condition. Furthermore, this message prevails as a core orthodoxy for most (even if not all) of evangelicalism, because it is consistent with the Biblicism that is proclaimed as the basis of authority for evangelical teaching. If the New Testament is studied carefully, that is the message that emerges most clearly. Many private interpretations come and go, and some last and become the bases

---

[9] I am grateful to Timothy Tennent for his comments on this passage. A resource for contemporary world evangelicalism is *Evangelicals around the World: A Global Handbook for the Twenty-first Century*, Brian C. Stiller, Todd M. Johnson, Karen Stiller, Mark Hutchison eds., (Nashville: Thomas Nelson, 2015).

[10] *Dynamics of Spiritual Life: An Evangelical Theology of Renewal* (Downers Grove, IL: InterVarsity, 1979), 256.

for various sub-movements. But the core biblical gospel message that can be found throughout the ages is something that keeps coming out near the top in the market of spiritual free enterprise, as one of those things proven to really work.

There is also another notable factor involved in fostering a degree of coherence in such an institutionally chaotic movement, and that is tradition. Tradition is something that evangelicals do not talk much about. They often present their Biblicist outlook as avowedly ahistorical and primitivist. Evangelicals are often taught as though they can skip over the many centuries of church history and tradition and get back simply to the practices of the New Testament church. Yet all such movements themselves depend upon traditions of interpretation, even if some of the traditions are of recent origin. And almost all draw on older traditions. The very idea of "the Bible alone" as an authority is a tradition inherited from the Reformation, and accentuated in the evangelical renewal movements since the eighteenth century. As older state-supported ecclesiastical authorities diminished, new movements pointed to the Bible as the source of their authority. Yet within the evangelical movement the authority of "the Bible alone" came with its own traditions and assumptions regarding interpretations and the functioning canon. Accordingly, even as innovative evangelical movements added their own emphases on holiness, the relation of law and grace, eschatology, gifts of the Spirit, and so forth, they also took for granted a sort of common core of evangelical orthodoxy. Although the actual content of Scripture helped dictate that common core, so did inherited tradition. The best example of this is that the vast majority of evangelicals are Trinitarians, and teach in conformity with the doctrines of the incarnation formulated by the early church councils. These are not doctrines that one would expect to be so overwhelmingly dominant if evangelicals depended simply on sitting down with "the Bible alone" and a completely open mind.

So here is our question: if the wider context is that these general dynamics of evangelicalism seem to generate a degree of coherence just on their own, what then do renewal movements such as Neo-evangelicalism contribute to such a project? The way I propose to answer that question is to view Neo-evangelicalism as inheriting a certain set of evangelical sub-traditions. Then its contribution is to mobilize energies to emphasize some of these, while it jettisons or diminishes the influence of others.

Neo-evangelicalism differed from most evangelical renewal efforts in that, as far as I can see, it did not seek to innovate. In that respect, we can contrast it with other evangelical movements such as Methodism, Disciple, Darbyism, and the various Holiness and Pentecostal groups, all of which came on the scene with some new doctrinal twist to offer. Neo-evangelicalism, by contrast, seems to have been a genuinely conservative movement that hoped to renew some aspects of the Protestant and evangelical heritage that had been lost or diminished.

With that in mind, we can inquire as to the principle traditions that Neo-evangelicalism inherited and how it hoped to modify or strengthen these. As I already suggested, one of the traditions Neo-evangelicals inherited was that revivalism, evangelism, and missions, all emphasizing individual conversion and commitment, were essential to the success of the church. They took these evangelistic goals as given and did not seek to change them. They wanted only to facilitate them as much as possible.

A second tradition that they took for granted was that revivalism and evangelism were not only urgent for saving souls but were also the best means for saving and extending Western civilization or Christendom. Harold Ockenga emphasized that theme in his inaugural address at Fuller Theological Seminary in 1947, "The Challenge to the Christian Culture in the West." In 1947, after the two terrible world wars, many cultural leaders were agonizing over what had gone wrong with Western civilization, and even in the cultural mainstream, some respected commentators were saying that the civilization needed to return to its Christian roots. For Ockenga and the Neo-evangelicals, such a cultural project was simply a given. What had gone wrong in Germany, the home of the Reformation, was first that Germans had turned away from "the convictions of historic primitive Christianity," and then turned toward rationalistic humanistic philosophies that led to cultural relativism. Now the United States was likewise in danger of turning to godless naturalistic philosophies.[11] Thus restoring the strength of traditional Protestant Christianity was essential for saving the nation.

That cultural program also had a political dimension. The leadership of the Neo-evangelicals was largely conservative Republican, although it included a few equally conservative southern Democrats. It was militantly anticommunist, antisocialist, and patriotic. Today all sorts of books point out that the movement was politically conservative and supported by big business, and so these arguments purport to uncover the roots of the later overtly political evangelicalism.[12] I think these works have indeed uncovered some of those roots, but often they fail to distinguish between the

---

[11] Harold Ockenga, "The Challenge to the Christian Culture of the West," Opening Convocation Address, Fuller Theological Seminary, October 1, 1947. www.fuller.edu/about/history-and-facts/harold-john-ockenga/

[12] Two recent examples are Matthew Avery Sutton, *American Apocalypse: A History of Modern Evangelicalism* (Cambridge: Harvard University Press, 2014) and Kevin M. Kruse, *One Nation Under God: How Corporate American Invented Christian America* (New York: Basic Books, 2015).

hidden and tangled networks of roots and the later lushly political branches. The Neo-evangelical movement was built on a white, northern European, educated, business-oriented leadership base, and so took for granted that Christian civilization thrived on free enterprise and that communism was its opposite that needed to be adamantly opposed. But while representatives of the movement made pronouncements on political topics, it was not anything like the later-mobilized political evangelicalism that emerged after the late 1970s. The new evangelicals wanted to be politically relevant, and it was important for Carl Henry, for instance, that *Christianity Today* be headquartered in Washington D. C. At the same time, partly in reaction to the liberal social gospel, Henry and others wanted to say that churches as such should stay out of politics. It was a fine distinction: individuals should be shaping the social order, but churches should keep to their spiritual functions.

While the political implications of the cultural task of rebuilding Western civilization were often ambiguous, the intellectual task was often conspicuous in the Neo-evangelical agenda. Ockenga identified godless naturalistic philosophies as the chief threat to Christian civilization, and so rebuilding excellence in Christian thinking was an essential countermove. In that task he followed the lead of his revered seminary mentor, J. Gresham Machen. Machen had argued that the intellectual task was so essential because "what to-day is the matter of academic speculation begins tomorrow to move armies and bring down empires."[13] But as a young pastor at Park Street Church, Ockenga found himself in a movement that had pitifully little intellectual firepower. Even the Reformed tradition that he embraced, which was the most intellectual wing of fundamentalist evangelicalism, was a battered remnant divided by fierce internal theological squabbles. During the mid-1940s, Ockenga organized several scholars' conferences held on the seaside near Boston. A total of perhaps twenty scholars attended at least one of these meetings, but there was not much more of a pool of outstanding evangelical scholars to draw on. Ockenga then helped found Fuller Theological Seminary in 1947, where he brought together as many accomplished evangelical scholars as he could find. The founding of *Christianity Today* in 1956 was one of the keystones in building an intellectual movement. Such a "thought journal" featuring serious articles could help educate both clergy and laity. Neo-evangelical leaders hoped to cap their efforts with the founding of a Christian university. But the attempt to establish "Crusade University" in the early 1960s soon faltered and had to be abandoned.[14]

---

[13]"Christianity and Culture," *Princeton Theological Review* 11 (1913): 7.

[14]Owen Strachan, *Awakening the Evangelical Mind: An Intellectual History of New-Evangelicalism* (Grand Rapids: Zondervan, 2015) provides a helpful account of these and related developments.

As that failure illustrates, the intellectual rebuilding of Neo-evangelicalism had been largely in the realm of theology, not in Christian thought generally. In 1960 there still were not a lot of accomplished evangelical scholars in fields other than theology. The theological rebuilding, however, was a real accomplishment. The theological traditions that Neo-evangelicalism had inherited were primarily a mix of Reformed theology and fundamentalism. The Reformed heritage emphasized intellect, while the fundamentalist side was often anti-intellectual.[15] But after the modernist controversies of the 1920s, both had fostered intellectual separatism. On the Reformed side, some of the best scholars followed Machen into a search for hyper-Reformed theological purity. On the fundamentalist side, Scofield Bible dispensationalism and literalist interpretations of Genesis 1–3 provided a wall of strict biblical authority to protect believers against any inroads of theological liberalism or evolutionary naturalism. The theological project of Neo-evangelical leaders such as Ockenga was to rebuild evangelical theology by drawing on a flexible non-separatist version of the Reformed tradition to correct the excesses of dispensationalism and other simplistic fundamentalist formulas. In that they were helped especially by their alliances with British scholars such as John Stott, J. I. Packer, or F. F. Bruce, who had not experienced the extremes of American fundamentalist battles and hence could help the movement recover its broader pre-fundamentalist Protestant-Augustinian roots.

In the long run this intellectual rebuilding has been remarkably successful. In the field of theology evangelicalism has developed many impressive intellectual centers that are robustly diverse, but in which there is usually a recognizable core that connects with mainstream Christian traditions. Perhaps even more remarkable is what has happened in the realm of Christian scholarship outside of theology in the past half century. In 1965 you probably could have fit all the well-published evangelical scholars into a single train car. Today the faculties of more than a hundred colleges of the Council for Christian Colleges and Universities are filled with impressive scholars and teachers who can hold their own in any intellectual setting. A good number of evangelical scholars have taken their places in mainstream American higher education.

In terms of heritages that Neo-evangelicalism helped to flourish, the most important for Christian intellectual life outside of theology was that of Abraham Kuyper, imported from the Netherlands largely through the Christian Reformed Church. The American Reformed heritage tended to be

---

[15] See Mark Noll, *The Scandal of the Evangelical Mind* (Grand Rapids: Eerdmans, 1994) for an insightful critique of the anti-intellectual heritage.

strong intellectually in the realm of the theological disciplines, but did not include a tradition of emphasizing distinctly Christian perspectives in other intellectual fields.[16] Neo-evangelical efforts to mobilize Christian scholars inevitably drew in some who had been shaped by the Kuyperian heritage. Those perspectives, emphasizing the integration of faith with all areas of learning, proved appealing to faculties of separatist Christian colleges that had been shaped by fundamentalist heritages. One could pursue intellectual rigor and yet remain distinctly Christian. These developments were not simply the outgrowth of Neo-evangelical efforts to mobilize evangelical scholars. They also reflected the demographics and economic growth of a movement in which increasing numbers have been attending college and going on to graduate schools. But the Neo-evangelical message that engaging in Christian scholarship and teaching is an important calling certainly helped lay the groundwork for these impressive developments. In marked contrast to its struggling state at the beginning of the Neo-evangelical era, the evangelical intellectual community today is simply one of the most vibrant that there is anywhere.

For that surprising work of God to have the positive future effects that it potentially could have, a number of things have to happen. Most important is that the intellectual community needs to stay in touch with the popular essence of evangelism, missions, and revival, as it did in the Neo-evangelical era—as signaled by the alliance of Ockenga and Billy Graham, for instance. Evangelicalism, because of its free market structure, is given to populist, simplistic, either-or formulas. In order to get beyond these, evangelical scholars need to stay in touch with their church communities and to signal that they are truly evangelical, and that they gently correct the tradition constructively, rather than trying to tear it down.

Such attitudes are essential for fulfilling another potentiality. That is, in providing models for the world evangelical communities that tie evangelicalism to the essentials of the whole Christian tradition. Certainly one of the most important accomplishments of the Neo-evangelical coalition was in the Lausanne Movement, beginning with the first International Conference on World Evangelization in 1974. John Stott, for instance, played a major role in that movement, promoting a "basic Christianity" that reflected the essential doctrines of churches through the ages. Today, American evangelical seminaries train thousands of world scholars and pastors who return to their countries to provide leadership there. Some from those nations,

---

[16] I offer some explanation of the reasons for this difference in "The Evangelical Love Affair with Enlightenment Science," *Understanding Fundamentalism and Evangelicalism* (Grand Rapids: Eerdmans, 1991), 122–52.

notably Korea, are themselves active in spreading substantial versions of the gospel internationally. There is also a great need for support of Christian educational institutions abroad, especially in Africa. All these tasks are extensions of the Neo-evangelical vision of tying evangelism to the deeper Christian theological traditions.[17]

As I said, that Neo-evangelical ideal—of tying evangelism to deeper Christian traditions—developed in reaction to some of the extremes of fundamentalism. One of the main dimensions of this reform of fundamentalism was to get away from the fundamentalist separatism that Ockenga and others saw as counterproductive. So the turn to the mainstream Christian theological heritage was to emphasize a version of evangelicalism that, while firmly against modernist departures from that tradition, would be inclusive of all sorts of evangelicals and other Protestant traditionalists.

That inclusivist effort was impeded by two major obstacles. One was residual fundamentalist defensiveness from within the movement. Many of the Neo-evangelical leaders and their constituents feared that the theological reforms were moving too fast and dug in their heels by insisting on affirmation of the "inerrancy" of Scripture as a test of fellowship. Although that issue continues to carry weight in some circles, its effects as a basis for dividing the movement have diminished in recent decades. Especially important, I think, is the wide recognition that the Bible can be inerrant only in what it intends to teach, and that way of putting it shifts many of the more divisive issues, such as the age of the earth or dispensationalism, into the category of hermeneutics.

In reflecting on what we can appropriate from the Neo-evangelical tradition today, I think it is important to keep in mind aspects of their outlook that do not translate well into the twenty-first century. The most important of these is their cultural and political program. In 1947, the idea of rebuilding the Christian civilization of the West seemed natural enough. But underlying that was an essentially conservative partisan political heritage. One example of the problem with that heritage was that the movement never had much success in bringing many African Americans into their coalition, despite the fact that the vast majority of African-American churches are evangelical by the usual definition. Most Mennonites did not fit either. The matter became especially problematic after the 1960s, when some younger evangelicals attempted to build an evangelical coalition on the political left. That "moral minority," as historian David R. Swartz has put it, was soon eclipsed by the dramatic emergence of the religious right and

---

[17] See Joel Carpenter, Perry L. Glanzer, and Nicholas S. Lantinga, eds., *Christian Higher Education: A Global Reconnaissance* (Grand Rapids: Eerdmans, 2014).

the "Moral Majority" in the later 1970s.[18] In the face of government support for rapidly changing American public mores, many evangelicals began to move the cultural political agenda from the background to the forefront of the movement. That prominent wing of the movement became largely about reclaiming America's allegedly Christian heritage, and was pretty closely identified with conservative Republican politics. Whatever the virtues of that agenda, one of its effects was that it limited the scope of the movement, and its prospects for being inclusive. It tended instead to accentuate divisions with Christians who held differing views regarding economics, foreign policies, and social agendas. Politics tended to overshadow everything else, to present its own simplistic either/or choices, and to deflect from the main purposes of the movement.

So today, in addition to learning about and benefiting from Neo-evangelicalism's combining of evangelism and theological-intellectual renewal as part of a worldwide movement, we can also learn from their greatest mistake. That was the mistake of thinking that they could restore evangelical Protestantism to a leading role in shaping American culture as a whole. In the 1940s and the 1950s, a time of great religious revival and public piety, it was quite understandable, even if it was a bit audacious, to take on such an agenda. At that time, it was still natural for ambitious white Protestants to think that they could recover a custodial role for the whole culture. Then, beginning in the 1960s, the culture veered in radically different directions, and the openly partisan politics of the culture wars seemed to many to be the only recourse.

By the second decade of the twenty-first century, when the public culture has turned resolutely away from traditional Christian mores, it should be clear that the days for evangelical Protestantism to be America's informal religious establishment are over. By now it should be apparent that churches should live up to their name as ecclesia, or called out communities. Whether we refer to our distinctiveness from the mainstream culture as "counter-cultural," the "Benedict Option," "the church in exile," or champions of "principled pluralism," we need to cultivate a consciousness that Christianity and American culture are entirely different allegiances—even if not entirely incompatible. Such a stance will also keep us more in tune with world evangelicalism, where evangelicals do not have a history of cultural control. Churches and their supporting institutions, especially the whole range of educational and charitable institutions, can still be cultural influences, but as responsible subcommunities that promote cultural pluralism and mutual

---

[18] *Moral Minority: The Evangelical Left in an Age of Conservatism* (Philadelphia: University of Pennsylvania Press, 2012).

tolerance. Their cultural influence can continue to be along the paths that Neo-evangelicalism set: that is, of promoting evangelism and missions that are tied to classic theological outlooks that provide alternatives to narrow sectarianism and simplistic populist innovations. Evangelical churches and their supporting institutions can also demonstrate (by the way they treat others) what it means to be a vibrant alternative community. Especially in their charitable institutions, evangelicals can demonstrate what it means for such an alternative community to be concerned not only for its own members but also for the welfare of its neighbors and of strangers.

6

BILLY GRAHAM AND THE SHAPING OF AMERICAN EVANGELISM: LEGACIES

Grant Wacker

Billy Graham's role in the shaping of American evangelism is a capacious topic that would take hours, if not days, to fully explore. This essay will focus on the more manageable but equally important question of his lasting influence. Indeed, it's one of the two questions reporters constantly ask me: "What is Billy Graham's legacy?" The other one is, "Will there be a successor for Billy Graham?" I will take up the second problem toward the end, for the two are closely related.

First, a few words about Graham's stature in the American religious landscape in the long second half of the twentieth century.[1] Though Graham is familiar to most students of the history of evangelism in (northern) North America, one recent Gallup poll reveals that 30 percent of Americans under the age of thirty have no idea who he was—or is. So it is worth remembering, as one *Wall Street Journal* writer recently said, "It's easy to forget what a big deal Graham was."[2] I will offer a few statistics and then a couple of anecdotes to make the case.

To begin with, Graham set countless records. With the possible exception of Pope John Paul II, he likely spoke to more people face-to-face than

---

[1]For documentation of the factual data in this paragraph, and most of the factual data and direct quotations in the remainder of this essay, see (except where noted) Grant Wacker, *America's Pastor: Billy Graham and the Shaping of a Nation* (Cambridge, MA: Harvard University Press, 2014), esp. 20–28, and Wacker, "Billy Graham's America," *Church History: Studies in Christianity and Culture*, 78:3 (September 2009): 489–511, esp. 490–95. I have provided documentation below for data and quotations not sourced in one of the publications noted above. See also Billy Graham, *Just As I Am: The Autobiography of Billy Graham* (Grand Rapids: HarperOne/Zondervan, revised edition, 2007). For a bibliographic essay on Graham scholarship, see Wacker, *America's Pastor*, 319–21.

[2]Barton Swaim, "The Gospel According to Billy Graham," *Wall Street Journal*, December 19, 2014, http://www.wsj.com/articles/book-review-americas-pastor-by-grant-wacker-1419026666.

any other person in history. Between 1945 and 2005—the main years of his public ministry—the number totaled 215,000,000 souls. Possibly one billion, perhaps two billion, additional people saw or heard him via electronic media, including radio, television, land lines, satellite dishes, feature length movies, and finally even social media. More than three million registered decisions for Christ, either for the first time or as recommitments. Starting in 1955, he scored a spot fifty-nine times on the Gallup poll's "Most Admired Man in the World" list. That's more than twice the number of the runner-up, Ronald Reagan, who scored a spot thirty-one times.

Graham knew eleven presidents in a row, from Harry Truman to George W. Bush. Barack Obama made twelve, if we count a pilgrimage to Graham's mountaintop home in Montreat, North Carolina, to visit the preacher after Obama became president. To be sure, Truman was not Graham's friend. In 1950, when Graham was only thirty-one, he botched an interview with Truman by innocently telling reporters the content of their private conversation in the Oval Office. Truman never forgave him. But all the other presidents were friends, and four of them very close friends. The latter group included Lyndon Johnson, Richard Nixon (for better or for worse), Ronald Reagan, and George H. W. Bush. Indeed, good evidence suggests that Johnson ranked as Graham's closest friend in his entire life outside Graham's immediate associates in the Billy Graham Evangelistic Association (BGEA). Graham was also close to the first ladies of Johnson, Nixon, Reagan, and Bush: Lady Bird, Patricia, Nancy, and Barbara. (That is an important yet untold story in itself.)

So whether we measure Graham's status by statistics or by his (almost certainly) unique access to the pinnacle of American power, his reach proved extraordinary. Martin Marty, one the greatest historians of the twentieth century, and a mainline Lutheran clergyman, recently commented that on the Mt. Rushmore of American religious leaders, three names were sure bets: Jonathan Edwards, Martin Luther King Jr., and Billy Graham. (With characteristic wit, Marty added, with a wink, "I haven't decided on the fourth one yet.")

Letters from ordinary people to Graham reveal his status, too. I will say more about them later. But here the point to notice is the sheer magnitude of them, running to millions posted during the six decades he strode the public stage. Children's letters are significant in their own way. During my research, my wife Katherine and I stumbled across a large cache of missives from children, sequestered in a store room in the BGEA headquarters in Charlotte, North Carolina. To the best of my knowledge, no one (except BGEA staff members) had ever read them. Among the hundreds we saw, one, posted in 1971, probably from a first- or second-grader, seemed to speak for all. After requesting a free book, the young author signed off, "Tell Mr. Jesus hi." The envelopes that carried letters from adults, now exhibited in a Billy Graham Library showcase, are likewise revealing. Some bore only a sketchy address, or a wildly inaccurate one, or none at all, but they all made it. One that I especially liked included a full and accurate address, but down in the lower left-hand corner the writer had scrawled, "In case of rapture, never mind." These stories alone tell us a great deal about the depth and breadth of Graham's interaction with popular culture.

One additional anecdotal illustration goes far to document Graham's influence beyond evangelical circles. It comes from Bob Dylan in the May 2015 *AARP Magazine*. Dylan, now 74, reflected on his life.

> When I was growing up, Billy Graham was very popular. He was the greatest preacher and evangelist of my time—that guy could save souls and did. I went to two or three of his rallies in the '50s or '60s. This guy was like rock 'n' roll personified—volatile, explosive. He had the hair, the tone, the elocution—when he spoke, he brought the storm down. Clouds parted. Souls got saved, sometimes 30- or 40,000 of them. If you ever went to a Billy Graham rally back then, you were changed forever. There's never been a preacher like him. He could fill football stadiums before anybody. He could fill Giants Stadium more than even the Giants football team. Seems like a long time ago. Long before Mick Jagger sang his first note or Bruce strapped on his first guitar—that's some of the part of rock 'n' roll that I retained. I had to. I saw Billy Graham in the flesh and heard him loud and clear.[3]

Despite Graham's Olympian status, his long-term impact—his legacy—is surprisingly elusive and hard to assess. The historian Steven Miller put it this way: "Graham's public persona was always [subtler] and [more] oblique than his strident platform rhetoric and vivid media profile seem to imply." Elsewhere Miller captured the point with brilliant succinctness: "Billy Graham may be America's most complicated innocent."[4] A line that the journalist David Brooks applied to President Dwight D. Eisenhower applied equally well to Graham: "He looked simple and straightforward, but his simplicity was a work of art."[5]

Though tracking Graham's legacy is more complicated than one might think, the evidence does offer warrant for good guesses. For clarity, I will break the legacy into five components. The first deals with doctrine, the sec-

---

[3] Dylan quoted in Grant Wacker, " 'He Brought the Storm Down,' Introduction," *American Pilgrim: Billy Graham, Religion, Politics, Culture*, edited by Andrew Finstuen, Anne Blue Wills, and Grant Wacker (forthcoming).

[4] Miller, "Complicated Innocence: A Case Study of the Billy Graham Image," in Finstuen et al., *American Pilgrim*.

[5] David Brooks, *The Road to Character* (New York: Random House, 2015), 67.

ond evangelical culture, the third American politics, the fourth the power of hope, and the fifth successors.

Doctrine

Beginning, then, with doctrine, it is important to notice that some claims remained fixed throughout Graham's career. By my count seven tenets persisted in his preaching decade after decade. Though they might be called evangelical boilerplate, they were boilerplate precisely because Graham made them so. He gave them the appearance of always having been there, since time immemorial.

1. Biblical authority

2. The triune nature of God

3. Original and universal sin—everyone everywhere is born with it

4. Salvation or new birth through faith in Christ's atoning death and miraculous resurrection

5. The necessity of moral and ethical growth after salvation, or, as many put it, sanctification

6. Mission—something so wonderful must be shared

7. A final destiny of heaven or hell (though over the years the emphasis increasingly fell more on heaven and less on hell).

But if those seven claims remained fixed, others changed, and the changes form an extremely important part of the legacy.

First of all, over the span of Graham's career he moved from biblical inerrancy and literalism to a larger and more dynamic sense of biblical infallibility. Simply put, the Bible is authoritative not because it is historically accurate in every detail but because it does what it promises to do: infallibly bring people to repentance and faith in Christ. In one way or another he said that he trusted the Bible because it worked in his own life and in the lives of the people who listened to him. From there, Graham moved backwards to a strong affirmation of biblical accuracy. Nonetheless, infallibility, not inerrancy and literalism, formed the baseline.

The second change related to Graham's understanding of conversion, or, as he preferred to call it, the new birth. In the early days he effectively called for a "this-moment conversion"—stand up, walk to the front, sign a decision card, join a church, and then boldly bear witness to your newfound faith.

His trademark radio and television programs went by the bracing title *Hour of Decision*. His popular magazine, which at one point enjoyed a circulation of six million, bore an even more bracing title, *Decision*. The point was clear. *Choose* Christ, right now, right here.

But over time Graham came to acknowledge that one could register one's faith in Christ in other ways. He allowed that many people, including his wife, Ruth, never experienced a single moment of decision. Rather they grew up "saved" and never saw themselves otherwise. More to the point, Graham grew to understand that the majority of people in his crusades were actually making not a first-time commitment but a *recommitment*. Of those, most had been members of churches at one time but had drifted away. Graham's preaching called them back, urging them to shoulder the responsibilities of a Christian life.

Graham's notion of the moral and ethical results that should follow the new birth also changed. He always retained the primary emphasis on individual conversion, that point should be emphasized, but he also came to appreciate the need for an intentional move from individual conversion to working for social structural reform. He knew that move did not take place automatically. In Adrian Weimer's chapter at the beginning of this book we see that white Puritan ministers, in the midst of all their intense devotional writing, reshaped their ministries in response to some of the worst atrocities of the age inflicted on Indians by their own communities during King Philip's War in the 1670s. Graham may not have known much about that tragic part of America's history, but he did understand the larger and longer problem. Converted hearts did not automatically produce converted hands. Though rarely the center of his message, he did increasingly call for civil rights laws to erase structural injustice and he urged whites to obey civil rights laws already on the books.

The next change pertained to hell. Simply put, Graham never denied it but he did redefine it. In the early days he, like most evangelists, portrayed hell in terms of fire, brimstone, and everlasting torment. But he soon felt that this evangelical chestnut simply was not biblical. Hell was separation from God's love. Reporters, accustomed to other evangelists' hardline position, sometimes pressed him. Graham responded in variety of ways but always (or almost always) to the same point: "I'm only going to go as far as the Bible does. What could be worse than separation from God's love?" The mature Graham left it there, in God's hands.

Graham's notion of mission broadened from a forthright verbal proclamation of the gospel to a more inclusive effort to bring as many people as possible into hearing range of the gospel. This point merits emphasis. Alienate as few as possible and attract as many as possible. That meant, among other things, reaching out to fundamentalists who had scorned him as too accommodating to liberals and Catholics. Yet here he enjoyed little success. As late as 1966 Bob Jones, president of Bob Jones University, would say that Billy Graham was doing "more harm to the cause of Jesus Christ than any other living man."

With far more success, Graham reached out to the mainline Protestants, Catholics, and Pentecostals. His principle was: "I'll work with anyone who will work with me if they don't ask me to change my message." Today the idea of evangelicals working with mainline Protestants, especially in charitable endeavors like interfaith shelters and campus ministries, hardly raises an eyebrow. But in the early 1950s, it did. The same point applied to working with Catholics. In the early 1950s the two traditions viewed each other with great wariness, but Graham cut through that hostility, beginning in Boston in 1950, by successfully drawing Archbishop—later Cardinal—Richard Cushing into public support for his meetings. In developing his relationship to Pentecostals, Graham never endorsed speaking in tongues as a necessary sign of Christian life, and he downplayed divine healing, apocalyptic premillennialism, and other markers of the Pentecostal tradition, but in a day when evangelical elites avoided Pentecostals, Graham embraced them.

Graham also increasingly called for an irenic approach toward world religions. He never trimmed his insistence on Christ as the only way to heaven, but he saw no point in *attacking* other people's traditions, as many evangelicals did. To be sure, in his early years Graham violated his own rules a time or two. But on the whole, and certainly in his later years, he scrupulously tried to avoid criticizing other preachers, denominations, Christian traditions, and world religions, including of course, Judaism. Repeatedly he said, in one way or another, "My job is to preach the gospel, not go into other cultures and disparage them."

Most controversially, he refused to speculate about the ultimate fate of nonbelievers. To reporters who asked, he would say something like, "That's up to God and I'm not going to play God." William Martin, the dean of Graham scholars, summed it up this way: "Part of Graham's change [came] from his wider exposure to a variety of peoples and cultures. If you have been everywhere and if you know everybody, it's hard to believe there's only one way."[6]

Let me now briefly talk about two other changes bearing on doctrine, ones that most historians have not said much about. Unlike many evangelicals, Graham sensed that some claims were simply more important than others. To a good extent he introduced the notion of scale to the evangelical

---

[6] William Martin, e-mail to the author, 12.07.15.

world. Pick your battles. Don't fight for everything. Then, too, Graham
legitimated the notion of discussion. There are essentials and nonessen-
tials, and deciding what is and is not essential should be the product of
exchange among brothers and sisters in Christ. That decision cannot come
from *Christianity Today* or from any ecclesiastical tribunal. Rather it must
be a product of conversation and consensus among evangelical believers
everywhere.

In sum, one of Graham's key legacies to us is the ability to combine a
fixed core, a still point in a turning world, with incremental changes about
how that core should be expressed and applied.

Evangelical Culture

Let us turn now to the second broad category, evangelical culture. The
short of it is this: Graham made himself a badge of credibility for evangelicals. This wasn't something he did intentionally, but he did it effectively in
several ways. One, he was not extreme, not by his own standards or by the
culture's. Graham brought evangelicals out of the cultural closet, out of the
margins, and taught them how to take a seat at the table of conversation in
the public square. Consider for example John Ashcroft: governor, US sena-
tor, and attorney general. Graham taught evangelicals like Ashcroft how to
engage the public sphere with good manners, regardless of partisan identification. In Graham's shadow, evangelicalism sometimes became more a
style than a theological position. One of the finest historians of American
religion, Samuel S. Hill, once said, tongue-in-cheek, "Billy taught evangelicals when to wear a neck tie." Along the way Graham also taught the press
that the differences between evangelicalism and fundamentalism were more
than theological.

Then, for many years, Graham effectively defined the center of the evangelical and to some extent even the general religious landscape. Evangelicals positioned themselves by their proximity to him. As George Marsden
once quipped, an evangelical could be defined as "anyone who likes Billy
Graham." The preacher taught many partisans that Christ did not die on
the cross to save sinners from cigarettes or gambling or dancing or playing
cards. Rather, Christ died to save people from our sinful natures and offer
everlasting life here and in the life to come. That insight gradually formed
the center of the evangelical landscape, at least in the most influential evangelical seminaries like Fuller, Trinity, Gordon-Conwell and, less directly,
Duke and Princeton. Graham was no Richard Baxter or John Bunyan, but
his preaching evoked a sense of where the heart of Christian commitment

should lie. He didn't smoke or drink or dance or play cards himself, but that wasn't the point. The point was to redeem humans from their own worst enemy within.

Graham also taught evangelicals the importance of a practical approach to daily Christianity. This pattern emerged not so much in his sermons or books as in "My Answer," a daily Q&A column that appeared in newspapers across the country. Graham didn't write the column himself but he approved the boilerplate that his editorial assistants used. It is striking how concrete the answers were. Most offered a heavy dose of conventional evangelical theology, but the theology usually marched in tandem with common sense guidelines drawn from biblical precepts. In Graham's mind, the guidelines worked because they came from the Bible and because they had stood the test of time. One of his favorites was "scrambled eggs can't be unscrambled." One woman asked if she should tell her husband about a sexual experience with another man many years back, before she was married. In so many words, Graham answered, "It might make you feel better but it will hurt him and hurt your marriage. Confess your sin to God, and then move on." Eggs cannot be unscrambled.

Graham embodied a pole-star of decency. Biographer Martin said it best: Graham represented Americans' "best selves." It is almost needless to add that Americans often didn't live up to their own highest values, but he did, and millions took notice. We might begin with Graham's commitment to marital fidelity, without compromises of any sort. That included any activity that might invite suspicion, such as traveling or dining alone with a woman outside the family. He was equally committed to financial transparency, again, with no compromises of any sort. After 1952 Graham and nearly all of his associates received a publically stated salary and lived within the protocol of publically audited records.[7] Absolute honesty about numbers reflected transparency in another way. Tell the truth exactly as it is, in every respect. And so, for example, reporters repeatedly asked about the number of converts. Graham's answers were always the same, in one way or another, "I have no idea. I can count *inquirers* but only God knows who the converts were." And finally, don't criticize. To be sure, Graham strongly criticized social/cultural trends he found destructive, but he rarely criticized other individuals or denominations or Christian traditions, and after the early 1960s he made a point never to criticize other cultures or religions.

---

[7]Because of revenue from record sales, George Beverly Shea's compensation was independently derived and not public. To the best of my knowledge, that arrangement was unique in the BGEA. I owe this information to historian Edith Blumhofer, who is working on a biography of Shea.

American Politics

These considerations bring us to American politics. I can't say that
Graham changed US political history as Lyndon Johnson, Ronald Reagan,
and Martin Luther King Jr., did, but he did change Americans lives in sub-
tler and, for many people, more profound ways. Leighton Ford, Graham's
brother-in-law and associate evangelist, put it perfectly: "Billy functioned
like an arrowhead."[8] On most things, the tip of the arrowhead pointed in a
progressive direction. To be sure, that orientation did not apply across the
board. He was always behind the curve on women's rights in general and
women's ordination in particular. He didn't oppose them, but he had very
little to say about the question.

On the landmark issue of civil rights, Graham represented uneven but,
on the whole, steady progress. As late as 1949, he endorsed segregation,
which was hardly unusual for a relatively comfortable white evangelical
growing up in the South in the 1920s and 1930s. But in 1950, he admonished
his own Southern Baptist Convention for its racism for refusing to admit
African Americans to its seminaries. By 1953, he was ready to make a more
dramatic move. All of his meetings until then had been segregated: blacks
on one side, whites on the other, often with a rope down the middle. That
was an evangelical tradition in the South, re-enforced by stalwarts like Billy
Sunday. Though the evidence is murky, it seems that halfway through a
meeting in Chattanooga, TN, in the spring of 1953, Graham walked out into
the audience, and pulled down the rope himself. The organizers apparently
resisted, but he pulled it down anyway. It is telling that in the next crusade,
in Dallas in May, the ropes went back up, but by the following year he had
come to a firm decision that the ropes would never go up again. They didn't.
Graham took vilification from his white friends and even received death
threats against himself and his family. In the early 1960s he backed off some,
in the face of Black Power and disorder in the streets. Temperamentally, he
was always disposed toward orderly process. But by the middle 1970s and
especially 1980s and 1990s he had re-embraced without compromise the
animating spirit, if not always the street tactics, of the civil rights movement.

In 1982, in the patriarchal cathedral in Moscow, Graham said that he
had undergone three conversions in his life: to Christ, to racial justice, and
to nuclear disarmament. Through the 1980s and 1990s, Graham carried
that demilitarization torch with growing vigor. He preached that civilization was on the brink of self-destruction, which was not God's will. He
called for discussion with the USSR of the two nations' differences. By any

---

[8] Ford, e-mail to the author, 12.08.15.

reasonable measure of things this move took enormous courage in an age when most Americans, not to mention most evangelicals, remained wary of Soviet intentions.

As for the culture wars, when they arrived in the late 1970s Graham resisted. He agreed with some conservatives' positions, but he also said that they didn't talk enough about poverty and hunger. Even if they did, Graham believed that partisan politics did not belong in the pulpit. For sure, he helped pioneer the cultural space that the Christian Right grew to inhabit. He insisted that there was a difference between partisan politics, which served the interests of the Democratic or the Republican parties, and moral politics, which served the long-range moral interests of the nation as a whole. Graham offered few guidelines about how to distinguish them, but he did offer examples. Discussions about the Panama Canal Treaties were partisan but discussions about racial injustice were moral. Apparently, he assumed that matters open to debate among reasonable people fit the former category while matters not open fit the latter.

Now I don't want to present Graham as flawless. He made some grievous mistakes, but how he dealt with those mistakes are a part of his legacy too. As many now know, in 1972 he had made odious remarks about Jews and the media in a putatively private meeting with President Richard Nixon in the Oval Office. When those remarks came to light in February 2002, he was mortified, and so were Americans in general and Jews in particular. Many Jews had considered Graham their friend. He apologized in print, repeatedly saying, in a variety of ways, "I don't know why I said it, I did not feel that way then or now, but there is no excuse." In the summer of 2002 Graham held a crusade in Cincinnati, the home of Hebrew Union College in 2002. He visited with a delegation of rabbis. He said that the things he had said that day long ago were "unforgivable"—but he asked them to forgive him, and by all appearances they did. One observer remembers that when the aging Graham entered the room the rabbis stood. Graham asked them to sit down, saying, "I am the one who should be on my knees." Unlike many Graham supporters, he did not try to spin his mistake. He faced it squarely and he tried to make amends.

The Power of Hope

The final legacy is how he preached about the possibility of a second chance in life. This one transcended doctrine, evangelical culture, and American politics. For lack of a better term I will call it the power of hope. Beyond commitments or recommitments to Christ stood Graham's message that no matter how badly you have messed up your life, Christ's willingness to forgive offers you a second chance. The evidence lies in the millions of letters that flowed into the Minneapolis (later Charlotte) BGEA office. A typical one, which I have fashioned from a systematic sampling of hundreds, ran like this.

Dear Dr. Graham,

I am writing to thank you for coming to our town last year. My husband and I wanted to go to all of your meetings but he took sick and so we got only to the last one, but I am very glad we did. Your sermon touched my heart. I was saved when I was 12. We went to a Baptist church and my mother taught Sunday school, but in high school I started smoking and met a good-looking guy and we fell in love. So I got a job at the post office and didn't go to college. He was Baptist too but we both drifted from the church. Later we got divorced. I think he was having an affair. Anyway, I found a wonderful man, Len, and we married and had two wonderful children. But he wasn't a Christian. Then you came to our town. Like I said, your message touched my heart. I made a new commitment to Jesus and Len got saved to. I hope you come back soon. I will be on the front row. I am enclosing ten dollars. Not a lot but all I can afford right now. We pray for you every day, and Ruth too.

Love,

Betty
Small Town, North Carolina
P.S. Please send me your book, *Peace with God*.[9]

American history brims with calls for a second chance. The ideal goes back to the very beginning. Puritans imagined themselves a "City on a Hill." Revolutionary firebrand Thomas Paine memorably declared, "We have it in our power to begin the world over again." Nineteenth-century Holiness folk proclaimed a Second Moment of Grace. The Statue of Lib-

---

[9] I crafted this letter carefully, over several drafts, in order to capture the style of writing and the demographic and spiritual profile of the typical writer, as well as the kinds of issues that kept coming up. The Billy Graham Center Archives prohibits copying or any use of the letters that might reveal the identity of their authors. For that reason, as well as my sense of an ethical obligation not to identify or quote letters that writers obviously intended for Graham or his staff—and not outside researchers—I have created a typical letter rather than quote or draw on quotations from actual letters in the collection. For additional details, see Wacker, "He Brought Down the Storm," in *American Pilgrim* and others.

erty invited Europe's huddled masses to "breathe free." The resonances of political movements and programs—Progressive Party, New Deal, Square Deal, New Frontier, Compassionate Conservatism, and Yes, We Can—all betokened Graham's instinctive sense that Americans were prepared to hear his message of a second chance. It was his legacy of hope.

Successor

Finally, will we see a successor to Billy Graham? The short answer is: no. That may sound dogmatic, especially coming from a historian, since historians have a lousy record for predicting anything. Still, I find the likelihood of a single-person successor difficult to imagine.

For one thing, people with his unique combination of "gifts and graces" come along rarely. The looks, voice, poise, timing, sincerity, humility, and ambition, both for himself and for God, defy the odds. But that is only the beginning. Part of the magnitude of Graham's achievement lies in the extraordinary (literally *extra-ordinary*) stamina that enabled him to stay on the public stage for more than sixty years. Staying in view that long was one thing; avoiding the pitfalls of self-aggrandizement was another. Though at times he succumbed to the allure of hobnobbing with people of great power, there was never a hint of personal moral deviance or self-enrichment.

Moreover, Graham spoke with authority across the years. The burning issues of the day paraded past him, one after another, and then disappeared. Yet his voice remained, somehow seeming to transcend them all. In the words of *Christianity Today* editor Ted Olsen, "It's one thing to be quick with a quote, as many were. But it's something more to command the moral respect that inspired enthusiasm for the second half of the twentieth century."[10] Graham knew the danger of hitching his wagon to the star of partisan and culture-war shibboleths, instead of focusing on truths that remained generation after generation.

Another reason to doubt that we will see a successor for Graham is that his closest associates, Cliff Barrows, George Beverly Shea, and Leighton Ford, were men of extraordinary talent in their own right. We often think of Graham by himself, marching solo across the religious landscape, but that is a serious mistake. In numerous ways his associates either performed crucial tasks he could not execute himself (Barrows and Shea), or provided a back-up for the times when he was unable to preach (Ford). All stayed with him all or nearly all the years of his ministry—a testament to Graham's

---

[10]Olsen quoted in Margaret Bendroth, "Billy Graham's Legacy," in Finstuen et al., *American Pilgrim*.

judgment about how to select top associates. (It is no small irony that Graham's judgment about associates did not always carry through to his choice of friends in the White House.)

But even if a person of Graham's gifts and graces should come along, the setting that created him and that he helped create has changed. Though the innovative means that he used—rapid transportation, electronic communications technology, low cost high resolution printing, inexpensive mass advertising, and even social media—are likely to grow increasingly sophisticated, it is by no means certain that a successor would possess the aptitude to deploy them.

Beyond that, a profusion of period-related questions arise. How does the virtual dissolution of the small nuclear family, gathered around a flickering television screen, change the equation? In an age of social media, would huge stadium crusades any longer work? The unprecedented devastation of World War II, the introduction of nuclear weapons, the specter of expansionist communism, the fragmentation and reconfiguration of society in the face of racial and gender injustice, and the rise of seemingly intractable culture wars are just a few of the factors that marked Graham's age in distinctive ways. Graham provided answers. Some of his answers were perennial responses to perennial dilemmas of the heart, but others were time- and place-specific. It is hardly obvious that Graham would have offered answers for 2015 in the same way that he offered them for the post–World War II era.

So what *will* happen? For one thing, we will see less-heralded or unheralded figures who might not even know who Graham was. Former *Newsweek* religion editor Ken Woodward once said that Graham's legacy will fall to a generation of barefoot evangelists around the world who never knew his name.[11] Woodward of course meant "barefoot" metaphorically: they will not be connected to the centers of power. They will not be friends of billionaires and presidents and kings as Graham was. And what will they look like? Drawing on wide reading in American religious history, the historian Margaret Bendroth perceptively predicts that they will not be white, let alone white Americans. They will appeal to multiethnic audiences. Less happily, all will be male. Yet like Graham, they will represent chastity, integrity, sincerity, ambition, humility, and hope. And they will not be doctrinally argumentative.[12] Debates about five-point Calvinism or the nuances of eschatology or speaking in tongues or women in the pulpit or gays in the pews will take second, third, or even tenth place behind the insistence on

---

[11] Kenneth L. Woodward, "Billy Graham Retrospective," *Daily Beast,* forthcoming.
[12] I draw the contours of this prediction from Bendroth, "Legacy," in Finstuen et al., *American Pilgrim.*

a life-changing experience with God in Christ that transforms every other aspect of their lives. That experience will provide working answers to perennial questions about how we find the road to life everlasting.

In *Pilgrim's Progress*, John Bunyan may have captured Graham's legacy with uncanny precision three centuries ahead of the event: "He had in his pocket a map of all the ways leading to or from the Celestial City; wherefore he struck a Light (for he never goes without his tinderbox)." Whoever Graham's successors may be, heralded or less heralded or unheralded, all will be living not only in Graham's shadow but also in his vision of world evangelism.

7

ARE THE SURPRISING WORKS OF GOD COMPLETELY SURPRISING?

Jim Singleton

The study of the history of revivals engages us from two perspectives. On the one hand, it seems to point to a serendipitous work of God, pouring down on what appears to be dry soil, an unexpected season of showers of anointing. From another perspective, however, there are those who begin to trace issues of a larger cultural change that could suggest preconditions for revival. Hence, what do we make of the cultural and religious climate of today? Could there be any winds of revival on the horizon? My focus will be to engage pastors on the level of this second perspective.

Many pastors love church history. We love learning about the many facets of spiritual awakenings. I am a prime example of this. I am a long-term pastor, and my own doctoral dissertation research was about how revivalism shaped a central understanding of evangelism in nineteenth century Presbyterianism.

As pastors, we want to know if there is anything in this history of awakenings that would propel us to anticipate another such movement in our day. Is there anything in our history that might suggest that we are about to have another awakening? Or are spiritual awakenings always utterly surprising, offering no way to anticipate them at all? More to the point, many of us who are pastors would like to know if we might be privileged to participate in one of these seasons of awakening.

There are places in the world where we still hear thrilling stories of awakening or revival. When the history of the twenty-first-century church is written, the church in China will be a major part of the story. What has been happening in China has been and will continue to be one of the thrilling stories of movements of people coming to faith. Mongolia has seen a wonderful wind of the Spirit since the fall of Soviet influence. Over the past twenty-five years a young church there has matured, and has a vision to reach the places that Genghis Khan once conquered, but this time with the sweetness of the gospel. And there are still fascinating movements of God's Spirit among many of the people groups of India, particularly those of the Dalit or "untouchable" caste. My old high school friend David Garrison has recently written of the amazing stories of God's movement in the Islamic world.[1] Certainly, the story of the movement of God's Spirit in Africa is staggering. The church on that continent has grown from ten million Christians in 1900 to over four hundred million today.

The face of Pentecostalism is the face of spiritual awakening in many places in the world. In 1906, Pentecostals numbered only a few handfuls of people. Now Pentecostals and Charismatics probably number half a billion people throughout the world, especially in Latin America. They are the fastest growing Christian group in the world.

For most of us who are American pastors it seems like the Great Awakenings and great movements of the Spirit have all been somewhere else, or in some other time. It is a little like arriving in Boston as a baseball fan and hearing all about the excitement of three recent World Series titles for the Red Sox (2004, 2007, 2013)—but seeing that the Red Sox have finished in last place in 2014 and 2015. Where are the vibrant times of renewal?

American Evangelicals did have a season of excitement in the 1970s and into the 1980s. Arriving on the campus of Gordon-Conwell Theological Seminary as a student in 1980, I could still feel the excitement of that era, even in New England, of all places. It was the time of the "Jesus People," or the "Jesus Movement." The Charismatic renewal was making a mark in mainline denominations. From California beaches to college campuses, something new had been happening.

Young Life was supplementing congregational ministry with youth in this turbulent era, and drawing many into new relationships with Christ. College ministries were reaching hundreds in the impressionable college years. InterVarsity Christian Fellowship (IVCF) sponsored a large missions conference called Urbana, which happened every three years between Christmas and New Year's. Many would point to Urbana as a place where a call to missions or ministry was discerned.

In June of 1972, Campus Crusade held a catalyzing event in Dallas called "Explo 72." It was held in the Cotton Bowl and was one of the first huge stadium rallies for Christ (eighty thousand in attendance). It also represented one of the first outdoor venues celebrating an emerging genre of Christian rock music, with performers like Larry Norman, Love Song, Andraé Crouch

---

[1] David Garrison, *A Wind in the House of Islam* (Monument, CO: WIGTake Resources, 2014).

and the Disciples, and even Johnny Cash. Writing for *Newsweek*, religion writer Kenneth Woodward called this a "Christian Woodstock." New music continued to change the way baby boomers worshipped throughout this pivotal decade through Keith Green, 2nd Chapter of Acts, the Maranatha Singers, and countless others. Chuck Colson and his book *Born Again* brought hope that such a renewal would impact Washington and the political arena. Billy Graham was still at his peak as a revivalist. What a thrilling decade!

Out of that era there was a new energy animating all kinds of congregations that drew baby boomers back to church. Chuck Smith's Calvary Chapel (Costa Mesa, California) was one of the first major churches populated by the initial waves of "Jesus People." Jack Hayford and his Church on the Way (Van Nuys, California) and Chuck Swindoll and First Evangelical Free Church (Fullerton, California) both had an explosion of growth and influence upon many other congregations. Grace Chapel in Lexington, Massachusetts, pastored by Gordon MacDonald, was another church emerging in that season. Bill Hybels and the Willow Creek Church near Chicago, and Rick Warren and Saddleback Community Church in California were creating models for congregations to imitate in reaching out to bring people back to the church. Both Willow Creek and Saddleback ushered in the new phenomenon of the megachurch. Many wondered if that excitement in the 1970s and 1980s would become another Great Awakening.

It was in 1978 that William McLoughlin, a sociologist of religion, posited the idea that we might be living in what he called the Fourth Great Awakening in the United States. His book *Revival, Awakenings, and Reform* provided an important way of thinking about religious movements.[2] McLoughlin wrote about common elements that he saw in the First and Second Great Awakenings. Like other writers, he also saw a Third Great Awakening in the late eighteenth century and early nineteenth century (1890–1920), which he believed followed a similar pattern. There is debate about whether the early twentieth-century revival had the culture-wide impact of an Awakening, but that debate is for another setting. When McLoughlin wrote in 1978, he believed he was seeing the same sets of conditions that suggested to him that we were then in a Fourth Great Awakening which he thought might continue until the 1990s.

Evangelicalism became a dominating force in American mainstream culture. It splashed onto the covers of major magazines. Evangelicals claimed their first president in 1976 in Jimmy Carter, who identified himself as the "born again" candidate. There was great optimism and hope in

---

[2] William McLoughlin, *Revival, Awakenings, and Reform* (Chicago: University of Chicago Press, 1978).

the air in evangelical circles in the 1970s and 1980s that we might be on the edge of something. Richard Lovelace and Garth Rosell were both helping students and faculty at Gordon-Conwell in that era to think through these possibilities of awakening happening again.

This Fourth Awakening, however, did not have the culture-changing impact of the First and Second Awakenings. The rich excitement of those decades has faded. Today the church in North America mostly feels quiet compared to the '70s and '80s. There are still some dynamic movements going in places, but they largely feel invisible for Christians as a whole. For instance, the Church of God in Christ (COGIC) has enjoyed an amazing growth story in the United States. It barely existed one hundred years ago, yet it is now the fifth largest denomination in the country. Further, there is real life among some new immigrant congregations, not only in Boston but around the country. And there is vibrant life in the micro-expressions of vitality in the church planting movement in the United States. Although it is too early to know the extent of influence church planting will have long term, we should keep our eyes on this movement. David Garrison defines a church planting movement as "a rapid and multiplicative increase of indigenous churches planting churches within a given people group or population segment."[3] Ed Stetzer says there are more than four thousand church plants a year in the United States. This is a significant number, blunted only, however, by the reality that it is also true that about four thousand older churches close each year.

Even with these pockets of spiritual vitality, it must be said that rarely is the church front-page news anymore. Nevertheless, many of us who are pastors still wonder if there is any indication of a renewal movement coming now. If so, are there signs we should be noticing? Will the Awakening be a total surprise or something we can anticipate and participate in? Are there warning signs we expect?

The Shape of North American Awakenings

To gain a perspective on these and other questions, we turn especially to the work of William McLoughlin mentioned previously. Again, McLoughlin believes that four religious awakenings have passed through this country. We might quibble about the dates and perhaps even about the extent of these movements, but his understanding is as follows: First Great Awakening

---

[3] David Garrison, *Church Planting Movements: How God Is Redeeming a Lost World* (Monument, CO: WIGTake Resources, 2004), 7.

(1730–1760), Second Great Awakening (1800–1830), Third Great Awakening (1890–1920), Fourth Great Awakening (1960–1990).

McLoughlin saw these awakenings unfolding in five definable phases or periods that he drew from the work of another sociologist, Anthony F. C. Wallace. Wallace's primary area of study was religious movements among Native Americans. In his most widely-known article, "Revitalization Movements," Wallace noted that revitalization movements can get triggered when "day to day behavior has deviated so far from the accepted (traditional) norms that neither individuals nor large groups can honestly sustain the common set of religious understandings by which they believe they should act."[4]

Wallace's work provided McLoughlin with an outline of a way to view awakenings. Wallace's five stages of spiritual awakening are as follows:

Stage One—Personal Stress
Stage Two—Cultural Distress
Stage Three—Rise of a Prophet
Stage Four—Early New Light Adopters
Stage Five—Persuasive Reaching of Mid-Adopters: Culture and Institutions
     Are Reshaped.

The first two stages are the problem stages where something is wrong. McLoughlin describes the beginnings of these movements in this way:

Awakenings begin in periods of cultural distortion and grave personal stress, when we lose faith in the legitimacy of our norms, the viability of our institutions, and the authority of our leaders in church and state. They eventuate in basic restructurings of our institutions and redefinitions of our social goals.[5]

He suggests that the net effect of an awakening would be "restorative—returning us to a faith in ourselves, our ideals, and our 'covenant with God' even while they compel us to reinterpret that covenant in the new light of experience."[6]

In stage one, the beginning of an awakening would be evident when there is widespread stress for all kinds of individuals. Somehow the way their life had been put together no longer appears to work. Another author on this subject, Mark Shaw, writes, "Prior to the outbreak of a revival, people in a given context feel that their maps of reality no longer work. The old ways appear to be dead ends. It could be because of globalizing forces such

---

[4] Cited in McLoughlin, *Revivals*, 12.
[5] McLoughlin, *Revivals*, 2.
[6] Ibid, 2.

as a colonial takeover, war, an economic roller coaster or an internal crisis destroys confidence in the shared worldview. Often a new dominant culture creates a crisis of confidence in a minority culture."[7] Shaw goes on to write,

> As historical moments, revivals begin with problems. Their soil is often that of social volatility and the failure of older forms of the faith or traditional religion to deal with that volatility. Out of the ashes of the old springs the new. New leaders emerge and form a movement that ends up clashing with the established powers. If the movement can resolve those clashes, it then moves outward to alter the social, spiritual, and culture landscape of the surrounding world.[8]

McLoughlin described the personal stress stage this way,

> People lose their bearings, become psychically or physically ill, show what appears to be signs of neurosis, psychosis, or madness, and may either break out in acts of violence again family, friends and authorities or become apathetic, catatonic, incapable of functioning.[9]

Today I think we certainly do see a lot of personal stress in this culture. The current popularity of guided meditation may be one measure of the severity of the stress this culture feels. Add to that our addictive behaviors and our deep relationship with consumerism that often yields financial stress. Of course, in every period the reality remains that we are sinners and we regularly mess up our own lives, but we might be in just the right context for a new answer to this world.

In describing stage two, McLoughlin writes,

> A religious revival or great awakening begins when accumulated pressures for change produce such acute personal and social stress that the whole culture must break the crust of custom, crash through the blocks in the mazeways, and find new socially structured avenues along which the members of the society may pursue their course in mutual harmony with one another.[10]

In 2015 there were grievous shootings at a church in Charleston, South Carolina. There were shootings at a small community college in Roseville, Oregon. The Boston Marathon bombings in 2013 shook that community. When these dislocations happen on a repeated basis, a society wonders what the roots are that hold the society together. For some there is a nativist urge to look back to a better era when the "taken for granted" world seems preferable to the present.

---

[7] Mark Shaw, *Global Awakening: How 20th-Century Revival Triggered a Christian Revolution* (Downers Grove, IL: InterVarsity, 2010), 25.

[8] Ibid., 29.

[9] McLoughlin, *Revivals*, 12.

[10] Ibid., 15.

You can think of other periods that preceded an awakening. England before the First Great Awakening was in a very dismal period as a culture. The church was at very low ebb. Thomas Carlyle described the country's condition as "Stomach well alive, soul extinct."[11] Deism was the new theological fancy. A philosophical morality was standard fare in the churches. Diane Severance writes,

> Sir William Blackstone visited the church of every major clergyman in London, but "did not hear a single discourse which had more Christianity in it than the writings of Cicero." In most sermons he heard, it would have been impossible to tell just from listening whether the preacher was a follower of Confucius, Mohammed, or Christ![12]

Prior to the Second Great Awakening there were challenges in the Atlantic seaboard with the Enlightenment worldview, and on the Western frontier with the stress of living in such dangerous areas. In the Third Great Awakening there were challenges from the devastating aftermath of a Civil War. There was a slowness to assimilate the rapid immigration from Ireland and Italy into the melting pot of American civilization. In all three periods there were problems—both in individual stresses and cultural challenges.

If there was a Fourth Great Awakening in the 1970s, we again see this individual stress which collected into societal stress. Desegregation exposed the nation's fear and strife in stunning ways. Youth Culture was challenging authority on multiple fronts. There had been major assassinations in the 1960s which stunned those who hoped for a world safe from fear. The United States was waging a war in Vietnam that millions of Americans found unjust. The traditional cultural ethic of self-denial in America was flipping in the '70s to a new cultural ethic of self-fulfillment. That change alone profoundly affected the family and the concept of the common good. Such conditions were sufficient for an awakening.

What about today? Are we in enough individual stress and cultural dysfunction that might be in advance of a renewal? We certainly see random violence haunting the land. We see dysfunction at the highest levels of government. We have just come through devastation in our banking system. Those kinds of traumas, which happen far too often, shake our vision of this culture. Pollution, climate change, and legalization of things long questionable in this culture are stressful to those wondering how our society will hold together. How do we affirm individual rights in a collective culture? How do we sustain the common good when individual freedom

---

[11] Diane Severance, "Evangelical Revival in England," *Christianity.com*. Salem Web Network.
[12] Ibid.

is the great yearning across the land? Do you think there might be enough cultural stress to open us up to a mighty wind again?

In stage three of McLoughlin's paradigm he points out that in each awakening people, or sometimes a person, have been raised up to point to a new light. McLoughlin points to the appearance of a prophet or prophets who see a new way of being that provides a path out of the cultural stress. We can think of a Moses in Egypt or a Martin Luther in Germany. Someone has to see a new way where the faith can provide dynamic light for the future.

In the First Great Awakening there was a cluster of prophets pointing to a new vision—Jonathan Edwards, George Whitefield, Gilbert Tennent, and Archibald Alexander. In England, John and Charles Wesley were such figures, together with Whitefield. In each case, these individuals used new techniques such as open air preaching, but they also employed new ways of understanding the conversion story. The result was a kind of leadership that catalyzed new avenues of understanding such that a culture moved forward.

During the Second Great Awakening the "prophets" were Timothy Dwight, Asahel Nettleton, James McGready, Charles Finney, Lyman Beecher, Albert Barnes, and a host of others. There were impacts throughout the field of missions that flowed from this awakening. The duration of this renewal allowed it to touch American culture in deep and significant ways.

The Third Awakening was dominated by professional revivalists like Dwight L. Moody, J. Wilbur Chapman, Billy Sunday, and Sam Jones. The new professionalism of revival was a central part of this movement. It is certain that many lives were impacted by these revivals, though the extent to which society changed is still in question.

What is needed to instigate a paradigm shift for spiritual awakening is someone to open new ways and share new light. Is that happening today? Is there a voice that is carving a new mazeway that fits today's variegated culture? Two decades ago we might have thought it was happening with some of the megachurch pastors who were leading the attractional church. Bill Hybels and Rick Warren have been massively influential both in their own congregations and in a host of congregations that are influenced by them. Yet, their ministry hasn't quite reached the point of revival. Another group of pastors comes from a more traditional bent—Tim Keller, John Piper, and Mark Dever. They have had wide influence, including the City to City Network of churches and 9 Marks publishing, but is it yet a movement? In a populist way, both Joel Osteen and Oprah Winfrey have wide-ranging spiritual influence, but their work has not created the kind of cultural change we call Awakening.

Do we have a set of people who are calling us with a new light akin to what happened before? This is not something that preachers can just invent. God must raise it up. Where will we expect a new awakening? The complexity of American culture now is quite different from previous awakenings. We don't have a monolithic culture in this country that could easily be reached all at once. A "one size fits all" approach likely will not work in this place. But where is the Holy Spirit beginning to move? There may be someone raised up at an academic conference or in a seminary classroom next week. Perhaps someone sitting in your congregations will feel that nudge like the prophets of old.

In the fourth stage, the prophets begin to speak and lead in such a way that a number of people are hearing a call to a new way of life that is bringing liberation. In previous renewal movements these new ways have captured those in transition, those aware of their needs, and those who are sensing that there is more to life. Today they are called "early adopters." There is often a release of emotionalism as stress is relieved and as solutions to their lives become visible. There also often come some judgmental elements which can cause a division.

By stage five, the larger culture grows to be accepting of the movement even if not all are touched by it. Many realize this is good for the culture. A new worldview or mazeway emerges and old institutions are restructured. McLoughlin writes,

> Finally, in the last phrase of a revitalization movement, the prophets succeed in winning over that large group of undecided folk who, though they have not themselves experienced the ecstasy of conversion, have been sufficiently impressed with the doctrines and behavior of the new lights to see the relevance of the new guidelines and to accept their practices.[13]

Meeting Current Challenges

Measuring awakening for today against this grid from McLoughlin requires understanding today's unique culture. Three social anomalies come to mind. First, the complexity of cultures—is it possible to have a culture-wide awakening when the country has such a broad mix of cultures? Second, post-Christian ethos—we do not have a precedent for a post-Christian culture experiencing an awakening. In all four previous awakenings there was a substantial Christian mindset and background to draw upon. That reservoir is drying up in this culture. Third, there is the prevalence of pluralism. Today there are so many religious choices in this country. Thus, to have

---

[13] McLoughlin, *Revivals*, 22.

one, like evangelical Protestantism, rise up and capture the culture would certainly require a surprising work of God.

In the Old Testament there are the great themes of exodus and exile. Evangelicals have certainly preferred the thought of exodus, of leaving behind bondage and heading toward a Promised Land of cultural acceptance, but post-Christian pluralism has put us in exile where we do not see a way to any leadership from the center. That is an unfamiliar approach for many of us. Evangelicalism is not a movement from the margins.

In conclusion, I have no prophetic word about what will break through in a new awakening for this country. But I offer eight words that may sustain us until the day when we do see new light dawning. First, *Keep Opening God's Word Faithfully*. Walt Kaiser reminded us in the first chapter of this book that a recovery of the Word of God has always been central to any awakening. That requires a steadiness in sticking to the ancient way of truth. A vital renewal movement will be one that centers upon God's Word.

Second, *Seek the Lord's Face Collectively*. So many Christians around the world can teach us about this. American Christians are not known for serious prayer together. We were in previous eras, but not now. We must return to seeking the Lord and keep praying for a fresh outpouring of the Holy Spirit.

Third, *Learn from Our Global Partners about This Challenge*. There are awakenings around the world and we must learn all we can from what God is doing in China and Latin America and Africa.

Fourth, *Do Not Despise the Day of Small Things*. We look for all the ways that God is moving among us even in small ways. Every renewal movement started with events that seemed small at the time. So let us faithfully do the things before us.

Fifth, *Utilize a Multi-Faceted Approach*. We will need church plants and we will need church replants and church revitalization. I think we continue to dream of every way to bring renewal one congregation at a time while we wait for a broader movement of the Spirit.

Sixth, *Continue a Kingdom Focus on Renewal*. Let us express both a Matthew 25 and Matthew 28 vision of what we are called to do. We remember that it is the Kingdom of God we yearn to see expressed in our midst—and a way of both sharing the gospel and expressing deep compassion

Seventh, *Bind Together in Solidarity—What Is Common?* God does great things when the people of God work in concert with each other. Unity is a great delight and a great stimulus for God's work. In this era of Exile we don't need to be seeing other congregations as competition, but partners in the calling of today. Let us find one heartbeat in each place for the ministry of the Kingdom.

Eighth, *Embrace the Humility of the Season.* We embrace the humility of a season when the church in our country is not thriving in many places. We are not to be arrogant or driven by worldly pride. Let us live into the calling we have and trust God with the next surprising renewal. I do pray that God will do it again and bring Awakening in our midst. And what a joy it would be to participate in such a movement of God's Spirit! May it be so!

8

Transported to Oz: The Mission Field, Mission Force, and the Surprising Work of God in America

Ed Stetzer

Introduction

What I hope to accomplish in this chapter is three-fold: to clear the air (so that we can understand our mission field), clarify God's mission force (so we can understand who the church is, and what it should do), and remind us that God is still at work in this mission field with His mission force. To do so, I will address three ideas: I will argue why people assume the "sky is falling," demonstrate that the Evangelical church's mission force has been relatively steady but still remarkably unengaged, and suggest how we might prepare ourselves to faithfully minister in a post-Christian culture.

Most of us remember the classic movie *The Wizard of Oz*—a tornado whisks a Kansas farm girl named Dorothy (along with her little dog, Toto) to the merry old Land of Oz. Once there, Dorothy finds Oz very different from her Kansas farm. Surrounded by singing munchkins, flying monkeys, and a handful of witches, Dorothy has to adapt to her new environment if she is to have any hope for survival.

Interestingly, the church in America has a parallel narrative. Like Dorothy, we have to acknowledge the reality that we are not where we once were, and in some ways, we have to adapt to a new environment. We are not in Kansas anymore. The church isn't facing flying monkeys or a wicked witch. Instead, we face what James Davison Hunter describes as the fading cultural hegemony of Christian America.

In his 1987 book *Evangelicalism: The Coming Generation*, Hunter, the Labrosse-Levinson Distinguished Professor of Religion, Culture, and Social

Theory at the University of Virginia, noted that American Evangelicals are fragmented on a host of issues ranging from theology to gun control.[1] He argued that this fragmentation—along with growing secularism, skepticism, and pluralism—has lessened Evangelicalism's cultural and political capital. As a result, Evangelicals will be marginalized, and no longer shape or influence American society as they have in the past.

Fast-forward to 2009. I call it the year of Christianity's predicted demise. That year marked the publication of the American Religious Identification Survey (ARIS), which reported a noticeable decline in the number of Americans who identified as Christian. In 1990, ARIS researchers found that 85 percent of Americans identified as Christians. In 2008, that number had dropped to 75 percent. A 10 percent decline over eighteen years is a Dorothy in Oz moment for America, to be sure.

That report inspired former *Newsweek* editor Jon Meacham's cover story entitled "The End of Christian America."[2] Based upon the findings of the ARIS study, Meacham predicted that the vision of "Christian" America—a vision held by many professing believers—was not only in jeopardy, it was replaced with a new vision of America. American Christianity's hegemony no longer exists.

Third, the late Michael Spencer, blogging under the pseudonym "the internet monk," wrote a series of blog posts, later republished in the *Christian Science Monitor*, warning of a dire future for Evangelicals. In a piece entitled "The Coming Evangelical Collapse," Spencer, a Baptist preacher who died from cancer in 2010, forecasted the following trends:

> Within two generations, Evangelicalism will be a house deserted of half its occupants. (Between 25 and 35 percent of Americans today are Evangelicals.) In the "Protestant" 20th century, Evangelicals flourished. But they will soon be living in a very secular and religiously antagonistic 21st century. This collapse will herald the arrival of an anti-Christian chapter of the post-Christian West. Intolerance of Christianity will rise to levels many of us have not believed possible in our lifetimes, and public policy will become hostile toward Evangelical Christianity, seeing it as the opponent of the common good.[3]

In recent years, the narrative describing the decline of Christian America has accelerated and continues to draw national interest. For some, the decline of Christian America is seen as a sign that the church is dying in the

---

[1] James Davison Hunter, *Evangelicalism: The Coming Generation* (Chicago: The University of Chicago Press, 1987).

[2] John Meacham, "The End of Christian America," *Newsweek*, April 3, 2009, http://www.newsweek.com/meacham-end-christian-america-77125.

[3] Michael Spencer, "The Coming Evangelical Collapse," *Christian Science Monitor*, March 10, 2009, http://www.csmonitor.com/Commentary/Opinion/2009/0310/p09s01-coop.html.

United States. As a result, like Chicken Little, more than a few Christian leaders fear "the sky is falling" and Christianity is dying in the West.

However, the problem is no real researcher—anywhere—believes this to be the case. The truth is, the sky is not falling, the church in America is not dying. Has our cultural environment changed? Yes. Is the church seemingly struggling and confused by the changing culture? Yes. Just like Dorothy transported to Oz, in a relatively short amount of time we have been transported to a new land.

The Mission Field: Making Sense of the Distorted Narrative

Those who claim that Christianity is dying in the United States often turn to anecdotal statistics to bolster their claims. Here are a few that are more common:

- **Divorce:** "The divorce rate is the same inside the church as it is outside the church."

- **Youth Attrition:** "86 percent of Evangelical youth drop out of church after high school and never return."

- **Pastoral Strife:** "1,500 pastors leave the ministry each month;" "80 percent of pastors feel unqualified and discouraged in their role as pastor;" "50 percent of pastors would leave the ministry if they had another way of making a living;" "70 percent of pastors constantly fight depression;" and "almost 40 percent polled said they have had an extra-marital affair since ministry."

All of these statistics are taken from the websites of reputable and well-meaning people. Do you know what all of these statistics have in common? They are not true.

Divorce

First, let's take a look at the divorce rate statistics. You can find statistics that self-identified Christians have the same divorce rate as Americans in general. That's not surprising, since most Americans (70–75 percent) identify as Christians. However, many in that 70–75 percent are what we would classify as nominal believers (something I will address later), which means they have a loose religious affiliation.

When we look at church attendance patterns, however, the statistics tell a different story. Those Christians who attend church on a weekly basis are much less likely to get divorced. The truth is that faithful Evangelicals, mainline Protestants, and Catholics divorce at a substantially lower level than the whole population.[4]

Youth Attrition

Second, 86 percent of Evangelical youth do not ultimately drop out of church. By contrast, it turns out that their faith is relatively resilient in subsequent generations. A University of Southern California study, published recently by Oxford University Press, actually shows a majority retention rate for Evangelicals, though mainline Protestants only retain about a quarter from generation to generation.[5]

Pastoral Strife

Third, the picture isn't as dire for pastors as some people suggest. According to a LifeWay Research study, most pastors love their job and don't see it as damaging to their families.[6] Nearly 8 out of 10 pastors (79 percent) disagree with the following statement: "Being in ministry has had a negative effect on my family." In addition, 93 percent of those surveyed "feel privileged to be a pastor." So, although pastors both face and recognize unique challenges in ministry, they love it and don't plan to leave. In fact, only around 1 percent of pastors in Evangelical and historically black churches leave the ministry each year.

Though I seek to undermine Chicken Little claims, my argument is not that all is well. Quite the contrary, I've written many books and articles that describe the challenges facing our churches. But facts are our friends,

---

[4] Ed Stetzer, "Marriage, Divorce, and the Church: What do the stats say, and can marriage be happy?" *The Exchange*, February 2014, http://www.christianitytoday.com/edstetzer/2014/february/marriage-divorce-and-body-of-christ-what-do-stats-say-and-c.html. The actual percentages are as follows: 34 percent of Evangelicals, 32 percent of mainline Protestants, and 23 percent of Catholics, a statistically significant difference from the rates for the general population.

[5] "Religion Runs in the Family: Vern Bengtson's research shows the surprising resiliency of faith as it passes from parents to children," interview by Amy Ziettlow, *Christianity Today*, August 2013, http://www.christianitytoday.com/ct/2013/august-web-only/religion-runs-in-family.html.

[6] Ed Stetzer, "That Stat That Says Pastors Are All Miserable and Want to Quit (Part 1)," *The Exchange*, October 2015, http://www.christianitytoday.com/edstetzer/2015/october/that-stat-that-says-pastors-are-all-miserable-and-want-to-q.html.

and the facts don't support the narrative that the church is dying or in steep decline.

Statistics indicate that Christian church attendance is slightly declining—not steeply declining, or that Christianity is declining in America (or could in the future). One of the most helpful sources of data on religion in the United States is the General Social Survey (GSS). The GSS, a long-term survey of America culture and demographics, uses the RELTRAD system to standardize religious classification. Based on RELTRAD, which is short for "religious traditions," there are four broad categories in American Christianity: Catholicism, Mainline Protestantism, Evangelicalism, and historic African-American churches.

The latest report shows that Protestant church attendance in the United States dropped from 23.2 percent in 1972 to 19.8 percent in 2014 (see Figure 1).

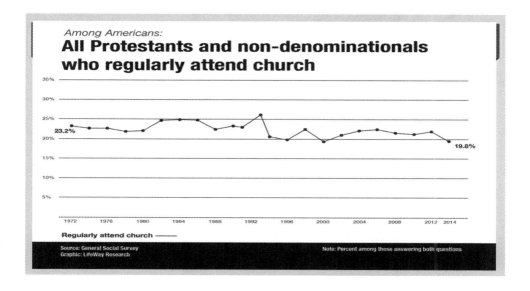

Figure 1

The GSS also reports a significant decline in the percentage of Americans who attend a Mainline Protestant church. In 1972, about three in ten (28 percent) Americans claimed a Mainline affiliation, while about one out of every eleven Americans (8.6 percent) claimed to regularly attend a Mainline church. In 2014, only 12.2 percent of Americans had a Mainline affiliation, while only 3.6 percent attended a Mainline church. (See Figure 2.)

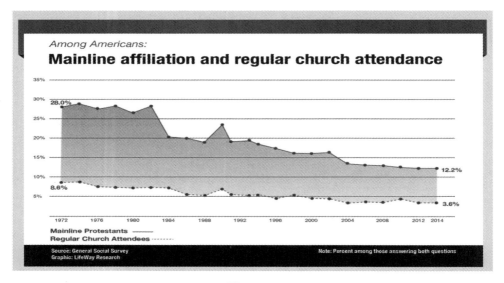

Figure 2

One of the most striking pieces of evidence for the decline of self-identified Christians comes from Pew Research's 2015 Religion Landscape study. That study, which included more than thirty-five thousand Americans, found that the percentage of adults (ages eighteen and older) who described themselves as Christians dropped by nearly eight percentage points over just seven years—from 78.4 percent in 2007 to 70.6 percent in 2014.[7]

That decline in Christian affiliation coincided with the rise of the "Nones" (those who claim no religious affiliation). Both the Pew and ARIS[8] figures show an increasing number of Americans have joined the Nones. According to Pew, about one in four Americans (23 percent) are now Nones.

According to Pew, "This is a stark increase from 2007, the last time a similar Pew Research study was conducted, when 16 percent of Americans were 'Nones.'"[9]

These statistics—an overall decrease in church attendance, a decrease in the number of people who describe themselves as Christians, and the

---

[7] "America's Changing Religious Landscape," Pew Research Center, May 2015, http://www.pewforum.org/2015/05/12/americas-changing-religious-landscape.

[8] The 2009 ARIS study found a rise in the "Nones," going from 8 percent to 15 percent. See Ed Stetzer, "The State of the Church in America," *The Exchange*, n.p., cited December 18, 2015. Online: http://www.christianitytoday.com/edstetzer/2013/october/state-of-american-church.html.

[9] "A Closer Look at America's Rapidly Growing Religious Nones," Pew Research Center, October 2012, http://www.pewresearch.org/fact-tank/2015/05/13/a-closer-look-at-americas-rapidly-growing-religious-nones/.

rise of the Nones—have led some to argue that the end of Christianity is near. Writer Hemant Mehta, best known as the "Friendly Atheist" blogger, says that those who disagree with that claim are just "rearranging the deck chairs on the Titanic."[10]

First, church attendance is one of the best statistical tools we have to gauge religious trends. These statistics are used by various people, with varying motives, to advance their narrative about the future of the church in American.

Some, who see Christianity as threat to the common good, want to promote the idea that the church is in a free fall. Others use bad news as a sales strategy for books and conferences: bad news sells; good news bores.

Others use these statistics as motivational tools. Claiming that Christians are threatened by divorce may make couples focus on their marriage. Telling parents that their children will leave the church may inspire them to support strong youth ministries. Warning churches that their pastors are underpaid and overworked—and might bolt from the ministry—may help churches' boards take better care of their shepherds.

Those may be good aims. But they often leave pastors, church leaders, and people in the pew with a distorted view of reality, at least when it comes to the church in America.

Second, though church attendance is among the best tools we have at our disposal to dialogue internally (among cobelligerents and like-minded Christians) and externally (often with hostile voices), these tools don't *literally* measure the vitality of Christianity *itself*. Part of the Chicken Little myth is alignment with an argument contrary to Matthew 16:18; God's mission force (the church) will never be stopped, not even if American church attendance trends suggest otherwise. These trends help Christians understand *how* to engage, not if they can engage or whether they should. Christianity is doing well, and will continue to exist, not because of its numbers and trends, but because of its savior.

Let me share with you four frames that more accurately capture the overall condition of Christianity in the United States:

Frame #1: Church attendance has slightly declined, but has remained relatively steady.

Back in 2013, the *Huffington Post* published an article entitled "Why Nobody Wants to Go to Church Anymore," inspired by a book written by

---

[10] Hemant Mehta, "Yes, Christianity Is Dying, and Conservative Leaders Are Avoiding the Most Obvious Solution," Patheos, May 18, 2015, http://www.patheos.com/blogs/friendly atheist/2015/05/18/yes-christianity-is-dying-and-conservative-leaders-are-avoiding-the -most-obvious-solution/.

Joani and Thom Schultz.[11] The post's author, Steve McSwain, criticized me for saying that the church is not dying. He went on to argue, based upon data from the Hartford Institute for Religion Research, that the church is in serious trouble. Among the statistics he cited: estimates that only 20 percent of Americans attend church each week and that more than four thousand churches shut their doors each year.

Chronicling church attendance data over time is important, in these cases. McSwain is partly right. Yes, based upon this research (Figure 1), the church in America has experienced a decline in attendance. And yes, many churches close their doors each year. However, although overall church attendance has declined by a few percentage points since 1972, it still hovers around the same rates as in the 1940s (according to Gallup). In 1940, 37 percent of Americans said "Yes" when asked by Gallup if they had been to church within the last week. In 2015, almost the same number (36 percent) said they'd been to church. So, it's silly to say that Christianity is dying—such claims are driven by a hostile agenda, not the facts.

Attendance is down, slightly, among Americans, but no one should suggest that it means "lights out" for the church; this is not an alarming trend, a so-called "steep decline," from a historical perspective.

Frame #2: Mainline Protestantism is hemorrhaging.

While overall church attendance is relatively stable, there is a segment of Christian churches that have taken a downward plunge. Protestantism is perhaps the best known through the "seven sisters" of the mainline churches. They include:

United Methodist Church
Evangelical Lutheran Church in America (ELCA)
Episcopal Church
Presbyterian Church (U.S.A.)
American Baptist Churches
United Church of Christ (UCC)
The Christian Church (Disciples of Christ)

In recent decades, these denominations have all experienced significant decline. As discussed earlier, in 1972 28 percent of Americans claimed to be part of a Mainline Church. In 2014, that figure dropped to 12.2 percent. This is no slight decline—this steep decline is a hemorrhage.

---

[11]Steve McSwain, "Why Nobody Wants to Go to Church Anymore," *Huffington Post*, December 27, 2015, http://www.huffingtonpost.com/steve-mcswain/why-nobody-wants-to-go-to_b_4086016.html.

This decline is based on a number of factors, including the so-called "birth dearth"—Mainline Protestants have fewer children per capita than Evangelical Christians, as sociologists Michael Hout, Andrew Greeley, and Melissa Wilde point out.

Mainline Protestants also have one of the lowest retention rates among American Christians.[12] Only 26 percent of those raised as Mainline Protestants remain in that tradition as adults—compared to 62 percent of those raised as Evangelicals. In other words, only about one in four children whose parents and grandparents were mainline Protestants are carrying on the family tradition.[13]

Frame #3: Nominal Christians and the growing "Nones" perpetuate a false narrative.

Pew Research noted that the number of people who self-identify as a Christian has dropped nearly 8 percent over the past seven years.[14] Part, though not all, is due to the decline among nominal Christians.

In the research world, we have a term for people who exaggerate (in a socially-desirable direction) when surveyed. It's called the "halo effect." The halo effect is the idea that people will answer things in ways that they think are affirmed by society.

In the past, when asked what faith they identified with, most Americans said they were Christian, even if they had no connection to a church. That's in part because being described as Christian was considered socially advantageous. Being Christian meant you were a good person. Being Christian meant you were a good neighbor, a trustworthy business operator. Today, because of the changing cultural landscape, more people find it preferable, or of equitable social value, to answer "None." There's less pressure and less benefit to identify with a specific faith in American culture. And, in my view, people who have no ties with organized religion are now being more honest. About one in four Americans and one-third of adults under the age of thirty are now religiously unaffiliated.[15] It's not that those interviewed are necessarily *less* Christian than they were, but that they describe themselves, finally, *more honestly* in regards to faith. That's actually a pathway forward for Christians to pursue, not a dead-end.

---

[12] Michael Lupka, "Mainline Protestants make up shrinking number of U.S. adults," Pew Research, May 18, 2015, http://www.pewresearch.org/fact-tank/2015/05/18/mainline -protestants-make-up-shrinking-number-of-u-s-adults.

[13] Vern L. Bengtson, *Families and Faith: How Religion Is Passed Down across Generations* (New York: Oxford University Press), 2013.

[14] Again, the research was based upon a survey of 35,000 Americans. See http://www .pewforum.org/2015/05/12/americas-changing-religious-landscape/.

[15] Ibid.

Frame #4: Christianity, noticeably, has lost its home-field advantage.

For most of our nation's history, Christians, and especially Protestants, have been America's "home team." In recent years, Christianity has been losing home-field advantage. How did Christianity lose its place of cultural prominence?

First, the fragmentation in American churches has diluted their cultural and political influence. According to the Hartford Institute for Religion Research, there are at least 217 different denominations in the United States. Additionally, there are scores of nondenominational churches. According to the 2010 Religious Congregation Membership Study, there are likely more than thirty-five thousand independent or nondenominational churches in the United States, representing more than 12.2 million members.[16]

Among those churches, there is a vast array of theological, missiological, cultural, and political differences. As a result, the church lacks both unity and uniformity. To borrow a phrase from James Davison Hunter, the church has lost a "binding address." And in order to speak with one voice and earn a hearing in culture, such a binding address is necessary. "The strength of culture [or in the church's case, subculture], then, is measured by the power of its address on people," Hunter writes. "Only when there is binding address is there the moral energy necessary to motivate men and integrate communities."[17] As a result, churches end up fragmented, fractured, and frustrated within a volatile and progressive culture.

Second, growing pluralism (the coexistence of various ideas, philosophies, religions, and authorities) in American culture has continued to marginalize the church. In some ways, the church has been drowned out amongst a sea of competing voices.

Although America was founded with a focus on free exercise of religion and principled religious pluralism, the kind of pluralism we experience today has left the American culture, in general, fragmented. Just as the church has experienced fragmentation and fracture because of its lack of binding address, so too has the broader American culture. As a result, American culture consists of various "plausibility structures" competing and living simultaneously beside others.[18]

---

[16] Hartford Institute for Religion Research, "Fast Facts about American Religion," accessed December 27, 2015, http://hirr.hartsem.edu/research/fastfacts/fast_facts.html#denom.

[17] Hunter, *Evangelicalism*, 210.

[18] James Davison Hunter, *To Change the World: The Irony, Tragedy, and Possibility of Christianity in the Late Modern World* (New York: Oxford University Press, 2010), 202. Peter Berger is noted for coining the term "plausibility structures." In his work *The Sacred Canopy,*

With this kind of environment, Hunter notes, "[O]ne is no longer enveloped by a unified and integrated normative universe but confronted by multiple and fragmented perspectives, any or all of which may seem, on their own terms, eminently credible."[19] The phrase "on their own terms" is key. Rugged individualism plays host to the virus of this new form of pluralism—the idea that what may be right for one group may be wrong for another—which fragments and fractures a society.

Third, there is a growing skepticism about institutions (in general) and religion (in particular). Hunter argues that this kind of skepticism leads us to "a place where we are always left wondering if nothing in particular is real or true or good."[20] I think he is correct.

In this section I have attempted to illustrate why some have distorted the narrative of the church in America by misusing good statistics, or using bad ones well. In addition, I have attempted to outline four frames that I believe represent a more accurate picture of the ecclesial and cultural landscape. In short: *the reality is that the church in America operates within a mission field where it has lost home-field advantage, and that's not necessarily a bad thing.*

That loss of prominence has led many cultural elites—media outlets, researchers, scholars, sociologists, and ecclesial antagonists—to argue that American Christianity is doomed. That claim, according to the research, does not hold up. However, the church in American is losing cultural influence, and is at risk of becoming irrelevant to groups with more social credibility. I understand why some assume the sky is falling, but with a closer look at the facts we can do better, and do better by the culture, than to perpetuate that assumption.

Berger describes a "plausibility structure" as a social construct that is created when what one believes is dramatized or demonstrated in their social action. In other words, what they believe is enacted in their daily life. See Peter Berger, *The Sacred Canopy: Elements of a Sociological Theory of Religion* (New York: Doubleday, 1967), 45. The culture war is a struggle between the competing plausibility structures. Lesslie Newbigin interacted with Berger's terminology and line of thought by arguing that for the gospel to engage a pluralistic and pagan culture, the church would have to not relegate the gospel to the private realm of beliefs or values, but it would need to hold and apply the gospel to both the public and private realms. See Lesslie Newbigin, *Foolishness to the Greeks: The Gospel in a Western Culture* (Grand Rapids: Eerdmans, 1986), 10–20.

[19] Berger calls this the heretical imperative, and argues that in modern Western culture people no longer acknowledge or accept a dominant or traditional "plausibility structure"; rather, they choose one for themselves. See Peter Berger, *The Heretical Imperative: Contemporary Possibilities of Religious Affirmation* (Garden City, NY: Anchor Press, 1979).

[20] Hunter, *To Change the World*, 205–6.

Accurately Measuring and Assessing the Mission Force

There is some growth, especially in one segment of the Protestant church. That group is Evangelicals.

What exactly is an Evangelical? The best working definition is the so-called "Bebbington quadrilateral," named for historian David Bebbington. According to Bebbington's definition, Evangelicals have four distinguishing characteristics: (1) a transformed life through following Jesus, (2) faith demonstrated through missionary and social reform efforts, (3) a regard for the Bible as the ultimate authority, and (4) a central focus on the sacrificial death of Jesus.

In 2015, the National Association of Evangelicals (NAE) and LifeWay Research created, and the NAE officially adopted, a joint statistical construct to help identify people with evangelical beliefs. Following Bebbington, but focusing only on beliefs, people are counted as evangelical when they strongly agree with four statements.

- The Bible is the highest authority for what I believe.

- It is very important for me personally to encourage non-Christians to trust Jesus Christ as their Savior.

- Jesus Christ's death on the cross is the only sacrifice that could remove the penalty of my sin.

- Only those who trust in Jesus Christ alone as their Savior receive God's free gift of eternal salvation.

About three in ten Americans would be evangelicals using this statistical measure.

In the United States, Evangelicals, like the Nones, are on the rise.

Using the RELTRAD tool, we can see that, according to the GSS, more people classify themselves as an Evangelical today than in 1972, and more people attend an Evangelical church on a weekly basis than in 1972 (see Figure 3).

If you look closely at the timeline from the GSS, you can see that church attendance for Evangelicals peaked in the '80s and '90s. Still, the percentage of Americans who attend an Evangelical church has increased dramatically since the 1970s.

I recently interviewed Greg Smith of Pew Research on their data. He explained:

> With respect to Evangelicalism in particular I would say that, particularly compared with other Christian traditions in the United States, Evangelicalism is quite strong. It's holding its own in terms of its share of the total population.

It's holding its own in terms of the number of Americans who identify with Evangelical Christianity. If you look at Christianity as a whole or Protestantism as a whole, the share of Protestants in the United States who are Evangelicals is, if anything, growing. So are there challenges for Evangelicalism and for Catholicism and mainline Protestantism? There's no question about that. Are any number of religious groups going to have to confront some of the generational patterns that we're seeing in these data? That's without question.[21]

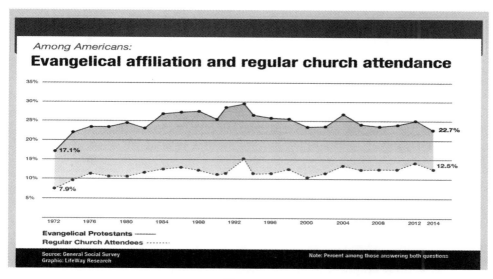

Figure 3

So, people who say that Evangelicalism is collapsing, dying, emptying, or whatever, are driven by something other than the numbers. This is not to say that, to quote the *Lego Movie,* "everything is awesome" among Evangelicals. But the reality is that Evangelicalism, as a whole, is not declining. In fact, one out of every eight Americans is a regular church-attending Evangelical—or, according to Pew, roughly 62.2 million people.[22]

Much of the growth among Evangelicals is due to the rise of nondenominational churches. From the established baseline in 1972–1976 of those who would classify themselves as nondenominational, nondenominationalism has experienced 428 percent growth. (See Figure 4.)

---

[21]"Religion in America: An Interview with Greg Smith of the Pew Research Center (Part 2)" by Ed Stetzer, *Christianity Today,* January 29, 2016, http://www.christianitytoday.com/edstetzer/2016/january/religion-in-america-interview-with-greg-smith-part-2.html.

[22]See GSS (General Social Survey) for one out of eight, http://gss.norc.org. For 62.2 million, see the Pew Research Forum, http://www.pewforum.org/2015/05/12/americas-changing-religious-landscape/.

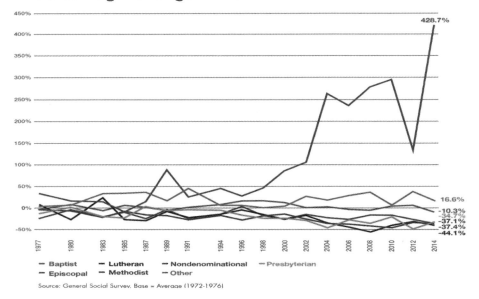

RISE OF NONDENOMINATIONALISM IN AMERICA

Percentage Change in Denomination

Source: General Social Survey. Base = Average (1972-1976)

Figure 4

Interestingly, nondenominationals in a few years will be, as a percentage, the largest group inside Evangelicalism. As of 2016, they comprise almost 30 percent of the total Evangelical population.

Outreach magazine's Top 100 (2015) reveals that 50 percent of the fastest growing churches and 46 percent of the largest churches in America are nondenominational.[23] And this does not take into account those churches that may affiliate with a denomination, but whose constituents may still view themselves as nondenominational. For example, many members and attenders of LifeChurch.tv, a multisite congregation with campuses across the United States, would not know they are affiliated with the Evangelical Covenant Church, a denomination descended from the Swedish dissenting movement.

Takeaways

There are at least four takeaways from the experience of American Evangelicals:

---

[23]"The 100 Fastest Growing Churches in America," *Outreach*, September 2015, http://www.outreachmagazine.com/wp-content/uploads/2015/09/15–100_PDF-Lists-Download.pdf.

Active Faith, Not Passive, Wins People

First, the group most known for more public and active faith—a faith that holds to the centrality of Christ's death and resurrection, conversionism, mission, and scriptural authority—has experienced overall growth in the last five decades. Evangelicals, at least by Bebbington's definition, turn their faith into action. They call people to repentance and faith, send and support missionaries, and commit to planting new churches. That's not exclusively an Evangelical, or Christian, reality—I could say much the same about Mormons. If churches desire to grow, they must challenge their members to activate their faith in a way that publically engages the culture and people therein.

Not Out of the Woods Yet

Despite their growth, Evangelicals face many challenges. One challenge is the decline of Evangelical denominations. These denominations seem to be declining in part because they overstated their size in the past. As a larger number of denominations become more accurate in reporting their membership and attendance, those denominations' decline will become clearer too. We'll also see denominations decline due to aging populations and declining birthrates. Nominal members will continue to drop out, while older congregations will struggle to adapt to a rapidly changing cultural context.

Another challenge is the influence of consumerism on churches. Many churches have become providers of religious goods and services, trying out the next best thing to attract bored Christians with lively and relevant experiences. Every new sermon series or program is advertised as the most exciting ever. As a result, believers are taught to look for God in the "epic" one-hour, weekend service rather than in day-to-day ordinary life. In other words, consumerism turns believers into spiritual junkies who live for the next spiritual high, rather than apostolic missionaries who live sent in their everyday lives. This will remain a growing challenge for Evangelicals who were influenced by the church growth movement (of the 1990s and 2000s), and who are now targeting a growing Millennial population whose most compelling apologetic is authenticity.

The Rise of the Evangelical Nones

Third, the rise in nondenominational affiliation has coincided with the decline of denominational loyalty. While denominations have many benefits (theological, methodological, and historical tradition, opportunity for close unity/fellowship, cooperation in missions/church planting, etc.), many newer churches have found it liberating to be an independent church—

detached from any denominational baggage (theological and methodological debates, in-fighting, and distraction from mission). In fact, many pastors
believe that they can be more effective by *not* advertising their denominational affiliation. This belief can be seen in the practice of newer churches
refraining from putting their affiliation in their name.

Certainly, the rise of the Nones within the broader American culture
and the rise of the Nones within Evangelicalism are interesting occur-
rences.[24] But perhaps they illustrate a particular cultural value shared by
many Americans—contempt for "labels." Many find labels restricting, con-
fining, offensive, or unfair. Thus, avoiding labels means freedom from judgment as well as liberty for individual expression.

The Emergence of Networks and Associations

Fourth, with the rise of nondenominationalism there has been a rise in
(nondenominational) networks and associations. There is some irony in this.
Although they don't affiliate with any denomination, many nondenominational
churches have formed, or are associated with, networks. And ironically, some
networks are likely to become denominations, or at least to act like denominations. For example, both the Vineyard and Calvary Chapel (early forerunners
of networks) basically function like denominations today. Additionally, other
networks and associations, such as A29 (Acts 29), ARC, Newthing, Multiply
Group, and Stadia, have been created to help fund and train church planters.
Furthermore, networks such as The Gospel Coalition, founded by D. A. Car-
son and Tim Keller, exist to encourage and educate Christians to "renew the
contemporary church in the ancient gospel of Christ."[25]

Networks and associations such as those listed above serve as community groups for leaders to find training, support, encouragement, and
fellowship—things that many feel bureaucratic, inefficient, and institutional
denominations cannot offer. Thus, it seems that at least for the foreseeable
future Evangelicalism will retain some level of influential presence using
nondenominational networks and associations.

A close look at the numbers reveals that Evangelicalism has fared better
than Mainline Protestantism over the last few decades. In reality, Evangelicalism embodies a mission force that has experienced some success, especially since 1972. Sure, some can point to sects of Evangelicalism and say
that Christianity is struggling; however, they cannot say—thanks in large
part to the rise of the Evangelical "Nones"—it is dying, or even declining.

---

[24] Another group of people within American culture that avoids being affiliated with
any one group is the "Independent" voter block.

[25] See "Overview," The Gospel Coalition, http://www.thegospelcoalition.org/about/overview.

Preparing Ourselves for God's Continued Work

Christianity in America isn't dying, nor is it thriving. That's the bad news, according to measures of religious affiliation and church attendance. However, the good news is that Jesus declared He is the rock upon which He will build His church and the gates of hell will not prevail against it. Jesus continues to build his church around the world—including here in America. Some research reveals that God is still surprisingly at work within our changed and changing culture.

As the church moves onward into this uncharted future, let me suggest some ways it can continue preparing itself as God's mission force within its mission field.

Understand the Culture

First, the church needs to understand the new cultural reality in which we live. We live in a day of increased complexity. Although 70–75 percent of Americans still claim to be "Christian," the "Christian" they claim is much different than what the Bible portrays.

I find it helpful to separate those who profess Christianity into three categories: *cultural, congregational,* and *convictional.*

Cultural Christians

This first category is made up of people who believe themselves to be Christians simply because their culture tells them they are. They are Christian by heritage. They stand to benefit in some way by being identified as Christian. They may have religious roots in their family or may come from a people group tied to a certain religion, such as southern Evangelicals or Irish Catholics. Inside the church, we would say they are Christians in name only. They are not practicing a vibrant faith. This group makes up around one-third of the 75 percent who self-identify as Christians—or about a quarter of all Americans.

Congregational Christians

The second category is similar to the first group, except these individuals at least have some connection to congregational life. They have a home church they grew up in, and perhaps where they were married. They might visit occasionally. Here, again, we would say that these people are not practicing any sort of real, vibrant faith. They are attendees only. This group makes up another third of the 75 percent—or about a quarter of all Americans.

These two groups make up what I call nominal Christianity. They are essentially "Nones in disguise." Their numbers will likely decline in the future.

Convictional Christians

The final group is made up of people who are actually living according to their faith. These are the people who would say they have been personally transformed by a personal relationship with Jesus and their lives have been increasingly oriented around their faith. Convictional Christians make up the final third of the 75 percent—or about a quarter of all Americans. The future American church will likely be built on this third group.

Strengthen Families with Faith

Along with understanding its cultural context, the church should also concentrate on strengthening the faith of the family unit. The vitality of tomorrow's church and its mission force will be predicated on the faithfulness of today's families. In other words, the family plays a major role in the participation of the coming generations' faith, as University of Southern California researcher Vern L. Bengtson describes in his book *Families and Faith: How Religion Is Passed Down across Generations.*[26]

Bengtson followed 358 families from 1970–2005 to see how they passed religion along to their children. In all, he and his team surveyed 3,500 family members from a variety of faiths. What they found at the conclusion of their study was that Mormons, Jews, Evangelicals, and Nones are the best at passing on beliefs to their children. (See Table 1.)

Table 1: Percentage of Parents Whose Children Had the Same Religion

Mormons	85%
Jews	82%
Evangelicals	62%
Catholics	43%
Mainline Protestant	26%

---

[26] Bengtson, *Families and Faith.* Data for Table 1 is taken from this study.

Bengtson expresses how important it is for children to see their parents exercise their faith. "If Christian parents speak about the importance of studying the Bible but never read the Bible," he told an interviewer, "then their child will see hypocrisy and turn away from their family's religion."[27] This may explain, partially, why many of the children of Congregational and Cultural Christian parents leave the faith. They simply do not see Christianity practiced faithfully. Thus, for the mission force (the church) to exhibit vitality in the future will require the strengthening of the parents' faith today. The church should take note and chart ways to focus on discipling the family unit.

Think Outside the Box

Third, the established church needs to think outside the box. I intentionally use the word "established" because existing churches tend to be less willing to think outside the box then new churches, who have no box (yet). According to research, a large majority of existing churches (across all denominations) are either experiencing decline or plateau. And many times it's due to a failure to change—to think outside the box.

By referring to "thinking outside the box," all I am suggesting is to be open to new ways in which God can work. Who would have thought thirty years ago that attendance at nondenominational churches would increase 428 percent? Although I defend denominationalism, nondenominationalism was a way to break out of the "denominational box." God has worked, and seems to continue to work, through nondenominationalism.

As the church moves into new cultural waters, it must be open to riding waves of new ideas and ways for God to work. As recently as today, one can be sure God is working in new ways and new places. He's working through missional incarnational communities, house church movements, new smaller networks and associations, third places, launching of new satellite campuses (multisite), and contemporary churches being planted in movie theaters and pubs.[28] Our culture has left (and continues to leave) the church; thus, we must look for new ways to go to where they are.

You're Not Supposed to Be Home

Fourth, Christians must realize their home isn't to be "won back" in America, but one day consummated in the future. Christians no longer

---

[27] Vincent Lim, "Professor's Book Challenges Prevailing Notions about Faith and American Families," *USC Social Work*, https://sowkweb.usc.edu/news/professor's-book-challenges-prevailing-notions-about-faith-and-american-families.

[28] See Henry Blackaby, *Experiencing God: Knowing and Doing the Will of God* (Nashville: B&H Publishing Group, 2008).

find themselves at home in American culture. In a short amount of time, the culture has changed so much that the church finds itself in a somewhat foreign environment. They are sojourners in a foreign land (1 Pet 2:11).

A church's or Christian's perspective on what their future home is shapes their posture and engagement with culture in the present. The current reality reveals that Christian perspectives are all over the map. For some, "home" is to reclaim the center, because they already feel like the church is being marginalized. They believe, in many cases, that God is judging America because of culture's drift toward secularism. Thus, they seek to "reclaim Christian America" through ad hominem attacks born out of resentment. They also seek to reclaim the center through evangelism. Oddly enough, they expect people—the very ones they attack and call out on Facebook and Twitter—to be open to the gospel.

For others, "home" is working for the common good. They feel like the church and the culture have enough in common to benefit one another. They react to those who want to reclaim the center by taking more of a retreat posture, through cultural accommodation. Accommodating the culture comes from their over-sensitivity to refrain from offending people even at the expense of the gospel. And that is why their posture and engagement is one of retreat.

Still others understand "home" to be the future New City of Jerusalem, which is the soon-coming consummated kingdom of God. However, their posture and engagement is one of recalibration given they are finding their bearings in this new cultural reality. For many, it will take time to understand how to pursue the mission of God within this new cultural reality.

Conclusion

As Dorothy was transported to Oz, the church has been swept up in a cultural tornado that has left it far away from home. This is one point the church has in common with Dorothy. Another point of commonality is the onward journey toward home. If you know the story of *The Wizard of Oz*, you know that Dorothy embarked on an adventure to see the wizard in hopes to get back home. However, home for Dorothy is quite different from the home the church should long for.

Dorothy longed to go back home to Kansas with Auntie Em and Uncle Henry on their nice quaint farm. Home for her was about regaining what she lost. But the church should have a different perspective about home. Home for the church isn't something to regain or reclaim; it's something much better, more glorious. Jesus is preparing our home, and at the divinely appointed time he will bring our home to earth in the form of a city (Revelation 21). Therefore, we march onward not to "reclaim" Christian America, but to embody and enact our future abode, the New City of Jerusalem—the consummated kingdom of God—in the here and now.

In this chapter I have explained why some suggest "the sky is falling" for Christianity in America. The way many use research—whether good research or bad—distorts the true picture of the church in America. Clearly, the ground is shifting. There's no doubt that some denominations, particularly those within Mainline Protestantism, have struggled greatly, and if they don't stop the metaphorical bleeding they will find themselves on life support in the next 20–30 years.

Additionally, some groups have experienced an increase in attendance and affiliation since 1972, namely nondenominational Evangelicalism, while others have experienced decline in their attendance and affiliation (most notably, the Southern Baptist Convention). However, based upon the research, the "sky" isn't falling for Christianity in America. Are there clouds and some storms? Sure. But the church's mission will not, cannot, be stopped.

In short, I believe the numbers reveal the reality that the church has been pushed further into the margins away from the center of societal privilege, and that many who would have at one time classified themselves as "Christian" are finding it easier to be honest and simply check "None." This is the new reality, but it's not a position we should lament.

In fact, Randall Balmer contends that "religion always functions best from the margins of society and not in the councils of power."[29] In response, we must engage in this new cultural milieu (mission field) by understanding the culture and the people therein. We must seek to live in this culture as a mission force that embodies and enacts the New City (kingdom) to come by sharing and showing the gospel of King Jesus. And finally, we must be open to God working in new, surprising ways that we may not be accustomed to. By doing these things, we can be prepared to navigate an Oz-like mission field in a way that exhibits the strength, vitality, and fruitfulness of God's mission force.

---

[29] Randall Balmer, *God in the White House: A History; How Faith Shaped the Presidency from John F. Kennedy to George W. Bush* (New York: HarperOne, 2008), 167.

9

THE AMERICAN CONTRIBUTION TO WORLDWIDE EVANGELICAL CHRISTIANITY IN THE TWENTIETH CENTURY

Mark Noll

On the night of Saturday, August 19, 2000, at the Roman Catholic World Youth Day in Rome, and after an address from Pope John Paul II, over one million young people from many countries watched a movie together.[1] The movie was the "Jesus" film, which had been first produced in 1979 and then aggressively distributed around the world by Campus Crusade for Christ International, an American evangelical para-church youth ministry founded in 1951.[2] The movie presents a minimalist depiction of the life of Christ, taken from the Gospel of Luke. It concludes with a direct appeal for viewers to recognize that Jesus, "the Son of God, the Savior, . . . wants to come into your life," and offers a model prayer that includes the statement, "I open the door of my life and receive you as Savior and Lord."[3] Ten weeks before the mass viewing of this movie in Rome, and halfway around the world in Chandigarh, Punjab state, India, Mr. Ashish Prabhash was first stabbed and then burned in his home, possibly by right-wing

---

[1] The original version of this paper, prepared for delivery in France, was published in a French translation as "L'influence amèricaine sur le christianisme évangélique mondial au XXe siècle," in *Le Protestantisme Évangélique: Un Christianisme de Conversion*, ed. Sébastien Fath (Turnhout, Belgium: Brepols, 2004), 59–80; it also served for trying out some ideas later published in my book *The New Shape of World Christianity: How American Experience Reflects Global Faith* (Downers Grove, IL: InterVarsity, 2009). I have welcomed the opportunity to return and revise the paper, which has never been published in English, as a tribute to Garth Rosell, whose scholarship on both earlier and later phases of American evangelical history dealt so insightfully with many of the themes treated in this paper.

[2] Paul A. Eshleman, "The 'Jesus' Film: A Contribution to World Evangelism," *International Bulletin of Missionary Research* 26 (April 2002): 68.

[3] "Jesus" (Inspirational Films/The Genesis Project, 1979; distributed by Campus Crusade for Christ, Liguna Niguel, CA).

Hindu militants. The murdered man worked for India Campus Crusade for Christ and was engaged in showing the "Jesus" film to rural villagers in his region.[4] Six years earlier four Rwandans who also worked with Campus Crusade in showing the film had been among the many victims in that nation's tragic genocide.[5] During the year 2000, videocassettes of the movie were distributed to two hundred thousand homes in Leicester, Carlisle, and the London borough of Lewisham, in the United Kingdom; plans were set in motion to deliver it to every household in Invercargill, New Zealand, one of the southernmost cities on the planet; and Campus Crusade released a DVD of the film that could be viewed with eight separate languages—Arabic, English, French, Japanese, Korean, Mandarin Chinese, Portuguese, and Spanish—thus providing versions understandable by over half the people in the world.[6]

The phenomenal scale of distribution of the "Jesus" film, to which we will return, suggests a number of important features concerning the American evangelical contribution to the recent world history of Christianity. The Campus Crusade film is representative of the globalization of trade, goods, and culture—as well as religion—in which the United States has played a leading part. It speaks of the large number of American volunteers who have left their own shores to work as Christian evangelists in other lands and of the relatively ample funding that has supported them. The film also illustrates a characteristically American alliance of advanced technology and evangelistic zeal. Perhaps most importantly, it displays the conversionistic and voluntaristic character of much American religion, as well as—in the case of Ashish Prabhash—the cultural disruption caused in some places where Americans have carried their conversionist, voluntaristic understanding of the Christian gospel.

As a contribution to the immense terrain of "world-wide evangelical Christianity," this study first examines the changing character of the twentieth-century American missionary force and surveys assessments of American missionary activity in other parts of the world. It then tries to explain why American-like forms of evangelical Christianity have expanded so rapidly during the second half of the twentieth century. The conclusion to which the study points is that while in recent decades world Protestant movements have come increasingly to take on some of the characteristics of American evangelicalism, the reason for that development has less to do

---

[4] *Financial Times* Asia Intelligence Wire from *The Hindu*, June 12 and June 17, 2000.

[5] *St. Petersburg Times*, August 6, 1994, 4.

[6] *Leicester Mercury*, Nov. 22, 1999, 13; *Southland Times* (N.Z.), June 5, 1999, 30; *Christianity Today*, Dec. 6, 1999, 22 (the DVD).

with the direct influence of American evangelicals themselves and more to do with the general transformation of world social orders in a pattern that American evangelicals had earlier experienced in the social history of the United States.

For the purposes of this study, "evangelicals" designates the modern descendants of pietistic and awakening movements in eighteenth-century Britain, America, and the Continent who continue to maintain the most prominent convictions of those earlier movements, or who promote beliefs and practices developing out of these movements. (Pentecostals and Charismatics are thus included as being descended, in the main, from Holiness offshoots of eighteenth-century Methodism.) In his useful summary of evangelical convictions, the British historian David Bebbington identifies four key ingredients: conversionism (an emphasis on the "new birth" as a life-changing experience of God), biblicism (a reliance on the Bible as ultimate religious authority), activism (a concern for sharing the faith), and crucicentrism (a focus on Christ's redeeming work on the cross, usually pictured as the only way of salvation).[7] "Evangelical" is a notoriously difficult word to define, especially since in the modern world many Roman Catholics also display at least some traditionally evangelical convictions, since many Protestants whom others label "evangelical" do not use that term for themselves, and since at least some traditionally evangelical denominations no longer promote the historic values of the movement.[8] But for the purpose of analyzing the American evangelical impact on the wider world, a definition that links historical continuity and contemporary convictions is probably the most useful.

Counting Missionaries

An examination of the American missionary force is one way to provide concrete information by which to assess the importance of American evangelicals for the United States' role in the world and the effect of American evangelicalism on world Christianity. To be sure, counting missionaries, except among well-organized hierarchical bodies like the Roman Catholic Church or the Church of Jesus Christ of Latter-day Saints

---

[7] David Bebbington, *Evangelicalism in Britain: A History from the 1730s to the 1980s* (London: Unwin Hyman, 1989), 2–17.

[8] For a discussion of the complexities of definition, see "Introduction," *Evangelicalism: Comparative Studies of Popular Protestantism in North America, the British Isles, and Beyond, 1700–1990*, ed. Mark A. Noll, David W. Bebbington, and George A. Rawlyk (New York: Oxford University Press, 1994), 3–7; and Mark A. Noll, *American Evangelical Christianity* (Oxford: Blackwell, 2001), 2, 12–15, 28–43.

(Mormons), is always a risky venture, at best. But throughout the twentieth century, international organizations and several American agencies tried to provide reliable information on the numbers, funding, and location of Christian missionaries. Despite problems of precision, a digest of that information, as summarized in the tables that follow, points toward definite conclusions.

Table 1: Overseas Missionary Personnel (World and United States)

	Total Prot. Missionaries	US Prots.	US % of total	US RC	US Mormons
1903	15,288	ca. 4,000	26%		
1911	20,333	ca. 7,900	39%		
1925	29,188				
1932				866	
1935		11,899			
1952		12,536			
1960		ca. 27,400			
1963				7,000	
1968		ca. 33,000		9,655	
1970				8,373	
1972	ca. 52,500	34,057	65%	7,691	13,000
1979		50,691		6,455	
1985		64,789		6,056	27,000
1991				5,595	
1999*		41,702+100,752		5,854	
2001	97,732	46,381	47%		

*N.B. Until the 1990s, efforts to count usually combined long term missionaries (career or more than one year) and short term missionaries (less than one year). The Protestant numbers for 1999 offer the number of long term missionaries and then the number of short term (less than one year) missionaries. The numbers for 2001 are for long term, career missionaries. Most Mormon missionaries are two-year appointees.

Sources: (total Protestants 1903, 1991, 1925) Harlan P. Beach and Charles H. Fahs, *World Missionary Atlas* (New York: Institute of Social and Religious Research, 1925), 76. (US Protestants 1903, 1911) Charles W. Forman, "The Americas," *International Bulletin of Missionary Research* 6 (April 1982): 54. (Roman Catholics) "Missions, Catholic (U.S.)," *New Catholic Encyclopedia, vol. XVII: Supplement: Change in the Church* (New York: McGraw-Hill, 1979), 428–29; *Mission Handbook 1991–1992* (Washington, D.C.: U.S. Catholic Mission Association, 1992), 28–29; Matthew Bunson, ed., *Catholic Almanac 2002* (Huntingdon, IN: Our Sunday Visitor, 2002), 447–48. (Protestants 1935, 1952) Joel A. Carpenter, "Appendix: The Evangelical Missionary Force in the 1930s," in *Earthen Vessels: American Evangelicals and Foreign Missions, 1880–1980*, ed. Carpenter and Wilbert R. Shenk (Grand Rapids: Eerdmans, 1990), 335–42. (1972) Edward R. Dayton, ed., *Mission Handbook 1973* (Monrovia, CA: MARC, 1973). (1979, 1985) Samuel Wilson and John Siewert, eds., *Mission Handbook*, 13th ed. (Monrovia, CA: MARC, 1986). (1999) A. Scott Moreau, "Putting the Survey in Perspective," in *Mission Handbook 2001–2003*, ed. John A Siewert and Dotsey Wellner, 18th ed. (Wheaton, IL: EMIS, 2001), 33–79. (2001) Patrick Johnstone and Jason Mandryk, *Operation World* (Carlisle, UK: Paternoster, 2001), 747.

Table 2: Number of US Agencies Founded

1900s	16	1950s	70
1910s	23	1960s	81
1920s	22	1970s	123
1930s	34	1980s	141
1940s	55	1990–1998	66

Source: *Mission Handbook 2001–2003*, 36.

As the first two tables indicate, the American proportion of the world-wide Protestant missionary force rose rapidly at the start of the twentieth century, grew steadily until reaching about two-thirds of the world total in the early 1970s, and still continues as a high proportion despite the recent surge in Protestant missionary volunteers from other countries. That surge is significant for the larger purposes of this paper, however, for it suggests that the number of Protestant missionary volunteers not from the United States has been increasing much more rapidly than the number of American volunteers. Table 2, which shows the rate at which new Protestant missionary agencies were created, indicates steady growth throughout the century, and then a special acceleration in the four decades after World War II. In the 1990s the pace slackened somewhat in the formation of new missionary organizations.

Table 3: Missionary Force 1972:
US Protestant, US Roman Catholic, British Protestant

	US Protestant	US R.C.	British Protestant
Africa	7,671	1,107	2,268
Asia	8,700	2,014	1,566
Europe & USSR	1,871	39	648
Latin America	9,592	3,429	648
Oceania	860	826	270
Total	29,290	7,415	5,400

Source: *Mission Handbook 1973*, 84.

Table 3, which presents comparative information for overseas missionary personnel for the year 1972, illustrates the world situation in greater detail. Britain, which at the start of the century had sent out the most Protestant missionaries, now trailed the United States by a factor of five. The number of American Roman Catholic personnel serving overseas was also larger than the British Protestant force. This same table also reveals the leadership of Protestants in American missionary ventures, since in the early 1970s the ratio of Protestant to Catholic missionaries was almost four to one, while the ratio of self-identified Protestants to Catholics in the United States as a whole was only about 2.4 to one.[9] Even considering the difficulties of precise enumeration, it is clear that American missionaries, especially American Protestant missionaries, had grown significantly by comparison to the missionary efforts of other Protestant countries.

The next tables indicate, in addition, that within the American Protestant missionary force, the number of evangelicals rose steadily throughout the century from a substantial minority to an overwhelming majority by the year 2000. In general terms, major American religious groupings reveal this general pattern throughout the century. Catholic missionary work (Table 1) began only in the early years of the century, rose steadily in number of participants until the late 1960s, and then declined gradually. Missionary activity of the mainline Protestant denominations dominated American missionary efforts at the start of the century, remained strong into the 1950s, and then trailed off significantly. By contrast, evangelical (and Mormon) missionaries made up only a minority of Protestant missionaries early in the century but continued to expand until they came to constitute all but a small fraction of American missionary efforts.

Table 4: U. S. Protestant Missionaries Serving Overseas

(A) Mainline Protestant Denominations

	1935–36	1952	1972	1999
Presbyterian Church (USA)*	2,100	1,805	1,005	772
United Methodist*	1,388	1,667	951	413
ABFMS	495	354	262	120+3
United Church of Canada	452		210	96
Protestant Episcopal	427	207	198	21+32
United Christian Missionary Soc.	173	213	673	
United Church of Christ			244	126

ABFMS = American Baptist Foreign Mission Society

*Methodist and Presbyterian totals for earlier years include numbers from denominations that later merged into the larger continuing denominations.

---

[9] The Gallup Poll in 1971 indicated that 65 percent of Americans identified themselves as Protestants and 26 percent as Catholics (2.5:1). For 1974, the same poll resulted in self-description results of 60 percent Protestant and 27 percent Catholic (2.2:1). *Religion in America, 1977–78*, The Gallup Opinion Index no. 145 (Princeton, NJ: American Institute of Public Opinion, 1978), 37.

(B) Evangelical Denominations

	1935–36	1952	1972	1999
Southern Baptists (1845)	405	855	2,507	4,562
Churches of Christ			1,623	2,168
Assemblies of God (1914)	230	626	967	1,543
Baptist Bible Fellowship (1950)			379	755
Christian & Missionary Alliance (1887)	447	667	803	726
Assoc. Baptists for World Evangel. (1927)			351	716
Baptist Mid Missions (1920)			511	612
Evangelical Free Church (1887)	32	101	181	ca. 600
Mission to the World—PCA				579
CBInternational (1943)				550
Church of the Nazarene (1908)	88	200	495	487
Seventh-day Adventists	1,240	1,107	1,546	514
Mennonite Board (1920)	52	109	454	200
(Swed.) Evangelical Covenant (1885)	38	123	94	92+15
Free Methodists (1885)	141	102	198	75

PCA = Presbyterian Church in America; CB = Conservative Baptists

(C) Interdenominational Agencies

	1935–36	1952	1972	1999
Wycliffe Bible Translators (1935)			2,200	2,930
YWAM (1961)			1,009	1,817
New Tribes Mission (1942)			701	1,514
Campus Crusade for Christ (1951)			114	973
TEAM (1890)	95	636	992	638
SIM (1893)			818	569
Frontiers (1972)				311
Gospel Missionary Union (1892)	42	120	288	163+34
OMF International (1865)			562	156
Operation Mobilization (1957)				171

YWAM = Youth With a Mission; TEAM = The Evangelical Alliance Mission; SIM = Serving in Mission (until the 1980s, Sudan Interior Mission); OMF = Overseas Missionary Fellowship (previously China Inland Mission)

Sources: Carpenter, "Evangelical Missionary Force"; *Mission Handbook 1973*, 89, 97–99; *Mission Handbook 2001–2003*, 51.

Table 5: Evangelical Proportion of US Protestant Missionary Force

(A) Throughout Twentieth Century

1935	40% (4,784 of 11,899)	
1952	49% (6,146 of 12,536)	
1999	91% (38,044 of 41,957)	

(B) In 1999

	Number of agencies	Combined budgets
Evangelical	1,019	$2.37 billion
Mainline	84	$0.52 billion
Other	10	$0.04 billion

"Evangelical" includes groups self-identified as independent, fundamentalist, Pentecostal, as well as evangelical.

Sources: Carpenter, "Evangelical Missionary Force"; *Mission Handbook 2001–2003*, 41.

Admittedly, the designations "evangelical" and "mainline" are fluid. But for the preparation of these tables "evangelical" designates the strongly conversionist groups that stress the four Bebbington characteristics. So defined, the mainline Protestant missionary force would always contain some evangelicals, but would often also stress humanitarian and development programs *instead of* evangelization. Many of the evangelical groups also do humanitarian and development work, but always *alongside of* rather than as a replacement for conversion.

Table 6: US Protestant Missionary Agencies

	Denominational	Non-denominational
1900	74%	26%
1940	55%	45%
1960	34%	66%
1980	26%	74%
1998	18%	82%

Source: *Mission Handbook 2001–03*, 39.

One additional trend is obvious from Tables 4B, 4C, and 6. Especially in the last half of the twentieth century, non-denominational evangelical missionary societies grew much more rapidly than denominational agencies. This development is significant because, in general, the nondenominational agencies tend to be even more aggressively conversionistic than the missionaries from evangelical denominations. In addition, funding for the non-denominational societies is completely entrepreneurial—those who want to be missionaries make contact with their own friends and with individual local churches and from these personal connections gather funds for their own financial support. If leaders of these nondenominational agencies envision large-scale projects (like Campus Crusade's "Jesus" film), their leaders must hustle up the money on their own. The contrast with fundraising among evangelical denominations is not in most cases great, since missionaries affiliated with evangelical denominations usually raise their own financial support in the same way. The major exception is the Southern Baptist Convention, which raises money for its missionaries collectively as a denomination and then as a denomination commissions and funds missionaries for their work. This much more corporate funding scheme, however, is standard among the missionary programs of the mainline Protestant denominations.

The larger point is that, with the exception of the Southern Baptists, the American missionary programs that are most conversionistic in their message are also the most voluntaristic in their methods. Precisely these most conversionistic and voluntaristic mission societies have come to dominate the American missionary force over the course of the last half century.

Many examples could be offered to illustrate the rapid growth and extensive spread of these evangelical missionary organizations. World Vision, an evangelical development and relief agency founded in 1950 to assist orphans in Korea and elsewhere in Asia, during the year 2001 raised 964 million dollars, with about 55 percent coming from American sources. To put that figure into comparative perspective, the income of the World Council of Churches in 1999 was about 27 million dollars (roughly 40 percent from Germany), or only one thirty-fifth of the World Vision total.[10]

Yet for sheer scale and reach, there has been as yet nothing to compare with Campus Crusade's "Jesus" film project.[11] The founder of Campus Crusade, Bill Bright, apparently was thinking about using film for mass evangelism even before the organization was founded in 1951. Bright's thoughts took concrete form when, in the mid-1970s, he met John Heyman, a Jewish filmmaker, who had established the Genesis Project in order to film all the narratives of the entire Bible. Heyman had completed short films of the first twenty chapters of Genesis and the first two chapters of Luke when he was urged to contact Campus Crusade for help in marketing the films to Christian groups. In 1979, Heyman finished his full-length feature on the life of Christ based on the Gospel of Luke, which was then released for commercial distribution. Two years later Campus Crusade secured distribution

---

[10] For World Vision, www.wvi.org/home (Mar. 6, 2002). The World Council of Churches figure was reported on its website as 45.4 million Swiss francs, www.genevabriefingbook.com/chapters/wcc.html (Mar. 6, 2002).

[11] Unless noted otherwise, information is from Eshleman, "The 'Jesus' Film."

rights and began its own effort, which in the words of the project's director was "to show the 'Jesus' film to every person in the world in an understandable language and in a setting near where they live."[12]

Over the last two decades of the twentieth century, steady fixation on this goal, energetic labor by translators and dubbers, a wide network of American and non-American workers, and a steady flow of primarily American donations combined for a staggering result. As of 2000, the film had been shown in every village of Mongolia with over 250 people. It had been shown in over 400,000 villages of India in fifty-one languages. It was available in eighteen different languages for showing in South Africa. Most of the population of Burundi and 40 percent of the population of Rwanda had seen the film.[13] Mother Teresa asked that the film be shown in all her houses for the dying in Calcutta. It was available for downloading in fifty-five languages from the internet, with Arabic being the most often requested language, after English.

In the aggregate, as of March 1, 2002, the film was available in 729 different languages, with an additional 253 translations under preparation; according to Campus Crusade's statistics, it had been viewed by 4,937,942,748 people in 236 countries; over 34 million videocassettes had been distributed; Campus Crusade was using 6,220 full-time workers in 2,797 teams to show the film in 108 different countries; and the film could be connected to the start-up of 115,000 new churches. The most active promoters of the film were the mission boards of two American evangelical denominations (Southern Baptist Convention, Church of the Nazarene), two American interdenominational agencies (World Vision and Operation Mobilization), and the Roman Catholic Church.

In the face of such a flood of data, it is important to remember how the American evangelical concern for documenting Christian work in this way looks to non-Americans. Already in 1926, for instance, Kanzo Uchimura, a Japanese Christian, wrote after visiting the United States,

> Americans are great people; there is no doubt about that. They are great in building cities and railroads. . . . Americans have a wonderful genius for improving breeds of horses, cattle, sheep and swine. . . . Americans too are great inventors. . . . Needless to say, they are great in money. . . . Americans are great in all these things and much else; but *not in Religion*. . . . Americans must *count religion* in order to see or show its value. . . . To them big churches are successful churches. . . . To win the greatest number of converts with the least expense is their constant endeavor. Statistics is their way of showing success or failure in

---

[12] Ibid., 69.

[13] Information on South Africa, Burundi, and Rwanda from Patrick Johnstone and Jason Mandryk, *Operation World: 21st Century Edition* (Carlisle, UK: Paternoster, 2001), 136, 552, 582.

their religion as in their commerce and politics. Numbers, numbers, oh, how they value numbers![14]

However regarded, American ventures like Campus Crusade's "Jesus" film shows the aggressiveness with which American Protestants—with evangelicals in the lead—have carried their message to other parts of the world.

Results of Missionary Efforts?

But what have been the effects of American missionary service on world Christian developments? More particularly, how important have American evangelicals been in the transformation of world Christianity that has taken place over the last century? That transformation—it is worth pausing to note—has involved a breathtaking series of structural changes in the geography, demography, and center of gravity for world Christian adherence.[15] When the great Edinburgh Missionary Conference was held in 1910, over 80 percent of the world's affiliated Christian population lived in Europe and North America. Early in the twenty-first century less than 40 percent of the world's Christian population lived in Europe, and self-professed believers in North America and Europe were among the world's least active Christians in terms of church attendance, Bible reading, and Christian education.

The surprises as well as the magnitude of developments in the twentieth-century history of Christianity can be illustrated by a series of comparisons. By early in the twenty-first century it is probable that more believers attended church in China than in all of so-called "Christian Europe." There were more Anglicans in Nigeria than in England, America, Canada, Australia, and New Zealand combined. Weekly attendance at the Yoido Full Gospel church in Seoul, South Korea (at least 500,000 in its various facilities) was more than the total membership of many substantial American Protestant denominations. As of 1999, the largest chapter of the Jesuits was in India, and not in the United States as had been the case for many decades before. There were more Roman Catholics in the Philippines than in any single country of Europe, including Italy, Spain, or Poland.

---

[14] Uchimura quoted in Andrew F. Walls, "The American Dimension of the Missionary Movement," in *The Missionary Movement in Christian History: Studies in the Transmission of Faith* (Maryknoll, NY: Orbis, 1996), 221–22.

[15] For comprehensive surveys, see David B. Barrett, et al., eds., *World Christian Encyclopedia*, 2 vols. (2nd ed., New York: Oxford University Press, 2001); Todd M. Johnson and Kenneth Ross, eds., *Atlas of Global Christianity* (Edinburgh: Edinburgh University Press, 2009); Jason Mandryk, *Operation World*, 7th ed. (Downers Grove, IL: InterVarsity, 2010); Brian Stiller, ed., *Evangelicals Around the World: A Global Handbook for the 21st Century* (Nashville: Thomas Nelson, 2015).

The 2001 edition of David Barrett's *World Christian Encyclopedia* provided broader evidence about the worldwide sweep of evangelical and evangelical-like movements. Using Barrett's narrowest definition of "evangelical," the *Encyclopedia* found that more "evangelicals" lived in the United States (40.6 million) than anywhere else in the world, but also that the next most populous "evangelical" countries were two where almost no evangelicals had existed one hundred years ago: Brazil (27.7) and Nigeria (22.3).[16] Of the next four countries where Barrett found the largest number of evangelicals, one was a historical center of evangelical strength (the United Kingdom, 11.6), but three had witnessed the growth of substantial evangelical populations mostly in the twentieth century (India, 9.3; South Korea, 9.1; South Africa, 9.1). Of the remaining twenty-four countries where Barrett found at least one million evangelicals, only three were in Europe (Germany, Romania, Ukraine) and one in North America (Canada). Fully ten of these others were in Africa (Angola, Congo-Zaire, Ethiopia, Ghana, Kenya, Mozambique, Rwanda, Tanzania, Uganda, Zambia), five were in Asia (China, Myanmar, Indonesia, Philippines, Australia), and five were in Latin America (Guatemala, Haiti, Mexico, Argentina, Peru).

Employing Barrett's more diffuse categories of "pentecostal," "charismatic," and "neo-independent" underscores more dramatically the world-wide distribution of evangelical-like Christian movements.[17] In the enumeration of these categories, Brazil led all the rest (79.9 million), followed then by the United States (75.2), China (54.3), India (33.5), South Africa (21.2), the Philippines (20.0), Congo—Zaire (17.7), Mexico (13.0), and then many other countries from Asia, Latin America, and Africa, as well as Europe.

A critical question, when considering the scope of American evangelical missionary activity and recent changes in world Christianity, asks where the United States has played a precipitating or only reinforcing role. Such questions open up a subject that is as complex as it has been understudied. The images of missionaries presented in American popular media are almost completely useless for answering this question, since their stock in

---

[16] The *Encyclopedia* defines "evangelicals" like this: "A subdivision mainly of Protestants consisting of all affiliated church members calling themselves Evangelicals, or all persons belong to Evangelical congregations, churches or denominations; characterized by commitment to personal religion."

[17] There is some overlap in the *Encyclopedia*'s enumeration between these three categories and the "evangelical" category. The *Encyclopedia*'s definitions are as follows: "Pentecostals" = Adherents of traditional pentecostal denominations. "Charismatics" = Baptized members affiliated to nonpentecostal denominations who have entered into the experience of being filled with the Holy Spirit; the Second Wave of the Pentecostal/Charismatic/Neocharismatic Renewal. "Neocharismatics/Independents" = Members of the Third Wave of the Pentecostal/Charismatic Renewal characterized by the adjectives Independent, Postdenominationist, and Neo-Apostolic.

trade is the emotive stereotype—whether, from different ideological angles, of innocence among primal peoples, repressed sexuality among mission imperialists, gnostic purity among missionary altruists, or some other purely Western type.[18] But even serious studies of popular missionary images touch only indirectly on the question of how much world Christian history is now being driven by American forces. It is one thing to ask how American missionaries have aided US economic and political interests; it is another to ask why forms of Christianity resembling American evangelicalism in at least some particulars now flourish in so many parts of the globe. More scholarship, unfortunately, has been attempted on the first question than the second.

On that first issue, a substantial literature has grown up around charges from anthropologists, journalists, and political radicals about American missionaries aiding American economic or political imperialism among indigenous peoples of Southeast Asia, Africa, the Philippines, and especially Latin America. The charges, which have been circulating at least since the early 1970s, reprise similar accusations that were once a stock in trade among critics of earlier British missionary activity.[19] The most serious of recent charges contend that the missionary complicity in US imperialism has resulted in ethnocide, or the deliberate destruction of indigenous peoples. Sometimes the accusations have been leveled against evangelical and fundamentalist missionaries in general, sometimes against particular mission organizations. Among the latter, special attention has been paid to two interdenominational organizations. The first is New Tribes Mission, which was founded in 1942 in order to bring Christian evangelism and Bible translations to previously isolated tribal groups. The second is the Wycliffe Bible Translators, an overtly evangelical agency seeking to create Christian churches among tribal peoples around the world. A particular point of contention for critics of Wycliffe is that its personnel also staff the Summer Institute of Linguistics, a self-described scientific organization that offers its services to governments around the world for the purpose of studying, recording, and transcribing previously unwritten languages.

---

[18] The film *Black Robe* (1991) is a rare exception to the stereotyping of missionaries and their work in popular culture, as witnessed for example, with great variation, in the films *The Mission* (1986), *At Play in the Fields of the Lord* (1991), and *The Mosquito Coast* (1986), or in novels like John Grisham, *The Testament* (New York: Doubleday, 1979), and Barbara Kingsolver, *The Poisonwood Bible* (New York: HarperFlamingo, 1998). For an assessment, see Jay Blossom, "Evangelists of Destruction: Missions to Native Americans in Recent Films," in *The Foreign Mission Enterprise at Home: Explorations in North American Cultural History*, ed. Daniel H. Bays and Grant Wacker (Tuscaloosa: University of Alabama, 2003).

[19] For thorough discussion, see Brian Stanley, *The Bible and the Flag: Protestant Missions and British Imperialism in the Nineteenth and Twentieth Centuries* (Leicester, UK: Apollos, 1990).

A lengthy parade of substantial writing made the charges of imperialistic ethnocide against these and similar missionary organizations.[20] The impetus for much of this literature came from a 1971 meeting in Barbados sponsored by the Programme to Combat Racism and the Churches Commission on International Affairs of the World Council of Churches along with the Ethnology Department of the University of Bern, Switzerland. This gathering issued a "Declaration of Barbados: For the Liberation of the Indians" that called upon all interested parties to end the destructive "acts of aggression directed against the aboriginal groups and cultures." The "Declaration" accused several Latin American states of promoting such acts and also implicated the work of missionaries, which "reflects and complements the reigning colonial situation." In particular,

> The missionary presence has always implied the imposition of criteria and patterns of thought and behaviour alien to the colonised Indian societies. A religious pretext has too often justified the economic and human exploitation of the aboriginal population. The inherent ethnocentric aspect of the evangelisation process is also a component of the colonialist ideology.[21]

In the wake of the "Barbados Declaration" a rush of writing followed that expanded on the document's analysis and reinforced its charges against missionary activity. In 1976, for example, Richard Arens edited a collection, *Genocide in Paraguay*, whose eight essays chronicled what the book's contributors called the intentional destruction of the Aché Indians. Critics of this book were, however, quick to point out that only two of its authors had ever visited the Aché themselves.[22]

More substantial was a colloquy from 1981, *Is God an American? An Anthropological Perspective on the Missionary Work of the Summer Institute of Linguistics*. This book included studies of Wycliffe/SIL work among Indian tribes in Bolivia, Brazil, Colombia, Ecuador, and Peru, and more general essays with titles like "The Summer Institute of Linguistics: Ethnocide Disguised as a Blessing" and "God is an American." The book's argument developed in these stages:

1. "The vast majority of the world's unwritten languages are spoken by ethnic groups without long histories of integration into state-level societies."

---

[20] For orientation to this literature, I am indebted to my colleagues Kathryn Long and Dean Arnold, and also to the splendid literature review provided by Jeffrey D. Webster and Thomas N. Headland, "Selected Annotated Bibliography: Conflicts Between Missionaries and Anthropologists and A Review of Missionaries' Reported Involvements in Human Rights," *Missiology* 24 (April 1996): 271–80.

[21] "The Declaration of Barbados," *Current Anthropology* 14 (June 1973): 268.

[22] Richard Arens, ed., *Genocide in Paraguay* (Philadelphia: Temple University Press, 1976). For criticism, Webster and Headland, "Selected Bibliography," 271–72.

2. The mission of Wycliffe/SIL is to reduce as many of these languages as possible to writing, to translate the Bible into these languages, and then to establish evangelical Christian churches among these groups. Wycliffe's rapid post-war expansion has made it a particularly important force among tribal groups, especially in Latin America.

3. Wycliffe's workers see themselves as fighting Satan. "Considering the social background of SIL members, [the] identification of Satan with Communism seems logical. Similarly there is an equally natural tendency for God to be transformed into an American."

4. Whether inadvertently or deliberately, Wycliffe/SIL, thus, perpetuates

> the various injustices suffered by the Indians at the hands of traders, cattle ranchers, professional hunters, rubber collectors, gold prospectors, oil companies, the army and other state institutions. The underlying force behind these diverse forms of encroachment is capitalism's attempt to resolve its internal contradictions by appropriating the Indians' labor-power, land, and resources. . . . The pressures brought to bear on Indian societies have made political and humanitarian assistance for the indigenous groups urgently necessary. This has been the opening of organizations like SIL. The missionaries have exploited the situation to advance their own goals rather than improve the position of the Indians. . . . In trying to solve "the Indian problem" SIL has become "the Indian problem." By implanting into Indian society its individualism and materialism, SIL has deprived them of exactly those social resources and values which could prevent their being totally "integrated" and destroyed. SIL's program tends to produce tribeless Bibles rather than Bible tribes. . . . The campaign against SIL is not against an organization that innocently translates Bibles, provides education or distributes medicine, but against its holy alliance with American ideology, international capitalism, and national "development plans."[23]

A more evenly balanced statement of these early indictments of American missionary work, and Wyclffe/SIL in particular, appeared two years later from David Stoll, who had also contributed an essay to *Is God an American?* His book is entitled *Fishers of Men or Founders of Empire?*[24] Stoll was a trifle less alarmed about SIL serving as a running dog lackey for American ideology and international capitalism. Instead, he was more concerned about what he described as the duplicity of the Bible translators in presenting Wycliffe to

---

[23] Quotations from Søren Hvalkof and Peter Aaby, "Introducing God in the Devil's Paradise," and Hvalkof and Aaby, " 'No Tobacco, No Hallelujah,' " in *Is God an American?*, ed. Hvalkof and Aaby (London: International Work Group for Indigenous Affairs and Survival International, 1981), 9, 11, 185.

[24] David Stoll, *Fishers of Men or Founders of Empire? The Wycliffe Bible Translators in Latin America* (London: Zed Press; Cambridge, MA: Cultural Survival, 1982).

North American supporters as a ministry of evangelism and SIL to Majority World governments as a scientific institution. Stoll worried especially that the latter activity often resulted in Wycliffe/SIL doing the bidding of right-wing oppressive regimes in the various countries in which it operated.

Throughout the 1980s and 1990s, other authors provided variations on these same themes—whether accusing New Tribes Mission and Wycliffe/SIL of slave trafficking in league with the CIA,[25] charging the New Tribes Mission of raiding, capturing, and imprisoning Ayoreode Indians of Paraguay in labor camps,[26] ascribing to the SIL a plot to destroy the Culina Indians' identity through the weapons of western capitalism,[27] or finding a sinister conspiracy at work in connections between Nelson Rockefeller's Big Oil and the widespread connections of the Wycliffe founder, Cameron Townsend.[28] An especially important contribution to this general indictment was provided by the second and third editions of a widely read book by anthropologist Napoleon Chagnon on the Yanomami of Brazil and Venezuela, in which he portrayed most of the missionaries with this tribe as blind to the Indians' best interests:

> In most cases reason and dialogue were not possible, for the missionaries were incapable of viewing the differences between "good" and "bad" in anything other than narrow biblical or theological terms, and could not appreciate the argument that the wanton destruction of a culture, if not its human bearers, was morally "bad" by some standards. Evangelism was by definition "good" in their terms if only a single soul was saved, and any price was worth paying to accomplish that end and any method legitimate.[29]

An expansion of this standard of critique, along with a shift in focus of its application, appeared in a full-scale indictment offered by a team of sociologists and religionists who saw a new global Christian fundamentalism leagued with an aggressive international capitalism and targeting, not this time isolated tribes, but the rapidly growing populations of the world's new great cities. With these modifications, the authors' bill of particulars sounded familiar:

---

[25] Norman Lewis, *The Missionaries: God Against the Indians* (London: Secker & Warburg, 1988). For comment, Webster and Headland, "Selected Bibliography," 275–76.

[26] Ticio Escobar, *Ethnocide: Mission Accomplished?* (Copenhagen: International Work Group for International Affairs, 1989). For comment, Webster and Headland, "Selected Bibliography," 274.

[27] Donald K. Pollock, "Conversion and 'Community' in Amazonia," in *Conversion to Christianity: Historical and Anthropological Perspectives on a Great Transformation*, ed. Robert W. Hefner (Berkeley: University of California Press, 1993), 165–97. Webster and Headland, "Selected Bibliography," 276, point out that Pollock never visited the Culina.

[28] Gerald Colby and Charlotte Dennett, *Thy Will Be Done: The Conquest of the Amazon; Nelson Rockefeller and Evangelism in the Age of Oil* (New York: HarperCollins, 1995).

[29] Napoleon Chagnon, *Yanomamö: The Fierce People*, 3rd ed. (New York: Holt, Rinehart and Winston, 1983), 205.

> For Christian fundamentalism in particular, the universalizing of the faith is intertwined with the homogenizing influence of consumerism, mass communication, and production in ways that are compatible with the creation of an international market culture by global capitalist institutions.[30]

The authors did recognize that some of the best-known promoters of the kind of religion that worried them included non-Americans like Reinhard Bonnke of Germany and Paul Yonggi Cho of South Korea. But they still tracked most of the money, energy, and motive force of "global fundamentalism" back to the United States.

The lengthy roster of works critiquing evangelical missionaries for promoting American-led global capitalism produced, as could only be expected, a host of formidable defenders. Those defenses are important for grasping the character of American evangelical activity in the world. But whether they—or the indictments—offer major assistance in fathoming the general course of Christianity in the non-Western world is a question that must be addressed separately after sketching the nature of that defense.

The defenders of American missionary practice made their case in weaker and stronger forms. Responsible apologists almost always grant that missionaries had in fact sometimes acted unwisely in how they linked the Christian gospel with the politics of American government, promoted capitalist exchange, or upset previously isolated tribal groups. But apologists have also made a number of effective responses.

In the first instance, critics of those who criticize the missionaries have found it fairly easy to expose the latter's ideological blinders. It was, for example, not an evangelical publication but a mainline Protestant periodical that attacked the Rockefeller-oil-Wycliffe conspiracy in these scathing terms:

> To call this book's logic specious would be too complimentary. It is replete with factual errors, logical inconsistencies, inflated language and historically unrelated facts. Only ideology or money (probably the former) could have motivated its authors to do such a hatchet job.[31]

In one of most ironic reversals in recent intellectual history, the anthropologist Napoleon Chagnon, who spoke so dismissively of missionary insensitivity to indigenous cultures, became a target of charges that, as an anthropologist, he assisted in the physical and cultural destruction of

---

[30] Steve Brouwer, Paul Gifford, and Susan D. Rose, *Exporting the American Gospel: Global Christian Fundamentalism* (New York: Routledge, 1996), 3.

[31] Elizabeth A. Cobbs, review of *They Will Be Done*, in *Christian Century*, November 1, 1995, 1022.

his jungle subjects.[32] It was pointed out shrewdly that the demonization of "global fundamentalism" resembled nothing so much as fundamentalist eschatology stood on its head:

> The book's outline thus oddly resembles the millenarian writings of the fundamentalists themselves. Both expect to see the world's commercial and financial systems controlled by a central power whether it is called the "investment classes" or the Antichrist.[33]

Most importantly, careful inquiries of supposed missionary malfeasance from anthropologists who were Christians themselves or sympathetic to Christianity convinced many neutral observers that much of the missionary bashing resulted simply from ideology *tout court*.[34]

Even more forthright defenses of missionary practice came from those who sought to demonstrate that missionaries have benefited rather than harmed the missionized. The many instances of such arguments include non-Christian Chinese scholars who bestow tempered words of praise on Protestant missionaries for the educational, medical, and technical assistance they brought to their country;[35] students of Central America who point out that some American missionaries have been strong advocates of indigenous human rights;[36] and other students of Latin American Indian tribes who believe they can show that contact with missionaries led to significantly better physical, intellectual, and social health.[37]

But the most compelling apologists for the missionaries are those who take a broad view of recent world history. They admit that missionaries have often been key agents for integrating indigenous people into wider social, economic, and political life, but then they contend that, since this kind of

---

[32] The charge was made most extensively in Patrick Tierney, *Darkness in El Dorado: How Scientists and Journalists Devastated the Amazon* (New York: Norton, 2000); for perspective, see Clifford Geertz, "Life Among the Anthros," *New York Review of Books*, February 8, 2001, 18–22.

[33] Joel A. Carpenter, review of *Exporting the American Gospel*, in *Church History* 66 (December 1997): 886.

[34] See especially two landmark essays, and the largely convinced responses of other anthropologists appended to the essays, Claude E. Stipe, "Anthropologists versus Missionaries: The Influence of Presuppositions," *Current Anthropology* 21 (April 1980): 165–79; and Robert J. Priest, "Missionary Positions: Christian, Modernist, Postmodernist," *Current Anthropology* 42 (February 2001): 29–68.

[35] Shen Dingping and Zhu Weifang, "Western Missionary Influence on the People's Republic of China: A Survey of Chinese Scholarly Opinion Between 1980 and 1990," *International Bulletin of Missionary Research* 22 (October 1998): 154–58.

[36] John Paul Lederach, "Missionaries Facing Conflict and Violence: Problems and Prospects," *Missiology* 20 (1992): 11–19. For comment, Webster and Headland, "Selected Bibliography," 275.

[37] Paul R. Turner, "Religion Conversion and Community Development," *Journal for the Scientific Study of Religion* 18 (1979): 252–60. For comment, Webster and Headland, "Selected Bibliography," 279.

integration has become all but inevitable for virtually all tribal peoples, it has been far better for the indigenous people that missionaries instead of other possible actors carried it out. The most well-reasoned response to Stoll's *Fishers of Men or Founders of Empire*, for example, was provided by a Wycliffe worker who admitted that "for me, man's relationship to God is the first principle of life," but who also argued that the Wycliffe message of evangelical Christianity would provide the "best way to bring those changes necessary to end oppression and human exploitation" that beset the Indians. Moreover, reducing indigenous languages to writing and teaching people to use their own printed languages provided a means of protecting such people from the totalizing forces of modern civilization: "The group that is forced into isolation from the rest of society through illiteracy is defenseless before the crush of 'civilization'; it is destined for destruction."[38] The issue was put even more sharply by a veteran missionary in Irian Jaya (New Guinea):

> Naive academics in ivy-covered towers may protest that the world's remaining primitive cultures should be left undisturbed, but farmers, lumbermen, land speculators, miners, hunters, military leaders, road builders, art collectors, tourists, and drug peddlers aren't listening. They are going in anyway. Often to destroy. Cheat. Exploit. Victimize. Corrupt. Taking, and giving little other than diseases for which primitives have no immunity or medicine. . . . We missionaries don't want the same fate to befall these magnificent tribes in Irian Jaya.[39]

Perhaps the most impressive statement of this argument came in the late 1980s from an anthropologist who, in fact, criticized severely the work of New Tribes Mission with the Yuqui people of Bolivia. That criticism notwithstanding, Allyn Stearman's conclusion was a strong, albeit round-about, defense:

> Had the Yuqui not been contacted by the New Tribes missionaries, the only people at the time willing to risk their lives in this process, it is certain that they would have been killed off or taken as [slaves]. . . . The fact of the matter is that very few people who do not have the driving zeal of the missionary are willing to put their lives on the line in a contact effort and to then devote the remainder of their existence to the difficult process of acculturation.[40]

---

[38] James Yost, "We Have a Mandate," *The Other Side*, February 1983, 25, 38. Yost was responding to David Stoll, "Wycliffe Bible Translators: Not Telling the Whole Story," ibid., 20–25.

[39] Don Richardson, "Do Missionaries Destroy Cultures?" in *Tribal Peoples and Development Issues: A Global Overview*, ed. John H. Bodley (Mountain View, CA: Mayfield, 1988), 117.

[40] Allyn MacLean Stearman, *Yuqui: Forest Nomads in a Changing World* (New York: Holt, Rinehart and Winston, 1989), 142); quoted in Webster and Headland, "Selected Bibliography," 277–78. For a superb account of how this nonbelieving anthropologist and the New Tribes Missionaries were later able to work together on behalf of the Yuqui, see Stearman, "Better Fed Than Dead: The Yuqui of Bolivia and the New Tribes Mission; A 30-Year Retrospective," *Missiology* 24 (April 1996): 213–26.

In a word, if the realm of the possible is limited to beneficent integration or destructive integration, missionary-led integration usually turns out to look beneficent.

Convincing as apologies have been for missionary activity, however, they do not directly answer the question of how American missionaries have affected the expansion of Christianity in the non-Western world. For that question, a still broader perspective is necessary. As a growing corps of solidly researched and carefully argued works have demonstrated, whether or not missionaries acted wisely, the primary agency in recent movements of Christianization has been not the missionaries but the new converts themselves.

One of the strongest points made repeatedly in this literature is that unusual hubris is required—among both supporters of American missionaries and their detractors—to presume that Westerners are primarily responsible for the mass expansion of non-Western Christianity. The following are only a few examples out of a rapidly expanding literature: From the beginning of Western contact, when the Yoruba of Nigeria accepted Christianity, they did so in the context of Yoruba problems and for Yoruba solutions.[41] When V. S. Azariah, the first Indian bishop of the Anglican church, promoted Christianity, and even distinctly British features of Christianity, he did so in order to advance Indian self-respect, Indian cultural advance, and even Indian nationalism.[42] Among the vast, incredibly diverse panoply of African Independent Churches (AIC), it is probably possible to find a few that take their marching orders from outside sources. But as a burgeoning literature records, these AICs are much more often genuinely independent—in how they join Christianity to traditional African religion, in how they practice Christianity in the context of their own existing social conditions, and in how they apply Christianity to plan for the future.[43] More generally, as Philip Jenkins has asserted, "there must have been a great deal more to Southern Christianity than the European-driven mission movement," or that Christianity would have contracted when European colonization came to an end. "We can suggest all sorts of reasons why Africans and Asians adopted Christianity, whether political, social, or cultural; but one all-too-obvious explanation is that individuals came to believe the message offered, and found this the best

---

[41] J. D. Y. Peel, *Religious Encounter and the Making of the Yoruba* (Bloomington: Indiana University Press, 2000).

[42] Susan Billington Harper, *In the Shadow of the Mahatma: Bishop V. S. Azariah and the Travails of Christianity in British India* (Grand Rapids, MI: Eerdmans, 2000).

[43] See, among many others, Allan Anderson, *Zion and Pentecost: The Spirituality and Experience of Pentecostal and Zionist/Apostolic Churches in South Africa* (Pretoria: University of South Africa Press, 2000); and Martinus L. Daneel, *African Earthkeepers: Wholistic Interfaith Mission* (Maryknoll, NY: Orbis, 2001).

means of explaining the world around them."[44] Jenkins' general observation has been reinforced by Lamin Sanneh on the specific subject of Bible translations. In Sanneh's impressive account of how Bible translation has invariably worked over the last two centuries, Western missionaries may think they can predict what new Christians will do with the freshly translated Scriptures, but the results when newly literate tribal peoples actually begin reading the Bible in their own tongues has regularly confounded missionary expectations. Unlike Islam, where the universal use of Arabic for the Koran creates a degree of international Muslim homogeneity, the translation of the Bible into myriad tongues has produced a breath-taking Christian heterogeneity. In Sanneh's summary, "I see translation as a fundamental concession to the vernacular, and an inevitable weakening of the forces of uniformity and centralization. Furthermore, I see translation as introducing a dynamic and pluralist factor into questions of the essence of the religion."[45]

In sum, even though American evangelicals have certainly been important actors on the contemporary world stage, it would be a fundamental mistake to regard evangelical missionaries as the controlling, hegemonic, sovereign agents of change in the recent history of world Christian history.

Explanation and Assessment

Observations by foreign visitors concerning religion in the United States offer an important insight for putting the relationship of American evangelicalism to world evangelical movements into clearer perspective. These insights feature accounts of how American circumstances have shaped the American practice of religion. Thus, for example, Claude-Jean Bertrand, writing in 1975, gave much credit to the churches for making the United States unique among the nations of the world, "the only one in history which has mixed all ethnicities and built the strongest power in the world without ever falling under the boot of a tyrant or a military caste." At the same time, Bertrand's research caused him to ask troubling questions about habits of American religious thought: "the laxity, the syncretism, the utilitarianism, this secularization, this nationalization of the church, are they compatible with a true faith in transcendent realities?"[46] Another visitor, Manfred Siebald,

---

[44] Jenkins, *Next Christendom*, 42, 43–44.

[45] Lamin Sanneh, *Translating the Message: The Missionary Impact on Culture* (Maryknoll, NY: Orbis, 1989), 53. For a parallel situation involving the translation of hymns, see Michael McNally, "The Uses of Ojibwa Hymn-Singing at White Earth: Toward a History of Practice," in *Lived Religion in America*, ed. David D. Hall (Princeton: Princeton University Press, 1997), 133–59.

[46] Claude-Jean Bertrand, *Les Églises aux États-Unis* (Paris: Presses Universitaires de France, 1975), 125–26. Author's translation.

professor of American studies at the Johannes Gutenberg Universität-Mainz, was more descriptive than prescriptive when he was asked in the summer of 1998 to explain why there were so many different Christian denominations in the United States. To Siebald, six factors were most important in shaping "the denominational pluralism of the USA": "the separatistic impulse, the separation of church and state, immigration, the westward movement, slavery, and revival movements."[47] Conspicuous by their absence in Siebald's account were the long-standing pillars of Christianity in Europe, including a sense of tradition, respect for hierarchy or inherited authority, and communal identity defined by religious-ethnic heritage.

Another French observer, Klauspeter Blaser, again highlighted the way in which American concepts of religion reflected more general conventions of American life. In his view, American Christianity has been marked specifically by what he calls "a combination of Puritanism and the Enlightenment," which "thinks of truth in terms of action and of tangible results more than as metaphysics or spirituality. Thought is oriented toward the realization of the man of the future, which corresponds to the American dream."[48] A thoughtful essay by Hartmut Lehmann added an insightful comparison with German religious life. In addressing the question of why the United States seemed to Christianize at the same time that much of Europe dechristianized over the last two centuries, Lehmann stressed the American combination of structural religious freedom and entrepreneurial religious activity:

> In the complex processes described here as christianization and dechristianization, in the United States and Germany, differences in the legal framework were effectively reinforced by differences in the religious context. In the United States factors such as voluntarism, revivalism, and pluralism created a cultural climate which favored the growth of religion and in which religious activism could easily be related to matters of justice and social reform. In Germany, factors such as the close cooperation between state and church, the suppression of nonconformism, and the domestication of active Christian groups produced a cultural climate in which religion was tainted with conservatism and with opposition to "progress."[49]

---

[47] Siebald quoted in Mark A. Noll, "Fazit," *Das Christentum in Nordamerika*, trans. into German by Volker Jordan (Leipzig: Evangelische Verlagsanstalt, 2000), 249. For Siebald's own academic assessment of religion in America, see his Habilitationsschrift, "'Prodigal Parable': Studien zur Parable vom Verlorenen Sohn in der amerikanischen Literatur" (University of Mainz, 1995).

[48] Klauspeter Blaser, *Les théologies nord-américains* (Genève: Labor et Fides, 1995), 14. Author's translation.

[49] Hartmut Lehmann, "The Christianization of America and the Dechristianization of Europe in the 19th and 20th Centuries," *Kirchliche Zeitgeschichte* 11 (1998): 12. A helpful response to Lehmann's essay was made by William R. Hutchison, ibid., 137–42. See also Lehmann, ed., *Säkularisierung, Dechristianizierung, Rechristianisierung im neuzeitlichen Europa: Bilanz und Perspektiven der Forschung* (Göttingen: Vandenhoeck & Ruprecht, 1997).

All such observations repeat, in modern terms, the seminal conclusion about American Christianity drawn by Alexis de Tocqueville in the 1830s as part of his assessment of democracy in the United States:

> On my arrival in the United States it was the religious aspect of the country that first struck my eye. As I prolonged my stay, I perceived the great political consequences that flowed from these new facts. Among us, I had seen the spirit of religion and the spirit of freedom almost always move in contrary directions. Here I found them united intimately with one another: they reigned together on the same soil.[50]

The relevant question posed by these foreign observations concerns the bearing of American circumstances on the development of Christianity in America. Outsiders in fact have often seen more clearly than Americans ourselves that American Christianity has been unmistakably American as well as Christian. More generally, expressions of religion in America—Catholic as well as Protestant, non-Christian as well as Christianity—have almost always reflected the following preferences:

- individual self-fashioning over communal identification;

- a language of choice and personal freedom alongside a language of given boundaries and personal responsibility;

- comfortable employment of commerce as opposed to cautious skepticism about commerce;

- a conception of religious organizations as voluntary bodies organized for action instead of inherited institutions organized for holding fast;

- an optimistic hope expressed in the creation of new institutions instead of a pessimistic skepticism about innovation;

- personal appropriation of sacred writings over inherited or hierarchical interpretation of those scriptures;

- a plastic, utilitarian attitude toward geography as opposed to a settled, geographically-determined sense of identity;

- a ready willingness to mingle different ethnic groups (in at least public settings and despite America's wretched history of slavery and its continuing ramifications) as opposed to strong convictions about ethnic purity; and

---

[50] Alexis de Tocqueville, *Democracy in America*, ed. and trans. Harvey Claflin Mansfield and Delba Winthrop (Chicago, 2000), 282. For a similar observation for Europe more generally, see ibid., 43.

- the innovations of the bourgeois middle classes instead of deference to traditional elites.

While it is certainly true, as asserted by Sébastien Fath, that "this heritage, this particular Protestant identity has profoundly molded contemporary American society, and the way in which it experiences social ties," it is also true, again in Fath's words, that "the social influence of a society of choice" has decisively shaped the character of American Protestantism, and also the character of Protestantism exported by evangelicals beyond American borders.[51]

The suggestion here depends heavily on the insights of Andrew Walls. In several essays, this perceptive missiologist has argued that two of the most significant developments in world Christianity during the nineteenth century were the successful adaptation of traditional European Christianity to the liberal social environment of the United States, and the use of the voluntary society as the key vehicle for Protestant missionary activity.[52] These developments were obviously linked since, by the start of the twentieth century, American Protestants had already developed the missionary voluntary society into the great agent of overseas evangelism that has been sketched earlier in this study. On the basis of Walls' observations, we can move to the critical assertion that an elective affinity existed between the kind of evangelical Christianity that became so important in the American setting and the American social movements in which it flourished— between, that is, a conversionistic, voluntaristic form of Christian faith and fluid, rapidly-changing, commerce-driven, insecure, ethnically promiscuous social settings.

If that affinity speaks to more than just American history, it provides a clue about the American evangelical role in recent world Christianity. Yes, American voluntaristic, conversionistic evangelicals have exerted an influence elsewhere. The more important reality, however, is not that world evangelicalization has been a simple product of American activity. It is, rather, that forms of conversionistic and voluntaristic Christianity have flourished

---

[51] Sébastien Fath, "Protestantisme et lien social aux États-Unis," *Archives de Sciences Sociales des Religions* 108 (Oct.–Dec. 1999): 6 (5–24).

[52] Walls, "The American Dimension of the Missionary Movement," and "Missionary Societies and the Fortunate Subversion of the Church," in *Missionary Movement in Christian History*, 221–40, 241–54; and "The Missionary Movement: A Lay Fiefdom?" in *Cross-Cultural Process in Christian History*, 215–35. For my own development of these themes, see *Das Christentum in Nordamerika*, which has also appeared in the United States with a title indicating its main arguments, as *The Old Religion in the New World: The History of North American Christianity* (Grand Rapids, MI: Eerdmans, 2002).

in other places where something like the nineteenth-century American social conditions have come to prevail—where, that is, social fluidity, personal choice, the need for innovation, and a search for anchorage in the face of vanishing traditions have prevailed.

Table 7: Evangelical Missionary Agencies: US and Non-US Personnel 1999/2001

	1999 US Personnel	2001 total Personnel	2001 from countries	2001 to countries	Largest contingent*
Denominationally based					
Southern Baptists	4,562	5,034	6	97	Asia 1904
Assemblies of God (1914)	1,543	3,546	58	153	Braz. 158
Christian & Miss. Alliance (1887)	726	1,652	17	61	Phil. 326
Baptist Mid Missions (1920)	612	1,065	2	44	Braz. 155
Baptist Bible Fellowship (1950)	755	905	1	79	Mex. 73
Assoc. Bapts. for World Evang. (1927)	716	850	3	46	Peru 54
Mission to the World—PCA	579	630	2	40	Mex. 58
CBInternational (1943)	550	630	1	46	Côte d'I 64
Church of the Nazarene (1908)	487	562	7	69	PapNG 53
Interdenominational					
Campus Crusade for Christ (1951)	973	15,218	118	135	E. Asia 3224
YWAM (1961)	1,817	11,808	132	144	Braz. 1068
Wycliffe Bible Translators (1935)	2,930	7,031	35	78	PapNG 547
New Tribes Mission (1942)	1,514	3,073	32	31	PapNG 547
Operation Mobilization (1957)	171	2,977	79	61	Asia 618
SIM (1893)	569	1,692	26	54	Ethiop. 160
OMF International (1865)	156	1,245	23	32	SE Asia 402
TEAM (1890)	638	862	23	40	Japan 101
Frontiers (1972)	311	692	33	63	Md East 190

*2nd largest contingent where largest is United States

Sources: *Mission Handbook 2001–2003*, 51; *Operation World*, 743–46.

Missionary statistics may help to clarify the general situation. As Table 7 indicates, while American interdenominational mission agencies have grown rapidly in recent years, the number of non-Americans working with American agencies has grown much more rapidly. By the year 2000 American-based agencies like Campus Crusade, New Tribes Mission, and YWAM—as well as agencies that have always linked Americans with Canadians and the British (like Wycliffe, OMF, SIM)—employed many times more non-Americans as full-time missionaries than Americans. To be sure, these figures could suggest that American leadership was now being exercised through proxies. But another set of numbers indicates that such an Americano-centric interpretation is too simple. At the start of the twenty-first century comparisons of evangelical and evangelical-like missionary movements worldwide showed that the ratio of commissioning local congregations to missionaries actually dispatched, is now much lower for evangelical churches in over thirty countries than in the United States. For example, where there is one cross-cultural missionary supported by every 0.7 evangelical churches in Singapore, by 2.1 churches in Hong Kong, 2.4 in Albania, 2.5 in Sri Lanka, 2.6 in Mongolia, 4.2 in South Korea, 4.9 in Myanmar, and 5.3 in Senegal, in the United States the ratio is 7.6 churches to one missionary.[53] The proper conclusion from this flurry of numbers would seem to be that, while the United States contains a whole lot of evangelical churches, those churches are not as proportionately active in cross-cultural missionary activity as many churches in the non-Western world.

As a Christian believer, I ascribe both the spread and vitality of Christianity to powers intrinsic in the faith itself. As a historian, however, I also know that the inner force of Christianity—in Christian terms, the work of the Holy Spirit—has assumed many different forms in many different cultures, of which the voluntaristic conversionism of American evangelicalism is only one. In the contemporary world, where so many regions have come to experience social circumstances resembling at least in some measure the social experiences of American history, it has not been so much American evangelicalism, but rather forms of Christianity analogous in their own circumstances to what American evangelicalism has been in the United States, that are making the difference.

---

[53] Johnstone and Mandryk, *Operation World*, 748–52. This compilation also shows a lower ratio of evangelical churches per missionary for fifteen European countries and Canada than for the United States.

10

EMERGING PARADIGM SHIFTS THROUGH THE GLOBAL REVITALIZATION OF CHRISTIANITY

Timothy C. Tennent

Introduction

Over the last six years, Asbury Theological Seminary has received a Luce grant to study Christian revitalization around the world. From Nigeria to Nairobi, from North India to the Philippines, from Costa Rica to California, from New York to New Zealand, this has been one of the most expansive examinations of the emerging new face of global Christianity ever conducted. We are finally moving from the remarkable statistical analysis of Todd Johnson and the "big picture" writings of Philip Jenkins to actual field-based studies of the world Christian movement in the twenty-first century. As it turns out, there is no such thing as a global Christian movement if, by that, one implies a monolithic new wave of Christian identity around the world. What we have, in fact, is a virtual explosion of very particularized Christian movements around the world. To give you a glimpse of the breathtaking pace of this, it might be helpful to note that at the turn of the twentieth century there were about one thousand six hundred distinct denominations around the world. By the turn of the twenty-first century, a mere fifteen years ago, we estimate that the number had exploded from one thousand six hundred to thirty-four thousand distinct denominations of Christianity around the world. However, what is truly stunning is what has happened in just the last fifteen years, as nearly ten thousand additional new Christian movements have arisen, bringing the current number to over forty-three thousand. In other words, every twenty-four months of this century the church has spawned more movements than it did in its first one thousand nine hundred years of existence. This is nothing short of breathtaking, with huge implications for the future of Christianity. If successfully crossing cultural, sociolinguistic, and geopolitical boundaries is one of the great markers of Christian vitality, then we can truly say that Christianity is alive and well in the twenty-first century.

Most current textbooks on world Christianity have underestimated the significance of what we are observing. This story is not merely about the shifting center of gravity of the world Christian movement from the West to the Majority world and the subsequent demise of the west-reaches-the-rest paradigm. That story is true, but the forces of globalization, immigration, technology, and the impulse of new church planting movements has rendered a far more complex and nuanced picture of what is happening. The major point to recognize, however, is that never before has the church had so many dramatic and *simultaneous* advances into *multiple* new cultural centers. It is not as if the story of our time was the withering away of Christianity in the West and the dramatic growth of an African church which will become the new standard-bearer of Christian vitality. Instead, we are now experiencing what John Mbiti calls multiple new "centers of universality."[1] Koreans, Chinese, Indians, Latinos, *and* Africans, among others, can all legitimately claim that *they* are at the center of the world Christian movement. We now have the collapse of the old center and the simultaneous emergence of multiple new centers. Furthermore, the very makeup of those arenas with strong histories of Christian identity, including the West and the Philippines, are themselves undergoing massive transformation. The emergence of new expressions of vitality even in the old centers (primarily through majority world witness even there) is sufficient testimony that Christian history can no longer be understood from only one vantage point, whether cultural, geographic, or confessional. The new reality of the Church is that it can only be fully appreciated from a very diverse, global perspective. The significance of the four hundred twenty thousand global missionaries who are crossing cultural boundaries is still not widely understood, but we do know that what was once primarily a western initiative has changed so that today only 12 percent of missionaries are coming from the western world.

This chapter will touch on just three major paradigm shifts which are upon us in light of our study of global revitalization movements.

(1) The Collapse of Christendom and the Emergence of a Fresh Encounter between Christianity and the World

Christendom refers to a political and ecclesiastical arrangement which reinforces a partnership between the church and the state. The state

---

[1] As quoted in Kwame Bediako, *Christianity in Africa: The Renewal of a Non-Western Religion* (Maryknoll, New York: Orbis Books, 1995), 157.

strengthens the church by promoting Christian hegemony over the religious and cultural life. The church, in turn, gives legitimacy to the state by supporting the ruler and tacitly implying divine approval of the actions of the state. In the context of Christendom, Christianity receives protection from the civil authorities. The classic phrase was *"Cuius regio, eius religio,"* broadly meaning that the faith of the ruler was the religion of the realm. The ruler was responsible for the spiritual welfare of his or her people; the ruler decides how they will worship; and in his or her dominion, uniformity of faith and practice was considered normal. To embrace a different faith was to be a "dissenter," with all of the explicit and implicit sanctions that term implied. Because of the connection with the state, Christendom often (even unconsciously) regards the Christian faith in territorial ways. To belong to the "realm" means, by definition, that you shared the faith of the "realm." Particular embodiments of the gospel were, therefore, linked to specific geographic regions.

Christendom has existed in both official, explicit ways and unofficial, implicit expressions, which we sometimes refer to as civil religion. Roman Catholicism has often retained this territorial perspective on Christianity. Protestantism, as well, originated as a movement within the larger context of European Christianity and, therefore, was born in the context of Christendom. This profoundly influenced the way the word "gospel" was understood. To be a Christian within Christendom is to see Christianity at the center of all public discourse. Evangelism occurs passively because Christianity is the prevailing plausibility structure. Christianity is the normative expression of religious faith and ethical action, and there are no major dissenting voices or alternative religious worldviews. Therefore, the gospel does not need to robustly defend itself against, for example, either secular atheism or some alternative religious worldview such as Islam or Hinduism. Islamic or Hindu counterclaims are virtually nonexistent in Christendom. Christendom-type Christianity's most frequent encounters with non-Christian faiths are engagements with a cultural "other" in military campaigns (such as the Crusades), or in sponsoring a missionary who, often unwittingly, transmits the gospel and the host culture in a single package.

Today the gospel is being rediscovered in the West and around the world apart from Christendom. It is even a bit ironic that Christianity in non-Christendom forms is emerging even in the face of the non-Christian versions of Christendom, most notably Islamic-dom or Hindu-dom— Islamic Sharia which merges mosque and State, or Hindu hegemony known broadly as Hindutva, but expressed politically through the RSS/BJP/VHP and the growing Bajrang Dal.

What are the implications of this for how the gospel is understood? Several examples can be given. First, the gospel is now reclaiming its long-denied right and renewed capacity to critique culture, not just accommodate it. Only when the gospel is freed from the chains of Christendom can it provide the necessary critique of the state and the prevailing culture which is required when the kingdoms of this world clash with the Lordship of Jesus Christ. We have lived so long in the cultural mainstream that it can feel quite strange to find ourselves on the prophetic margins, but this is actually our native home. We just haven't been here for a long time. Second, the gospel must become more robust in responding to very specific challenges which hitherto went unnoticed. In a Christendom context, the challenges of unbelief or from other religions are distant and remote. Therefore, the gospel gradually becomes domesticated and weakened. Today we are witnessing the rise of many new challenges all around us: postmodern relativistic secularism, the rise of Islamic fundamentalism, and the seeping pluralism of Hinduism, to name a few. These challenges will inevitably force faithful Christians to become far more articulate about what constitutes genuine Christian identity. Third, evangelism has to become more intentional, and one cannot assume that any of the dominant Christian paradigms of the last century are widely understood. Even basic religious categories like "God" or "sin" or "faith," which once sat very comfortably within the security of a mono-religious discourse, must now be explained and clarified.

Tertullian famously once asked, "What has Athens to do with Jerusalem . . . what has the academy to do with the church?"[2] Tertullian envisioned a culture with the revelation of God's word at the center. Divine self-disclosure is seen to supersede all other knowledge and discourse. In this sense, "Jerusalem" represents a society framed by revelation and, therefore, theological and cultural stability. "Jerusalem" represents a congregation of the faithful gathered to hear God's word, the centrality of the pulpit, and the one-way pronouncements which are issued "six feet above contradiction." In contrast, "Athens" is the place of religious pluralism and dialogic speculation. Today, we must recognize that we are no longer proclaiming the gospel from the "Temple Mount" of our "Jerusalem." Instead, we are seeking to persuade the gospel into people's lives in the midst of the raucous, pluralistic, experimental, skeptical environment of the "Mars Hill" of their "Athens." There are competing deities and revelations which clamor for attention. The gospel which we proclaim is largely "unknown," and our witness may need to find collaborative help from general revelation to gain a hearing for the gospel.

---

[2] Tertullian, *De Praescriptione Haereticorum* 7.9.

(2) The Emergence of a Fourth Branch of Christianity

We can no longer conceptualize the world Christian movement as simply belonging to Roman Catholic, Protestant, or Eastern Orthodox communions. We are witnessing enormous changes in Christian self-identity, which, in turn, influence how the Christian message is understood and shared.

The early followers of Jesus were simply known as "The Way." The term "The Way" referred to a small movement *within Judaism* which regarded Jesus as the fulfillment of Jewish hopes and expectations. In this early period there was no concept of Christianity as a separate religion. The earliest followers of Jesus were Jews, and they understood Jesus and His message within that context. However, with the dramatic influx of Gentile believers, it became necessary to reconceptualize what it meant to be a follower of Jesus Christ. Therefore, it was in Antioch, the home of the first major Gentile ingathering of believers, that the followers of Jesus were "first called Christians" (Acts 11:26).

In AD 330 the Emperor Constantine relocated the capital of the Empire to Byzantium in the East, renaming it Constantinople (modern day Istanbul). Gradually, the church developed two distinct traditions, one eastern and Greek and the other western and Latin. Conflicts between these two traditions over the authority of the Pope and the western insertion of the *filioque* clause[3] into the Nicene Creed eventually disrupted the church's unity. The "Great Schism," which formally separated Roman Catholic from Eastern Orthodox, occurred in 1054. From the eleventh century onward, it was necessary for Christians to reconceptualize the church, taking into account these very different expressions of Christianity, each with their own traditions, doctrinal emphases, understanding of ecclesiology, liturgy, and so forth.

The sixteenth century witnessed the culmination of a long-standing dissent movement within the church that finally broke out into what became known as the Reformation. Once the Reformers officially severed their ties with Rome, and the movement grew in size and scale, it became necessary for Christians to once again reconceptualize the church in new ways. The current threefold configuration has served the church for nearly five hundred years.

The point of this discussion is not to provide an overview of church history as much as it is to recognize that the identity of the church has gone through major upheaval and transformation over time. If you grew up in the late twentieth century, even a cursory glance at most church history texts will confirm that since the time of the Reformation, the Christian church has been broadly conceptualized as falling into three major divi-

---

[3] A reference to the phrase "and the Son" which was added to the Nicene Creed's affirmation about the Holy Spirit: "who proceeds from the Father *and the Son.*"

sions: Roman Catholic, Eastern Orthodox, and Protestant. This is a basic conceptual grid which dramatically influences how we understand the world Christian movement, and every student of church history learns it quite early on. Indeed, one's self-identity as a "Roman Catholic" or "Protestant" or "Orthodox" believer carries with it the enormous weight and force of history, the legacy of past decisive struggles, and the peculiarities of our own doctrinal and liturgical distinctiveness.

Because of the territorial legacy of Christendom discussed earlier, these three divisions are also used to identify ethnic, cultural, and political orientations which have very little to do with the Christian gospel, but remain crucial to one's self-identity. The struggle between the Republic of Ireland and the six Protestant counties of Northern Ireland that belong to the United Kingdom is a classic example. The breakup of former Yugoslavia into Catholic Croatia, Islamic Bosnia, and Eastern Orthodox Serbia was determined largely by the association of ethnic particularity with religious identity.

However, the dramatic shift in the center of Christian gravity makes this tripartite framework increasingly untenable. It is time for another major reconceptualization of the church. Millions of new Christians are pouring into the church throughout the Majority World. Many of these new Christians cannot be easily categorized under any of the traditional headings. The basic practice for many years has been to regard any group which was not explicitly Roman Catholic or Eastern Orthodox to be, by default, Protestant. However, as the numbers grew, it became increasingly problematic to lump every non-Roman-Catholic, non-Eastern-Orthodox Christian movement into the "Protestant" camp when they clearly have no link whatsoever to any European "protest" movement. Yet, equally, they are not related to the Pope or to the magisterium in Rome, nor are they submitted to any Eastern Orthodox Patriarch.

Many of these new Christians belong to various independent, Pentecostal-oriented movements. Others belong to independent, prophetic movements that are difficult to classify. Some of these movements are currently only quasi-Christian, but are moving toward orthodoxy. Other quasi-Christian movements are emerging as independent groups outside the boundaries of historic orthodoxy. Still others claim to be following Christ from within the boundaries of Hinduism or Islam, a phenomenon known as "insider movements," which has received considerable attention in missiological literature over the last decade.

In response to these trends, the 1982 edition of the *World Christian Encyclopedia* added several new categories, including "non-white indigenous" and "crypto-Christian." The 2001 edition of the same work changed the name of the "non-white indigenous" category to "independent" and added an additional category of "hidden" believers. The encyclopedia also reclassified millions of believers from the "Protestant" category to this new "independent" category.[4]

If the numbers of those in this "independent" category remained small, then perhaps the traditional tripartite division might find a way to survive the twenty-first century. However, the "independents" are easily the fastest growing segment of global Christianity, and must become a central part of our larger conceptual framework. At the turn of the twentieth century, the largest blocks of Christian affiliation were the Roman Catholics at 266 million, followed by Eastern Orthodox at 115 million and Protestants at 103 million. At the turn of the twentieth century it is estimated that there were less than 8 million "independent" Christians in the entire world. However, in the opening decade of the twenty-first century, there were 1.1 billion Roman Catholics, 432 million independents, 386 million Protestants, and 252 million Orthodox. Thus, independent Christians now form the second largest segment of Christian identity.[5]

This new Christian mega-block is not easy to categorize. The other major branches were largely defined because of a historical separation with Roman Catholicism that emerged due to particular, identifiable historical developments. This brought a certain kind of cohesion, historically and doctrinally, to these movements that, in turn, forms the main backbone of the narrative which is rehearsed and, in time, shapes and forms the identity of the movement. However, in the case of the independent churches there is no single, pervasive point of identity. It is true that there are certain broad trends which are sometimes cited. For example, sometimes it is noted that the independent churches are normally lay led, without formal training and with very informal leadership structures. Others point out that they are frequently Pentecostal/charismatic in their experience, rely heavily on powerful, prophetic figures for guidance, and have little sense of the larger sweep of church history. Still others point out the emphasis which is sometimes placed on certain legalistic taboos, idiosyncratic liturgies, doctrines, and worship practices, or missionary zeal. The point is that there is no single galvanizing "mark" of these new Christians.

---

[4] The 1981 edition projected 154 million Christians in the "non-white indigenous" category (p. 6). The name of this category was changed to "independent" in the 2001 edition and the number of Christians in this category was revised to 385 million "independent" believers. The *World Christian Encyclopedia* also found "hidden" believers within Hinduism in seven countries and "hidden" believers within Islam in fifteen countries.

[5] David B. Barrett, Todd M. Johnson, and Peter F. Crossing, "Missiometrics 2008: Reality Checks for Christian World Communions," *International Bulletin of Missionary Research* 32, no. 1 (January 2008): 29. The estimated 423 million Christians classified as "Independent" does not include an additional 36 million Christians who are classified as "marginal" Christians.

Nevertheless, the term "independent" seems an insufficient and some-what inaccurate descriptor, even though it is a vast improvement from "crypto" or "marginal" Christian.[6] It will probably take several more de-cades before it becomes evident if there might be enough shared perspec-tives, or some grand narrative which will carry enough ballast to galvanize these various independent strands to recognize larger points of coherence, connectedness, and identity. For example, what distinctive features might be found in movements as diverse as the Asian house church network, the African Initiated Churches of the Apostolic variety, the Fourth Watch in the Philippines, the City Harvest church in Singapore, the Fill the Gap Healing Centers in South Africa, the Meiti in India, the Cooneyites of Australia, and the Igreja ev Pente of Brazil? Eventually, leaders from these various independent movements will find ways of describing themselves as they interact with other segments of the global church. As dialogue increases, they may discover deeper points of convergence. Until then, phrases like the independent churches, the Majority World Church, the house churches, the indigenous churches, the emerging Global South churches, or the Younger Churches will continue to be used. The important point is that, whatever nomenclature we use, this "fourth branch" of Christianity must become central in our understanding of the twenty-first century church and what it means to be a participant or global player in God's mission in the world.

(3) The Seismic Shift from Modernity to Postmodernity

The final paradigm shift I want to examine is how Christian revitaliza-tion movements are shaping the transition from the context of modernity to postmodernity. Peter Kuzmic, the internationally-renowned leader from Eastern Europe, once commented that the most defining word of our time is the word "post." We live in a *post*-communist, *post*-Christendom, *post*-denominational, *post*-western, *post*-Enlightenment and *post*-modern world. There seems to be a growing consensus that there is a crisis occurring within modernity which may signal the end of, or a major modification in, the Enlightenment project. This crisis has been described as postmodernism, and is already having a profound influence on how the gospel is being un-derstood and communicated by evangelicals.

One of the earliest writers to recognize the collapse of modernity and the movement toward a post-Enlightenment world was the French phi-losopher Jean-François Lyotard in his 1979 article entitled *The Postmodern*

---

[6]The word "independent" implies sovereignty and self-sufficiency, both of which cannot properly be applied to a church which, by definition, is submitted to the authority of Christ.

Condition: A Report on Knowledge.[7] In the article, he coined the word "postmodern" in the way that it is used in today's discourse. He stated that the fundamental shift of our time is a growing crisis of truth.[8] In the modern world, there was a belief in an overarching truth—whether informed by a Christian worldview or a secular belief in progress and the perfectibility of humanity. Lyotard argued that modern societies produced order and stability by generating what he called "grand narratives" or "master narratives." These grand narratives provide a clear sense of *telos*, of destiny. Within these narratives, intellectual reflection was like embarking on a journey with a clear destination—the pursuit of truth.

In contrast, the *post*modern context is marked by a collapse of all grand narratives. Postmodernism marks the movement away from claims to objectivity, and a greater emphasis on fragmented forms and discontinuous narratives. In short, the very notion of truth as Truth has begun to collapse. There is no longer a cohesive "canopy of truth" or meta-narrative which gives meaning and purpose to our civilization. We are left only with our personal narratives. The only "truth" which remains is what is true "for me," with little courage or confidence remaining to state anything that is true for everyone or speaks about objective truth. To use the language of Lesslie Newbigin, in postmodernism there are no more "public facts." All we have left are "personal preferences."[9]

Looking back from this perspective, it is easy to see how the evangelical understanding of the gospel has been influenced by Enlightenment thinking. On the positive side, the gospel benefited from trust in meta-narratives and the idea of a final, all-encompassing *telos* to which all of human history was moving. The Christian meta-narrative and final goal of history may have been different than that of the Enlightenment, but at least the paradigm was there to build on. On the negative side, the overemphasis on reason sometimes produced hyperrational expressions of Christianity. Furthermore, the deeply embedded notions of human progress often caused evangelicals to not take sin seriously enough and to render the gospel as nothing more than the greatest "self-help" plan.

How is postmodernism influencing the evangelical understanding of the gospel? What implications does this have for Christian mission? How do we inhabit a postmodern world where Christianity is regarded as merely

---

[7] Jean-François Lyotard, *The Postmodern Condition: A Report on Knowledge* (MN: University of Minnesota Press, 1985).

[8] This trend and its implications for the contemporary church have been expounded brilliantly by David F. Wells. See, especially, his *No Place for Truth* (Eerdmans, 1993) and *Above All Earthly Pow'rs: Christ in a Postmodern World* (Eerdmans, 2005).

[9] This is one of the central arguments in Lesslie Newbigin's *Foolishness to the Greeks* (Grand Rapids: Eerdmans, 1986).

one local story among many? How do we respond to the postmodern lack of confidence about any claim to a universal story which gives a "canopy of meaning" to the entire human race, or that gives insight into the origin, the purpose, and indeed the destiny of the human race?

It is clear that postmodernism poses a number of serious challenges to the gospel. First, postmodernism erodes the very concept of objective truth rooted in God's self-revelation. Therefore, the authority of the Bible, the trustworthiness of expository preaching, and the call to repentance, to name just a few, all come under suspicion. Second, postmodernism's emphasis on personal narrative separate from any overarching meta-narrative has further pushed the church toward a privatized understanding of the gospel. Under the sway of postmodernism, the gospel loses its historical, missional, and cosmic dimensions, and through a radical kind of reductionism becomes merely a prescription for obtaining personal peace. Third, postmodernism's emphasis on the autonomy of personal choices has further pushed the church toward a full acceptance of marketing strategies for attracting new believers, business models for long-term planning and strategy, and a general entertainment orientation, because in this new world the "consumer is king." Once the gospel must be made "fun," there is little room for the prophetic imagination, the cost of discipleship, and the call to repentance.

On the other hand, there are Christian thinkers who argue that postmodern thinking, on the whole, is really a reaction to the Enlightenment project, more than a rejection of the category of truth per se. Carl Raschke, for example, in his *The Next Reformation: Why Evangelicals Must Embrace Postmodernity*, sees postmodernity as the necessary check to the autonomous individual and the overreliance on human reason. Post-modernity is not necessarily the total abandonment of the correspondence theory of truth, inevitably leading to philosophical nominalism, rejection of all absolutes, and finally total relativism and nihilism. Rather, through this reading, postmodernity is calling out for more room for mystery, a deep longing for community, and the reawakening of the modern consciousness to the power of story and narrative. This is precisely the point which Richard Lints makes in his "The Vinyl Narratives: The Metanarrative of Postmodernity and the Recovery of Churchly Theology."[10] Christianity flourished prior to modernity, so we must believe that Christianity can flourish—at least potentially—in the absence of modernity, that is, in a new postmodernity.

While the emergence of postmodernism does pose a potentially grave threat to the entire notion of truth, I do think that strategically we must also

---

[10]Richard Lints, "The Vinyl Narratives: The Metanarrative of Postmodernity and the Recovery of a Churchly Theology," as found in Michael S. Horton, ed., *A Confessing Theology for PostModern Times* (Wheaton, IL: Crossway Books, 2000), 99.

recognize the positive potentials in the sunset of the Enlightenment project. The great task which is before this generation of Christian leaders is to
reconstruct the great meta-narrative for a postmodern world, and through
that, proclaim anew the preeminence of the Lord Jesus Christ! We must
take advantage of the awakened openness to the power of narrative and tell
a bigger story—the grand meta-narrative of the redemptive story of God,
the *missio dei*. We have to get serious about our theological discourse and
put an end to minimalistic approaches. Evangelicals have become experts
in finding a thousand new ways to ask the same question, "What is the *least*
one has to do to become a Christian?" This is how the high ground of sote-
riology in the New Testament got reduced in the Alan Race categorization
as a discussion about some minimalistic bar to declare someone justified.
We are the ones who have boiled the entire glorious gospel down to a single
phrase, a simple emotive transaction or some silly slogan. It is time for a
new generation of Christians, committed to apostolic faith, to declare this
minimalistic, reductionistic Christianity a failed project. It is wrong to try to
get as many people as possible to acknowledge as superficially as allowable
a gospel which is theologically unsustainable.

The good news is that the global emergence of Christian revitalization
is helping the church to regain confidence in the truth of the gospel of Jesus
Christ. We are receiving a long-needed, fresh understanding of the rule and
reign of God as the great eschatological fact to which all history is moving. The wonderful thing about the biblical vision of the eschaton is that it
simultaneously trumps the modernist notions of human progress as well
as the postmodern malaise about any ultimate meaning at all. We need a
renewed call to repentance, a *metanoia* about what it means to be the people
of God called to mission. Finally, we are discovering that deeper ecumenism
which looks beyond our own institutional aggrandizement and discovers
the overarching unity that can move the church forward in the face of the
challenges of our day.

Conclusion

These three themes are merely the beginning of this new, global conversation which our consultations have just begun to explore. If time permitted,
we could explore the implications all of this has for theological formulation,
or global ecumenism, or mission to the Islamic world, or the role of the
gospel in African nation building. The horizon is vast, the opportunities are
breathtaking. We, as a global church, have much work to do, but we can still
say with our Lord that the harvest is truly plentiful. Thanks be to God. Amen.

11

AWAKENINGS AND REVIVALS IN THE CONTEXT OF GLOBAL CHRISTIANITY

Todd M. Johnson and Cindy M. Wu

Since the inception of the church, awakenings and revivals have been an essential part of the Christian experience.[1] Wherever Christianity has been planted and has grown cold over time, there has been the need for rekindling the faith. Awakenings have also resulted in the spread of Christianity to peoples and languages where it has not previously been present. At the beginning of the Christian movement, awakenings more frequently pushed the boundaries of the faith into new areas. Once Christianity was well established in Europe, awakenings normally revived Christians in their largely Christian context. Over the past one hundred years, and especially today, the global context of Christianity has created new opportunities for renewal, both in Christian contexts and in contexts where most people belong to other religions.

With this in mind, we can ask a series of questions about the context in which Christians find themselves today: How many Christians are there, and where do they live?[2] What languages do they speak, and what

---

[1] This chapter is derived from Todd M. Johnson and Cindy M. Wu, *Our Global Families: Christians Embracing a Common Identity in a Changing World* (Grand Rapids, MI: Baker Academic, 2015), Chapters 1, 2, 7, and 8.

[2] The starting point in any analysis of religious adherence is the United Nations' 1948 *Universal Declaration of Human Rights*, Article 18: "Everyone has the right to freedom of thought, conscience and religion; this right includes freedom to change his religion or belief, and freedom, either alone or in community with others and in public or private, to manifest his religion or belief in teaching, practice, worship and observance." The full text of the UN resolution can be found in Paul M. Taylor, *Freedom of Religion: UN and European Human Rights Law and Practice* (Cambridge: Cambridge University Press, 2005), 368–72. For the purposes of this article, we are adopting the United Nations definition of a Christian as one who self-identifies as such. Under this rubric, our global Christian family is made up of all who consider themselves Christians, whether they fit into our ideals of what it means to be a Christian or not. This view doesn't make any of us any less committed to our tradition but

denominations or networks do they belong to? What does the global Christian family look like? In the Western world, we typically think of a family as a nuclear family—mother, father, and a couple of children—while the Christian family is more of an extended family—a vast assemblage of aunts, uncles, cousins, and other relatives.

Ever since the first century, the Christian family has reflected a broad and far-reaching collection of people related by faith. Christians have never spoken just one language, represented just one ethnicity, or lived in just one country. Christians are individuals who have distinct ethnic identities, speak identifiable languages, and make their homes in specific geographic locations.[3] In fact, throughout the history of Christianity, the Christian message has often been embraced by whole villages, tribes, or peoples. At other times the number of Christians has declined in a particular place, either because they died or because they left their faith. In the many ways the story is framed, our global Christian family has a long and illustrious lineage.

From the shores of Galilee in the first century to the remotest villages in the Himalayas today, followers of Jesus Christ have gradually spread to virtually everywhere in the world. There have been approximately 8 billion Christians since the time of Christ (out of 38 billion human beings).[4] As of the end of 2015, the world's 2.4 billion Christians constitute 33 percent of the global population.

The long view: two thousand years

When we take a long view of Christian history, stepping back and considering two thousand years of Christian growth and decline, the demographics (or numbers) of Christians in this story are striking. Utilizing clues from historical records, we can track the numbers of Christians in every continent of the world across the entire history of Christianity.[5] The global percentage of Christians has gone up and down over time. Some high and low points are the years 700 CE (Christians make up 20 percent of the world's population), 1000 CE (17 percent), 1300 CE (23 percent), 1600 CE (18

---

it does mean that we are looking beyond our own network and expressing concern for all who call themselves Christians. This is how we use the term "Christian."

[3] For a detailed enumeration of Christians past, present, and future see David B. Barrett, George T. Kurian, and Todd M. Johnson, *World Christian Encyclopedia: A Comparative Survey of Churches and Religions in the Modern World*, 2nd edition (New York: Oxford University Press, 2001), 2 vols.

[4] David B. Barrett and Todd M. Johnson, *World Christian Trends* (South Pasadena: William Carey Library, 2001), 97.

[5] A detailed analysis can be found in Todd M. Johnson and Kenneth R. Ross, eds., *Atlas of Global Christianity* (Edinburgh: Edinburgh University Press, 2009), 212–13.

percent) and 1900 CE (24 percent). Asia had the most Christians for at least the first seven hundred years. Then by 1000 CE, Europe had that distinction, and has held it to the present. In 2015, three continents (Europe, Africa, and Latin America) all had approximately the same number of Christians. In a few short years, Africa will have the most Christians by far. In addition, Asia and Latin America will each have more Christians than Europe!

We can also group totals of Christians by Global North and Global South for the entire history of Christianity. By Global North, we are referring to Europe and Northern America; by Global South, we are referring to Africa, Asia, Latin America, and Oceania.[6] For at least the first nine hundred years (until about 920 CE), Christians in the Global South outnumbered those in the Global North. Christians were all southerners[7] at the time of Christ, gradually becoming more northern until 1500, when fully 92 percent of all Christians were northerners (Europeans). This percentage began to decline gradually until 1900, when it was 83 percent. After 1900 the percentage declined precipitously (or from the southern point of view, rose meteorically). If these trends continue, by 2100 over three-fourths of all Christians will be living in the South.[8] This represents a return to the demographic makeup of Christianity at the time of Christ (predominantly southern), but also a vast extension of Christianity into all countries as well as into thousands of peoples, languages, and cultures. The percentages are shown in Graph 1.1, "Christians by Percentage in the North or South, 33–2100 CE."

The short view: 115 years

After 1900, something profound happened to the European dominance of global Christianity. Churches outside Europe and the Americas that had taken root in the nineteenth century grew rapidly in the twentieth century.[9] Africa, in particular, led this transformation, starting with only ten million

---

[6] Global North is defined in a geopolitical sense by five current United Nations regions (53 countries): Eastern Europe (including Russia), Northern Europe, Southern Europe, Western Europe and Northern America. Global South is defined as the remaining 16 current UN regions (185 countries): Eastern Africa, Middle Africa, Northern Africa, Southern Africa, Western Africa, Eastern Asia, South-central Asia, South-eastern Asia, Western Asia, Caribbean, Central America, South America, Australia/New Zealand, Melanesia, Micronesia, and Polynesia.

[7] Ancient Palestine is located in the present-day UN region of Western Asia, defined above as part of the South.

[8] Note as well that many of those Christians living in the North will be Southern Christians who have emigrated there!

[9] Latin America was already ninety-five percent Christian (Roman Catholic) in 1900. The changes in Latin America since then refer to the growth of Protestantism and Pentecostalism.

Graph 1.1 Christians by percentage in North or South, 33-2100 CE

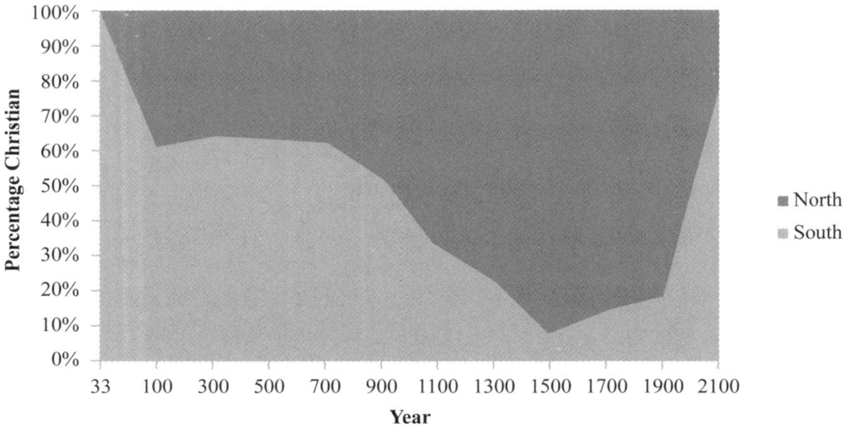

Source: *World Christian Database, October 2013.*

Christians in 1900, rising to three hundred and eighty million by 2000, and expected to grow to over five hundred and sixty million by 2015. In a real sense, this expansion was itself the result of a series of awakenings, including the East African Revival and the establishing of thousands of African Christian indigenous movements.[10] Table 1.1 below shows the changing status of Christianity by continent over the past 115 years.[11]

This table illustrates several important trends. First, over the past 115 years Christianity changed very little as a proportion of the world's population. In 1900 it was 34.5 percent of the global population, and in 2015 it was 33.0 percent. Second, one can see that Christianity has been growing more rapidly than the population in the Global South. Third, it has been growing more slowly than the population in the Global North. These two trends help to explain the rapid demographic shift of global Christianity to the South. While 82 percent of all Christians lived in the Global North in 1900, today nearly 65 percent of all Christians live in the Global South. This tells us that, without any further information to the contrary, one should look to the South for the majority of awakenings.

---

[10] See Kevin Ward and Emma Wild-Wood, eds., *The East African Revival: History and Legacies* (London: Ashgate, 2012) and David B. Barrett, *Schism and Renewal in Africa: An analysis of six thousand contemporary religious movements* (Nairobi: Oxford University Press, 1968).

[11] The methodology and sources behind these estimates are explained in detail in Todd M. Johnson and Brian J. Grim, *The World's Religions in Figures: An Introduction to International Religious Demography* (Oxford: Wiley-Blackwell, 2013).

Table 1.1 Christians (C) by United Nations continent and Global North/South, 1900–2015

Region	Population 1900	C 1900	% 1900	Population 2015	C 2015	% 2015	C 1900–2015	Population 1900–2015
GLOBAL SOUTH	1,135,392,000	98,674,000	8.7%	6,220,532,000	1,559,890,000	25.1%	2.43%	1.49%
Africa	107,808,000	9,918,000	9.2%	1,166,239,000	569,861,000	48.9%	3.59%	2.09%
Asia	956,196,000	21,914,000	2.3%	4,384,844,000	379,511,000	8.7%	2.51%	1.33%
Latin America	65,142,000	62,003,000	95.2%	630,089,000	581,730,000	92.3%	1.97%	1.99%
Oceania	6,246,000	4,839,000	77.5%	39,359,000	28,787,000	73.1%	1.56%	1.61%
GLOBAL NORTH	484,233,000	459,457,000	94.9%	1,104,251,000	860,433,000	77.9%	0.55%	0.72%
Europe	402,607,000	380,645,000	94.5%	743,123,000	579,789,000	78.0%	0.37%	0.53%
North America	81,626,000	78,812,000	96.6%	361,128,000	280,644,000	77.7%	1.11%	1.30%
Globe	1,619,625,000	558,131,000	34.5%	7,324,782,000	2,420,323,000	33.0%	1.28%	1.32%

Source: *World Christian Database*, www.worldchristiandatabase.org, 2013.

Note: C 1900–2015 and Population 1900–2015 represent the annual average growth rate of Christians and population over the 115-year period.

Christian traditions and movements

Table 1.2 below illustrates additional changes over the 115-year period from 1900–2015. Of the major traditions in Christianity, Roman Catholicism represents just over half of all Christians. Catholics' percentage of the global population grew slightly, to almost 17 percent today. This rise, however, masks a steep decline in adherents in Europe, accompanied by a simultaneous rise in Africa, Asia, and Latin America. Since 1900, Orthodox and Anglicans have declined as percentages of the population, both within Christianity and globally. Orthodoxy, decimated by the rise of communism in Europe, dropped from over 7 percent of the global population in 1900 to 4 percent today. At the same time, the Orthodox fell from 21 percent to less than 12 percent of all Christians. Anglicans (along with Roman Catholics) lost many adherents in the Global North while gaining in the Global South. In 1900, Anglicans represented 1.9 percent of the global population, dropping to 1.3 percent in 2015. Over the same period, the percentage of Anglicans among Christians fell from 5.5 percent to 3.9 percent. Protestant Christians have grown slightly as a percentage of all Christians. Their share of the global population, however, decreased from 6.4 percent to 6.1 percent in the same period. Independents, on the other hand, increased their shares of the total Christian community and of the global population. Independent Christians, especially in Africa and Asia, represented only 1.6 percent of Christians in 1900, but rose meteorically to over 17 percent by 2015. Their share of the global population also increased, from 0.5 percent to 5.7 percent. While awakenings have traditionally been found among Protestants, in the future one should look for awakenings in all traditions, particularly the Independents.

Movements within Christianity and across the traditions likewise experienced changes in size and percentage over the 115-year period (see table 1.2 below). Evangelicals and Renewalists can be considered part of previous and current awakenings—though both Protestants and Pentecostals have a narrative of "dead" faith that requires an awakening or revival to rekindle it.

Religions in the world today

While Christianity is shifting to the South, the global religious landscape is also changing. Four trends for the 115-year period are immediately apparent: (1) Christians' percentage of the world's population declined slightly; (2) Muslims have experienced the most significant change in proportion for any of the large religions; (3) Buddhists' and Chinese folk-religionists' combined share of the global population shrank by over half in that period; (4) agnostics and atheists experienced the largest percentage growth, from less than one percent of the world's population to well over eleven percent.

Table 1.2 Christian (C) traditions and movements, 1900 and 2015

	Name	Adherents 1900	% world 1900	% all Cs 1900	Adherents 2015	% world 2015	% all Cs 2015
Traditions	Anglicans	30,578,000	1.9%	5.5%	94,226,000	1.3%	3.9%
	Independents	8,859,000	0.5%	1.6%	418,168,000	5.7%	17.3%
	Orthodox	115,855,000	7.2%	20.8%	282,967,000	3.9%	11.7%
	Protestants	103,028,000	6.4%	18.5%	449,419,000	6.1%	18.6%
	Catholics	266,566,000	16.5%	47.8%	1,239,808,000	16.9%	51.2%
Movements	Evangelicals	80,912,000	5.0%	14.5%	328,582,000	4.5%	13.6%
	Renewalists	981,000	0.1%	0.2%	643,661,000	8.8%	26.6%

Source: *World Religion Database*, www.worldreligiondatabase.org, October 2013.

Note: Percentages do not add up to 100 percent because of double-counting between traditions.

Two other profound changes are noteworthy when comparing the strengths of religions globally in 1900 with those of 2015. First, sub-Saharan Africa was predominantly tribal religionist in 1900; by 2015 tribal religionists had been displaced as a majority bloc, with either Christianity (introduced from the south) or Islam (from the north) now forming the majority in almost all provinces. Second, Eastern Asia has gone from a majority of Chinese folk-religionists to a plurality of agnostics and atheists.

Another important trend to note is that Christians and Muslims together are claiming an increasing percentage of the world's population. If we were to go back to 1800, these two together would represent only about thirty-three percent of the world's population. Projections for 2100 show this increasing to sixty-six percent. So, in 1800, Christians and Muslims were one third of the world's population—by 2100 they are expected to count for two thirds. Surely the relationship between these two religions is a significant one.

Religiously affiliated vs. unaffiliated

Despite attempts to depict the twentieth century as a "secular" century, most of the people who lived during that period were, in fact, affiliated with a religion. In 1900, well over ninety-nine percent of the world's population was religiously affiliated. By 2015, the figure had fallen below eighty-nine percent, but this 115-year trend hides the fact that the high point for the nonreligious was around 1970, when almost twenty percent of the world's population was either agnostic or atheist. The collapse of Soviet Communism in the late twentieth century was accompanied by a resurgence of religion, making the world more religiously affiliated in 2015 than in 1970. While religious affiliation is not a direct indication of how religiously active people are, political scientists Pippa Norris and Ronald Inglehart point out,

> The publics of virtually all advanced industrial societies have been moving towards more secular orientations during the past fifty years. Nevertheless, the world as a whole now has more people with traditional religious views than ever before—and they constitute a growing proportion of the world's population.[12]

This resurgence of religious affiliation continues in the present (even though the number of atheists and agnostics continues to rise in the Western world), and the current growth of religions of all kinds in China (where the vast majority of the nonreligious live today) indicates that the future of the world is likely to be a religious one.

Anticipating the future of Christian awakenings

What does it mean for the future of awakenings that the proportion of Christians in the Global South continues to increase while the world becomes more religious? Churches in the South are on the whole more traditional, conservative (theologically but not necessarily politically), and apocalyptic

---

[12] Pippa Norris and Ronald Inglehart, *Sacred and Secular: Religion and Politics Worldwide* (Cambridge: Cambridge University Press, 2004), 5.

(concerned with end times) than churches in the North, which can seem to represent a more theologically liberal outlook.[13] As historian Philip Jenkins observes, "The denominations that are triumphing all across the global South are stalwartly traditional or even reactionary by the standards of the economically advanced nations."[14] Part of this dynamic is explained by the rise of the Pentecostal/Charismatic Renewal during the twentieth century.[15] Christians in this broader movement now number well over six hundred million, with most members concentrated in Africa, Asia, and Latin America.[16] Churches in the North might easily dismiss this rapidly growing movement in the rest of the world as primitive or underdeveloped were it not for that fact that an increasing number of southern Christians are emigrating to the North, bringing conservative, charismatic Christianity with them.

Awakenings move South

Until now, Western scholars have written the dominant theories and histories of awakenings, but the massive movements of Southern Christianity, whether they be Catholic, Orthodox, Protestant, Anglican, or Independent, will likely chart the future of Christian awakenings. The Northern church would do well to take on the posture of learning as British missiologist David Smith advises,

> We are witnesses to the emergence of new centres of spiritual and theological vitality as Christians from the southern continents add their insights to the church's total knowledge of the incomparable Christ. In the present transitional stage we are moving *from* a Christendom shaped by the culture of the Western world, *to* a world Christianity which will develop new spiritual and theological insights as the biblical revelation is allowed to interact with the many cultures in which Christ is now confessed as Lord.[17]

---

[13] Unfortunately this typology of South as conservative and North as liberal is somewhat imprecise and simplistic. For example, over fifty million Independents belong to white-led movements, e.g., Vineyard churches in the United States. The typology is most useful, then, in understanding the broadest trends as they relate to North-South Christian relations.

[14] Philip Jenkins, *The Next Christendom* (New York: Oxford University Press, 2002), 7.

[15] The three waves of Renewal are defined as (1) Pentecostals, those affiliated with Classical Pentecostal denominations, such as the Assemblies of God; (2) Charismatics, individuals in the mainline churches (Roman Catholic, Lutheran, Methodist, etc.) who have entered into the experience of being filled with the Holy Spirit; and (3) Neocharismatics, individuals who emphasize the gifts of the Spirit but who are members of Independent or postdenominational churches, such as Chinese house churches or African Independent Churches. See Barrett and Johnson, *World Christian Trends*, Part 5 "Georenewal," 265–90.

[16] See Todd M. Johnson, "Status of Global Mission, 2013, in the Context of AD 1800–2025", in *International Bulletin of Missionary Research*, Vol. 37, No. 1, January 2013, 32–33.

[17] David Smith, *Mission After Christendom* (London: Darton, Longman and Todd Ltd, 2003), 61.

"They speak in many tongues"

The rapid growth of Christianity in non-Western, non-English-speaking countries also implies that the language of Christians is changing. Already by 1980, Spanish was the leading language of church membership in the world (because of Latin America, not Spain).[18] European languages dominate the top ten, including English (2), Russian (4), German (6), French (7), Polish (8), and Ukrainian (9). But languages of the Global South are moving up the list: Portuguese (3, due primarily to Brazil), Chinese (5), and Tagalog (the Philippines) (10), with Amharic (Ethiopia), Korean, Yoruba (Nigeria), Igbo (Nigeria), and Cebuano (the Philippines) not far behind. Of course, Christians in Africa, Asia, Latin America, and Oceania worship in numerous languages besides Spanish, Portuguese, Chinese, and Yoruba. Thus, the translation of the gospel into indigenous languages and cultures has become increasingly important.

Western scholars will also have to recognize and seriously consider writings in non-English and non-European languages. There is a great need for Christian scholarship in these languages to be translated into English, French, German, Spanish, and other Northern languages. Apart from the shift away from Northern languages as the dominant languages of Christianity, there is also a need for a change in the perception of missions as a Northern phenomenon. For the past several hundred years, Christians in Europe and the United States have been "the church" and the rest of the world has been "the mission field." The shift of Christianity from Europe to the Southern Hemisphere means that Africa, Asia, and Latin America can no longer be seen as the periphery. Instead, Christian mission to the whole world will require participation from all Christians—North and South—to be successful.

The poor are still with us

Another daily reality for Southern Christians is poverty. Much of the Global South deals with serious issues of poverty and a lack of access to proper health care. Countries that have been hardest hit by AIDS—such as Botswana, Zimbabwe, and Swaziland—are also countries where Christianity is flourishing. Without access to the necessary medical care, accounts of healing and exorcism found in the Bible are taken more seriously.

---

[18] See Global Table 7 "Affiliated Christians (Church Members) Ranked by 96 Languages each with over a Million Native Speakers, AD 1980" in David B. Barrett, *World Christian Encyclopedia* (New York, Oxford University Press, 1982), 10. An updated table appears in the *Atlas of Global Christianity*, 213.

David Smith describes these churches as "overwhelmingly charismatic and conservative in character, reading the New Testament in ways that seem puzzlingly literal to their friends in the North," and as "largely made up of poor people who in many cases live on the very edge of existence."[19] Thus the growth of Christianity in poorer regions implies not only an alternate *reading* of the Bible, but indeed a different *experience* of the Bible. For the poorer Christian communities in the South, meeting the social needs of people is integral to Christian witness, theology, and ministry. For the Western church and missionaries, poverty and AIDS in the South cannot be ignored. Assistance must be granted with humility and in acknowledgment of a crisis *within* the Church.

Increasing religious diversity

At the same time that Christianity is shifting to the South, Christians are living in increasing religious diversity, which is particularly apparent in the Global North where secularization and immigration continue to transform the religious landscape. "Religious diversity" is present at two levels: intra-religious and interreligious. Intra-religious diversity encompasses the diversity found within a given world religion (for example, traditions such as Roman Catholicism, Orthodoxy, and Protestantism within Christianity), whereas interreligious diversity describes the degree of overall diversity of world religions (Christianity, Islam, Hinduism, Judaism, and so on) in a given population or geographic area. Here we are primarily addressing levels of interreligious diversity.[20]

Although Asia remains the world's most religiously diverse continent, its religious makeup has changed markedly over the last century. In 1900, more than half of Asia's population was Chinese folk-religionist or Buddhist; today, these two religions together total only one-fifth. Tribal religions declined from 5.6 percent of the population in 1900 to 3.7 percent today. These declines were the result of gains by Muslims and Christians. However, greater proportional gains were made by agnostics and atheists, especially in China.

These religious changes in Asia are not entirely surprising, considering the inherently pluralistic nature of the continent; in a sense, to be Asian is to be interreligious.[21] It is also common for Asians to cross national boundaries

---

[19] Smith, *Mission After Christendom*, 131.

[20] For a complete survey of the intra-religious diversity of Christianity, see Johnson and Ross, *Atlas of Global Christianity*, parts II and III.

[21] Peter Phan, *Being Religious Interreligiously: Asian Perspectives on Interreligious Dialogue* (Maryknoll: Orbis Books, 2004), 117, 127.

in search of employment, such as the large Indian and Filipino migrant worker communities in various Persian Gulf countries. The World Bank estimates that three million Indonesian women work abroad, primarily in Malaysia and Saudi Arabia, and mostly in domestic work.[22]

In sum, most of us are living with greater religious diversity than did our parents or grandparents.

Relating to other Christians

Throughout history and around the world today, Christians face questions about how churches should be organized and how different traditions should relate to each other. This is especially true in the context of revivals and awakenings. Do these events separate Christians or bring them together? From a theological point of view, we are primarily concerned with how differences are brought together to achieve unity in the Christian family. The challenge we face is figuring out what truths we share in the wider body of Christ, while also articulating our differing positions as legitimate differences within our global family. Asbury Seminary president Timothy Tennent summarizes his position when he writes,

> In the context of global Christianity we must first and foremost see ourselves as Christians proclaiming the apostolic faith and only secondarily as Reformed Christians, Pentecostal Christians, Dispensational Christians, or Arminian Christians. We must learn to think of ourselves as members of a massive global Christian movement that is looking more and more like John's vision in Revelation 7:9, which encompasses people from every nation, tribe, people, and language.[23]

Others are more sanguine. Sebastian and Kirsteen Kim write, "We do not expect a single world Christianity, a world church or a global theology, but we hope for ongoing conversation between Christians, churches, and theologies from around the world."[24]

The twentieth century witnessed a concerted effort to deal with the divisions among Christians. From the World Missionary Conference in Edinburgh, Scotland, in 1910 to the General Assembly of the World Council of

---

[22] Nisha Varia, "Asia's Migrant Workers Need Better Protection," *Human Rights Watch*, September 2, 2004, http://www.hrw.org/news/2004/08/31/asias-migrant-workers-need -better-protection.

[23] Timothy Tennant, *Theology in the Context of World Christianity: How the Global Church Is Influencing the Way We Think About and Discuss Theology* (Grand Rapids: Zondervan, 2009), 269.

[24] Sebastian Kim and Kirsteen Kim, *Christianity as a World Religion* (London: Continuum, 2007), 229.

Churches in Busan, South Korea, in 2013, great efforts toward "ecumenism" have been made, with varying levels of success, to bring together Christians of diverse stripes. The word "ecumenism" is derived from the Greek word *oikoumene*, used in the New Testament to mean the whole inhabited world (or the Roman empire). The term eventually came to refer to the whole Christian church. In contrast to this, we have noticed how natural it is for churches to use the word "church" in reference to themselves.

Missiologist Lesslie Newbigin was one of the twentieth century's great advocates for Christian unity. In 1953 he wrote,

> For myself, I do not believe that we can be content with anything less than a form of unity which enables all who confess Christ as Lord to be recognizably one family in each place and in all places, united in the visible bonds of word, sacrament, ministry and congregational fellowship, and in the invisible bond which the Spirit Himself creates through these means, one family offering to all men everywhere the secret of reconciliation with God the Father.[25]

He continued, "The church is one, and in this broken world must live in mission as a community of reconciliation. The church can fulfill its mission—its purpose—only as it makes plainly visible the unity in love that God wills for all who are incorporated in it."[26]

Relating to people of other faiths

At the same time that Christians need to learn to get along with one another, Christians need to learn to get along with those who do not follow Christ. As we have mentioned, the world is both increasing in diversity and increasing in engagement with diversity. Yet Buddhists, Hindus, and Muslims still have relatively little contact with Christians. Over eighty-six percent of these religionists do not personally know a Christian.[27]

You might agree with the idea of engaging deeply and getting along well with others, but questions linger: How do we increase contact with non-Christian religionists? How do we hold fast to a strong Christian identity while engaging with them? And how do we achieve common ground in light of such a plurality of beliefs?

One of the chief concerns of Christians who are willing to engage is how to do so without capitulating on core beliefs. Some cluster on one side

---

[25] Lesslie Newbigin, *One Body, One Gospel, One World: The Christian Mission Today* (London: International Missionary Council, 1958), 55–56.

[26] W. Richey Hogg, *One World, One Mission* (New York: Friendship Press, 1960), 147.

[27] http://www.gordonconwell.edu/resources/documents/12007PersonalContact.pdf.

of a spectrum of attitudes toward religious engagement, wanting to have a strong faith identity. They might resort to hostility as a safeguard against influences that make them doubt or dilute their faith. Christians who cluster on the other side of the spectrum are benevolent and more tolerant in their attitudes toward other beliefs, but might be perceived by other Christians, as well as other religionists, as having a "weak" faith identity. Historian Lamin Sanneh describes the spectrum this way: one side demonizes other religions while the other romanticizes them.[28]

Rather than having to choose between a strong faith identity with a hostile attitude or a weak faith identity with a benevolent attitude, we advocate for holding to a Christian identity that is strong *and* benevolent, maintaining a strong identity that is not ashamed of the gospel (Rom. 1:16), but that at the same time offers a benevolent outlook that treats others civilly (Col. 4:6).[29] In order to do this well, we need to study other religions and worldviews, especially from original perspectives. We need to engage with others in dialogue, being willing to listen and receive others without judgment. And we need to foster authentic friendships for more than just utilitarian purposes. While it would obviously please us to see every knee bow down before the Lordship of Jesus Christ, evangelism and conversion should not be our sole motive for dialoguing about faith. If it is, we will be tempted to give up if we do not see results. True engagement is fueled by love (Matt. 22:39).

Any discussion about interreligious engagement must not neglect those who do not adhere to a particular faith, or maybe profess no faith whatsoever. Nonreligious and antireligious movements have gained prominence in the postmodern era, with the growth rate of atheists and agnostics rising dramatically in some areas of the world in the past century, as well as those looking for "spirituality, not religion."

Engagement means caring

We have looked at how our world is changing and how those changes have impacted the global church. Those changes inevitably impact the way we view ourselves, inside and outside the church. We also believe that Christians who see themselves as part of a global Christian family will naturally

---

[28] Lammin Sanneh, "Secular values in the Midst of Faith: A Critical Discourse on Dialogue and Difference," in Viggo Mortensen, ed., *Theology and the Religions: A Dialogue* (Grand Rapids: Wm. B. Eerdmans, 2003), 147.

[29] McLaren, *Why Did Jesus, Moses, the Buddha, and Mohammed Cross the Road?* (Brentwood, TN: FaithWords, 2012), 41.

be concerned for their global human family as well, and that one of the most impactful awakenings that can take place is Christians rising up to respond to the needs of the world. Christian service is a testimony to the world of the power of God's love and care, and our selfless commitment to service has great potential to stir up a hunger for God. Christians have great gifts to utilize for all of God's creation.

Conclusion

All of these factors point toward a future for awakenings and revivals that will be more focused on Africa, Asia, and Latin America, while, at the same time, occurring in closer proximity with people of other religions and no religion. What is certain is that awakenings will not be drawing on a dominant Northern cultural, linguistic, or political framework. Christianity is a phenomenon not of Western uniformity, but of ever-increasing global diversity. Episcopal priest Paul-Gordon Chandler writes, "It is like the canvas of a beautiful painting with contrasting and complementary colors. The foundation for our unity as Christians throughout the world is not our likeness but our diversity."[30] The unanswered question for Christians from both the North and the South is how well we will work, minister, and grow together as a family in the context of this astonishing diversity.

---

[30] Paul-Gordon Chandler, *God's Global Mosaic: What We Can Learn from Christians Around the World* (Downers Grove, IL: InterVarsity, 2000), 15.

Contributors

Gwenfair Adams is Associate Professor of Church History and Director of Masters of Arts in Spiritual Formation at Gordon-Conwell Theological Seminary. As the Director of the Masters of Arts in Spiritual Formation, Dr. Adams teaches courses in the history and practice of Christian spirituality. Her interests are focused in the history of worship and the arts in the church. She is also the designer of LifeStory Exegesis (Story Spirituality™)—a model of spirituality that can be used in spiritual formation, direction, discipleship, and counseling. Bringing together theology, historiography, and literary theory, it engages the structure of the Creation-Redemption meta-narrative to provide a framework that shapes the understanding and effective living of one's life. Her book, *Visions in Late Medieval England: Lay Spirituality and Sacred Glimpses of the Hidden Worlds of Faith* (2007), explores the impact of visionary accounts in sermons, saints' legends and religious instruction manuals on the worldview and piety of the medieval laity.

D. Kevin Adams is Senior Pastor of East Baptist Church, Lynn, Massachusetts. He was born in Llanelli, South Wales, and is one of three brothers, all of whom are in full-time Christian ministry. Having become a Christian at the age of seventeen, he went on to be theologically trained at Bangor University where he earned a B.D. in theology and then went on to research the 1904 Revival and twentieth-century evangelism in Wales. He worked as Pastor for eighteen years at the Ammanford Evangelical Church, South Wales. His writing includes work on a film exploring Welsh Revival history and two books, including *Diary of Revival: The Outbreak of the 1904 Welsh Awakenings*.

Charles E. Hambrick-Stowe is Pastor of the First Congregational Church, Ridgefield, Connecticut. He previously served as academic dean and professor of Christian history at Northern Seminary (Lombard, Illinois) and director of the Doctor of Ministry program at Pittsburgh Theological Seminary. He served as pastor of two churches in Maryland and Pennsylvania over a twenty-two-year period. Dr. Hambrick-Stowe is the author or editor of six books and numerous articles in the field of American religious history.

David Horn is the Director of the Ockenga Institute of Gordon-Conwell Theological Seminary. His responsibilities involve oversight over multiple centers and programs involved in the seminary's commitment to offering theological education to a variety of constituencies beyond the traditional student body. He also has direct oversight over the Shoemaker Center for Church Renewal and the Compass Program. Dr. Horn writes and speaks on issues related to practical theology and sociology of religion. Previously, he served on the pastoral staff of First Congregational Church in Hamilton, Massachusetts, and continues to be actively involved in the leadership and teaching ministries of the church.

Gordon L. Isaac is the Berkshire Associate Professor of Church History and Advent Christian Studies at Gordon-Conwell Theological Seminary and the Director of the ThM Degree Program in Christian Thought. He regularly offers seminars on Martin Luther, Dietrich Bonhoeffer, and Symbolics. He has lectured internationally and has written articles and chapters in books on a wide array of topics. His book *Left Behind or Left Befuddled: The Subtle Dangers of Popularizing the End Times* (2008) traces the sociological and theological underpinnings of the Dispensational movement and its ethical consequences. His current research interests focus on the spirituality of Martin Luther, particularly as contained in the three rules for doing proper theology: prayer, meditation, and spiritual trial.

Todd M. Johnson is Associate Professor of Global Christianity and Director of the Center for the Study of Global Christianity at Gordon-Conwell Theological Seminary, where he researches the status of Christianity and world religions in every people, language, country, and city. Dr. Johnson is widely accomplished in the demographic study of Christianity and world religions. His PhD work in developing quantitative tools to analyze the past, present, and future of global Christianity has been put to fruitful use throughout his career, both at Gordon-Conwell and elsewhere. Dr. Johnson is also visiting Research Fellow at the Institute on Culture, Religion, and World Affairs at Boston University. He co-leads the International Religious Demography project and is co-editor of the World Religion Database (Brill 2008) at wwww.worldreligiondatabase.org. Dr. Johnson has also worked in numerous ecclesiastical posts relating to missions and evangelization. He is a member of the Lausanne Strategy Working Group as well as the Missions Commission of the World Evangelical Alliance.

Walter C. Kaiser Jr. is President Emeritus and Colman M. Mockler Distinguished Professor Emeritus of Old Testament and Old Testament Ethics at Gordon-Conwell Theological Seminary. He also served as the seminary's President from 1997–2006. Dr. Kaiser taught Bible and archaeology at Wheaton College, Wheaton, Illinois, and taught at Trinity Evangelical Divinity School in several capacities. In addition to teaching in the Old Testament Department, he was Senior Vice President of Education, Academic Dean, and Senior Vice President of Distance Learning and Ministries. Dr. Kaiser currently serves on the boards of several Christian organizations. He has published work in numerous commentaries and scholarly journals and has written many books, including *Toward an Old Testament Theology*; *Ecclesiastes: Total Life*; and *Hard Sayings of the Old Testament*.

George M. Marsden is a distinguished historian of American religion. His biography of Jonathan Edwards won numerous significant prizes. Among his other books are *The Soul of the American University, Religion and American Culture,* and *Fundamentalism and American Culture*. Dr. Marsden studied at Haverford College, Westminster Theological Seminary, and Yale University. He has taught at Calvin College, Duke University, and the University of Notre Dame, and is now scholar in residence at Calvin College. He lives with his wife in Grand Rapids, Michigan.

Mark Noll is Francis A. McAnaney Professor of History at the University of Notre Dame. He is a member of the American Academy of Arts and Sciences, and in 2006 he received the National Endowment for the Humanities medal at the White House. Dr. Noll's research is focused on the history of Christianity in the United States and Canada. He teaches courses in the Civil War era, general Canadian history, and the recent world history of Christianity. He is currently working on a book that combines narratives about the Bible in American history. His recent books include *Protestantism—A Very Short Introduction* (2011), *The New Shape of World Christianity: How American Experience Reflects Global Faith* (2009), and *God and Race in American Politics: A Short History* (2008).

Jim Singleton is Associate Professor of Pastoral Leadership and Evangelism at Gordon-Conwell Theological Seminary. He previously served on Gordon-Conwell's faculty as adjunct professor in Presbyterian polity and history at the Hamilton campus in 1991. The son of a Presbyterian pastor,

Dr. Singleton's call to ministry began early in his high school years and intensified in college. His particular interests lie in evangelism and the mission of the local church. Prior to his current post at Gordon-Conwell, Dr. Singleton served as senior pastor of churches in Texas, Washington, and most recently First Presbyterian Church in Colorado Springs, a downtown congregation of 4,200 members. He has taught at several seminaries around the world, including ones in Virginia, Texas, Washington, Moscow, and Zambia.

Ed Stetzer, PhD, is President of LifeWay Research and Missiologist in Residence at LifeWay Christian Resources, Nashville, Tennessee. He is the Senior Fellow of the Billy Graham Center at Wheaton College, and also serves as Visiting Professor of Research and Missiology at Trinity Evangelical Divinity School, Visiting Research Professor at Southeastern Baptist Theological Seminary, and has taught at many other colleges and seminaries. Dr. Stetzer is a contributing editor for *Christianity Today*, a columnist for *Outreach* magazine, and is the Executive Editor of *The Gospel Project*, a curriculum used by more than 1 million individuals each week. He also serves as Preaching Pastor of Grace Church in Hendersonville, Tennessee, a congregation he planted in 2011.

Timothy C. Tennent is President and Professor of World Christianity at Asbury Theological Seminary. Prior to this post, Dr. Tennent was the Professor of World Missions and Indian Studies at Gordon-Conwell Theological Seminary, where he served since 1998. Ordained in the United Methodist Church in 1984, he has pastored churches in Georgia, and served in several of the largest churches in New England. Since 1989, he has taught annually as an adjunct professor at the New Theological College in Dehra Dun, India, and he is a frequent conference speaker around the country and throughout the world, including in numerous countries in Asia, Africa, and Europe. Dr. Tennent is the author of numerous books and articles, including *Building Christianity on Indian Foundations, Christianity at the Religious Roundtable, Theology in the Context of World Christianity*, and *Invitation to World Missions: A Trinitarian Missiology for the Twenty-First Century*.

Grant Wacker is Gilbert T. Rowe Professor Emeritus of Christian History at Duke Divinity School. He specializes in the history of Evangelicalism, Pentecostalism, world missions, and American Protestant thought. He is the author or co-editor of seven books, including *Heaven Below: Early Pentecostals and American Culture* and *America's Pastor: Billy Graham and the Shaping of a Nation*. From 1997 to 2004, Dr. Wacker served as a senior editor of the quarterly journal, *Church History: Studies in Christianity and Culture*. He is past president of the Society for Pentecostal Studies and of the American Society of Church History, and a trustee of Fuller Theological Seminary. Wacker is a lay member of Orange United Methodist Church in Chapel Hill, North Carolina.

Adrian Chastain Weimer is Assistant Professor of History at Providence College. A historian of colonial America and the early modern British Atlantic, Dr. Weimer earned her PhD from Harvard University in 2008. Her recent book, *Martyrs' Mirror: Persecution and Holiness in Early New England*, explores how seventeenth-century New England Protestants imagined themselves within biblical and historical narratives of persecution. Her current research focuses on the crisis of religious and political authority in 1660s New England, exploring how a sacralized charter and a politicized church became grounds for resistance to empire in the early years of the Restoration.

Cindy M. Wu serves as Research Associate for the Center for the Study of Global Christianity at Gordon-Conwell Theological Seminary. She has served in church-planting contexts in China, Mexico City, Houston, and Boston. She lives in Houston, Texas.